THE IMMIGRANT HERITAGE OF AMERICA
SERIES

Cecyle S. Neidle, Editor

THE ORIENTAL AMERICANS

by

H. Brett Melendy
University of Hawaii

Twayne Publishers, Inc. :: New York

For

Brenda, Darcie, Lisa

and

Marian

Preface

THE IMMIGRATION OF THE CHINESE AND THE JAPANESE TO the United States has added immeasurably to this country's cultural heritage. Those who study the movement of people from these Asian nations to the United States are soon impressed with their capacity for hard work in the face of economic and social adversity and their ability to advance economically. When they began to establish homes, they created Chinese and Japanese cultural microcosms from which their children ventured to become Americans. The second generation retained much of its own culture while accepting certain aspects of the dominant society. Generally, they strove to meet the standards of American society. Many third-generation Asian Americans subsequently condemned them for this; in turn some of the newer generation has striven to recapture their Asian heritage.

The Asian immigrants and their descendants disprove the concept of the Melting Pot. The Chinese and Japanese did not wish to amalgamate with the dominant society, and most certainly white Americans of the nineteenth and twentieth centuries made it abundantly clear that they were opposed to Asian immigration and settlement.

This study is intended as a general survey of Chinese and Japanese immigration rather than a comprehensive study. Fortunately, many excellent monographs dealing with specific aspects of Chinese and Japanese immigration already exist for those who desire in-depth information. The purpose of this book is to review the history of the Chinese and Japanese immigration, to recount the hostile discrimination they encountered, and to show the accommodation of five generations of Chinese and three generations of Japanese to life in the United States.

The research for this book centered in California but much of the material was obtained elsewhere. I am indebted to the Library of Congress, the Foreign Affairs Section of the National Archives, and the libraries of the University of Hawaii, University of Oregon, and University of Washington for their assistance.

In particular, I am indebted to the Bancroft Library at the University of California, the California State Archives, the California Section of the California State Library, the San Jose State College Library, and the Stanford University Library. Materials were also consulted at the California Historical Society, the Public Archives of Hawaii, the Hawaiiana Collection of the University of Hawaii, the public libraries of Eureka, San Francisco, San Jose, California, and Honolulu, Hawaii.

I am pleased also to acknowledge the assistance of the American Philosophical Society and the San Jose State College Foundation through their awards of research grants. Among those who particularly helped in my research were John B. Tompkins and Robert H. Becker of the Bancroft Library; Allan R. Ottley of the California State Library; Robert L. Lauritzen, Christie Simpson, and Mildred B. Nelson of the San Jose State College Library; and Mrs. Helen Murrie of the Eureka Public Library.

Appreciation is extended to the following publishers who have given permission to use material to which they hold the copyrights: Allyn and Bacon, Inc. for *Japan: A Concise History,* by Milton Meyers; California Historical Society for "The Chinese in California," *California Historical Society Quarterly,* by Henryk Sienkiewicz; Chinese Historical Society of America for *A History of the Chinese in California;* University of Chicago Press for *Resident' Orientals on the American Pacific Coast,* by Eliot Mears; University of Hawaii for *The Hawaiian Kingdom,* by Ralph S. Kuykendall; University of Hong Kong for *The Chinese in the United States of America,* by Rose Hum Lee; Pardee Lowe for *Father and Glorious Descendant;* and William Morrow and Co. for *Nisei, The Quiet Americans,* by Bill Hosokawa.

It gives me pleasure to acknowledge the contributions of Professor Roger Daniels of the University of Wyoming for his critical review of the manuscript and Cecyle S. Neidle, Editor of the Twayne Immigrant Heritage of America Series, for her many excellent suggestions and patient editing.

Finally, this book could not have been completed without the tolerant understanding of my three daughters, and my wife, who has served as in-house critic, editor, and typist; my debt to her cannot be adequately measured.

H. Brett Melendy

Honolulu, Hawaii
June, 1971

Contents

List of Tables

Introduction:
Part of the Mainstream

THE PEOPLE OF THE UNITED STATES OF AMERICA HAVE LONG accepted the fact that they are a nation of immigrants. One of the country's strengths has been its ethnic and national multiplicity. Many white Anglo-Saxon Protestant Americans, however, have opposed unrestricted immigration as being inimicable to the nation's vitality. The history of American immigration is the story of hope, ambition, and beginnings for newcomers on the one hand and fear, prejudice, and repression by nativists on the other.

Emigrants from China and Japan joined the stream of arrivals to American shores at a time when European immigration was changing. Those Americans already here by the 1850's had created an economic-political power structure. Many leaders of the establishment were torn between their need for inexpensive labor and their unreasoning xenophobia.

At the time of the greatest Chinese and Japanese immigration to the West Coast, southern and eastern Europeans had already effected many changes in eastern urban America. A hallmark of any nineteenth- or twentieth-century industrial city was the concentration of new immigrants speaking strange languages, adhering to different national and ethnic customs, working for low wages, and demonstrating a much higher level of fecundity than did older generations of Europeans.

The United States Immigration Commission, created by Congress in 1907, undertook an investigation of the nature of immigration. The report, extended through forty-one volumes, reinforced existing views and solidified the appellation of "old" and "new" immigrants. The "old" immigrants had built the nation, according to the rhetoric of the report, and believed they had amalgamated into a single American people. The more recent arrivals, the commission stated, had not contributed in a similar manner and they did not appear to blend easily with groups already here.

The decade of the greatest Chinese immigration was the 1870's when 123,201 arrived. These years witnessed also the height of anti-Chinese agitation. During the same decade a total of about 2,800,000 immigrants from all sources migrated to America with about 2,270,000 coming from Europe, 81 percent of the total. The Chinese contributed 4.4 percent.[1] Thirty years later, anti-Japanese prejudice grew apace with increased immigration from the Island Empire. From 1901 to 1910, almost 8,800,000 new arrivals came from all nations. A little more than 8,100,000 came from the major fountainhead, Europe, while fewer than 130,000 came from Japan. Europeans accounted for 92 percent of the total while the Japanese share was 1.4 percent.[2] The significance of these figures is seen in the rampant hysteria and discrimination aimed against the Chinese and Japanese. Those "old" immigrants who had turned into xenophobes found these two Asian peoples an unwelcome addition to the mainstream of immigration and worked hard to eliminate them from the United States.

The Chinese and Japanese emigrating to this country remained small in number and never posed any serious threat. Yet their arrival coincided with the growing xenophobia aimed at all foreigners and because they were color-visible minorities, these Asians suffered greatly from prejudicial discrimination.

West Coast anti-foreign reactions, buttressed by eastern racial views, led to enactment of the 1882 Chinese Exclusion Act. At that time most Americans still thought of their country as a refuge for Europeans. Nevertheless, an important restrictive precedent had been established. In 1885, for example, when unskilled Italians and Slavs were utilized as common laborers, the Knights of Labor, calling for regulation of such immigration, compared these new arrivals to Chinese "coolies." The union wanted the exclusion legislation to include these unwanted Europeans. During the 1890's, organizations such as the Immigration Restriction League, concerned about protecting the "old stock," organized against the Asians and the new European immigrants.

At the dawn of the twentieth century, nativist organizations were increasingly sounding the tocsin of alarm, warning of the rising threat. The Japanese immigrant added a new dimension to the fears of white supremacists. Coupled with the nativists' racism was organized labor's opposition to the influx of immigrant labor. By World War I, the two groups had allied to push their program of restriction. In 1917, a literacy test for all immigrants became law while other Asians joined the Chinese in being excluded from the right of immigration.

The climax of this hostile anti-immigrant movement came in 1924. What had started in 1882 against the Chinese was now extended to the Japanese. Certain European immigrants deemed not desirable were closely controlled, virtually to the point of exclusion. Racial and ethnic regulation became the nation's immigration policy. The 1924 immigration act codifying the anti-foreign feelings of many Americans was indeed humiliating to certain European countries, and it was equally so to the immigrants from China and Japan who for some seventy-five years had been in the forefront of those newcomers who had had to bear the brunt of racial and economic discrimination.

Part I

The Chinese Americans

CHAPTER 1

The Homeland

FROM ABOUT 1850 UNTIL THE UNITED STATES CONGRESS limited immigration in 1882, Chinese emigration to the United States came primarily from the Kwangtung Province in southeastern China. The lives of these southeastern Chinese, living under different climatic conditions than those of northern China, were regulated by a rice economy. Northern China, the seat of government, imposed its will upon the South. Each region spoke different dialects, the inhabitants of each not being able to understand the language of the other.

China, long a land of mystery to the Western world, is, with India and the Near East, among the world's oldest civilizations. Its influence has been felt throughout Asia; its culture has contributed greatly to those of Korea and Japan. China's imperial system emerged slowly over a period of some 1,700 years. During most of this time, Confucian ideas helped to create a system of life for the people. During the time of several dynasties, from 1523 B.C. through 220 A.D., a governmental system consisting of loosely knit tribes developed into an empire. After a period of 370 years of political disunion, two strong dynasties, Sui and T'ang, reasserted imperial rule and extended China's authority over more territory.[1] At the same time, Chinese society evolved slowly. Some Westerners have viewed this coming and going of dynasties as manifestations of a backward nation.

In 1206, the Mongols, a nomadic people led by Genghis Khan, started their march through Asia. They established a world empire which lasted until the fourteenth century.[2] Chaotic conditions followed until the Ming Dynasty emerged to rule from 1368 until 1644.[3] As the power of the Mings declined, the Manchus marched from Manchuria to gain control of China in 1644. They created the Ch'ing Dynasty which stayed in power until 1912.[4] It was at the point of explosive conflict between China and the Western world in the nineteenth century that the power of the Ch'ing Dynasty gradually weakened. If China had been left to her own devices, a new dynasty might well have emerged. Pressures from imperialistic Western powers hastened the collapse.[5]

As indicated, the bulk of Chinese emigration to the United States came from China's southeastern coast, first principally from Kwangtung Province and later from the southern part of Fukien Province. The cultural differences which developed over the centuries were determined in large measure by China's geography.

North China, with its major city of Peking, China's traditional capital, is an arid region, hot and dusty in the summer and subject to Siberian cold in the winter. The area, similar in many ways to the American Midwest, has major crops of wheat and millet. Annual rainfall seldom exceeds twenty-five inches. North China is dotted with farming villages where, as in South China, man has fought nature for centuries to produce food for thousands of people. Northern villages located at about one-mile intervals had to produce food in each square mile of land for at least 1,000 people.[6] North China is one of four areas of high density population. The other three are the mountain plain of Szechwan in the West, the lower Yangtze Valley from Hankow to Shanghai, and the Pearl River Delta in the Kwangtung Province.[7]

Kwangtung is separated from the Yangtze River Basin to

the north by a mountain mass. Kwangsi Province to the east historically buffered Kwangtung against inland influences. Kwangtung's irregular coastline with several small harbors, however, lay open to maritime intruders. Because of the warm water, fish do not abound as they do along the north coast. Consequently there are few fishing villages.[8]

The Pearl River Delta is traversed by the Chu Kiang (Pearl River), Si Kiang, Pei Kiang, and Tung Kiang. The Si Kiang, or West River, is the major eastern waterway moving from Kwangsi to the ocean at the point where the Portuguese colony of Macao is located.[9] The delta is about 2,900 square miles in area with 75 percent of the land classified as agriculturally usable. It is interlaced with waterways, both natural and man-made. The alluvial flow settling around old islands has created mountains and hills.[10]

The Pearl River is formed by the joining of the three major rivers upstream from Canton, the province's principal city. The Pearl River flows by Whampoa, the historic China Trade anchorage, into a large estuary about forty miles in length, before it enters the Pacific Ocean. On the northeast shoulder of the estuary sits Hong Kong, the British imperial commercial center.

With the Tropic of Cancer twenty-one miles north of Canton, the delta's climate is tropical. Kwangtung has long hot summers from April to October, followed by cool dry winters and two months of foggy, muggy weather. The rains come with the monsoons during the summer months. Annual rainfall averages range from seventy inches on the coast to forty inches inland.[11]

Because of climate and terrain, the farmers engage in "wet farming," utilizing those flat lands which can be irrigated. These alluvial lands, rich in mineral deposits, return high crop yields. Rice is the dominant crop with two harvests a year. Even so, it is necessary to import additional rice to meet the needs of the province.

In the days of the Manchu, sugar cane alternated with

rice as a crop. Cane was also grown at higher elevations. Ducks were raised during the winter in the dormant rice paddies. Vegetables, bananas, litchi, mangoes, peaches, plums, and oranges supplemented the diet.[12] Extensive mulberry plantations, irrigated and drained by canals, were found on lands above tide level. In these waterways fish were an additional cash product. Each year, the harvested mulberry leaves were sold to those engaged in sericulture, one of Kwangtung's major cash crops. Silk production was important to both internal and external commerce.[13]

Intensive cultivation of available land, necessary for survival, tied the Chinese family to the soil. For countless generations, families had lived in the same village. The village, with its mud and bamboo houses sheltering approximately 1,000 residents, was the center of life. As farmers worked in nearby fields, they could see dark trees shading similar villages. In the delta, there was less than one-half acre of food-producing soil per person.[14] Anything that curtailed productivity spelled disaster.

Canton, focal point for commercial and cultural developments in Kwangtung Province, was, like other cities east or west, a place of fascination, excitement, poverty, and misery. In the 1850's, Canton's narrow streets, on which the houses and businesses of merchants and artisans were situated, teemed with street peddlers and laborers moving goods to and from the Thirteen Factories on the waterfront. The city, traversed by both canals and streets, had its old section set off by a six-mile-long wall.[15]

With the relative isolation of Kwangtung from the rest of China, the Pearl River Delta people developed several different dialects. The official language of China is Mandarin, the Chinese dialect normally taught in United States colleges. Interestingly, and tragically, most Chinese in the United States do not understand this dialect. They almost universally speak either Sze Yup, Cantonese (the dialect of

Canton, Hong Kong, and Macao), or Chungshan (the dialect used heavily in the Hawaiian Islands).[16]

Like their Northern countrymen, the Kwangtung Chinese had always engaged in the ageless struggle against the forces of nature. The Chinese, completely dependent upon nature, became fatalistic about the puniness of man. Their art and religion bear out the awe in which nature is held. At the same time, living in close proximity to many people has made them highly social individuals. Out of these pressures developed a different concept of man than that held by industrialized Europeans.[17]

China's agrarian society depended upon human hands and backs to provide the muscle of production. In the villages, the family, not the individual, was the key to survival. It was essential that sons be produced to help combat the forces of nature. Equally important, sons were necessary to care for senior members of the family.[18]

From the days of the Shang and Chou dynasties this simplistic but practical view of human existence—hammered out through experience—became formalized through the thought and writings of Confucius. Confucius's doctrine, based on his concept of family organization, regulated human activity and formed the basis for the Chinese empire. He believed that the prime need of man was to resolve problems of peaceful coexistence and harmony with the universe. This resolution was best accomplished by serving one's parents with filial love during the lifetime of the parents and an obligation to venerate and to make sacrifice to one's ancestors.[19] Confucian thought, which provided order to family and empire, was not a philosophical system addressing itself to the afterlife or the supernatural. Its basic concern was with man's present place in the universe. Confucianism became intertwined with Buddhism and Taoism, each acting as counterpoints or as complements to the others.[20]

Taoists reacted against the Confucian social order, holding that one should surrender oneself passively to Tao or the way of the universe. Taoism provided peasants, surfeited with the ordered life of Confucianism, with an outlet for their needs and fears of the phenomena of nature and accompanying superstitions. The peasants knew when their men danced with the ornate dragon's head during the New Year's celebration and firecrackers were exploded that evil spirits were warded off. Nature's dynamism provided many examples of supernatural forces with which to reckon. The Chinese peasant was more interested in the impact of Taoism upon his present life than he was concerned about any theological doctrine of rewards and punishments in the hereafter.[21]

Buddhism was a third major force shaping Chinese lives. Village women particularly were ardent supporters. Imported from India centuries before, those interpretations held by the Mahayana school had the greatest impact upon China. Attainment of Nirvana—a blissful afterlife to which prayers and good works would convey the soul—became possible after a cycle of transmigrations and purgatorial interludes. Buddhism, taken in conjunction with the other two religio-philosophical systems, developed a morality and religion with which the Chinese were at ease.[22] In the nineteenth century, Western missionaries found few people dissatisfied with Chinese religion. Christianity never became a viable alternative, a point of view hard to understand by Westerners.[23]

The meaning of family was constantly impressed upon young Chinese. Family members paid respect to the tablets commemorating ancestors who had made family survival possible. The common goal of family support and sacrifice lay at the heart of the Confucian family system.[24] The cement that held the family together was the land—the source of life. The assets—land, farm implements, housing—were jointly held.

The Cantonese knew that the Emperor, the Son of Heaven,

lived in the distant North. Confucianism had great impact upon the governmental structure. The government was likened to the village family with the Emperor the family leader. All owed a sense of loyalty to the Emperor, particularly his "adopted sons," those civil servants who held office because of him.

Scholars believed that the Son of Heaven, standing between Heaven and the people, could intervene in man's struggle against nature. If tragedy befell the country, the fault was laid at the door of the ruler. If the Emperor conducted himself properly, he would be able to govern through goodness. Adherence to morality led to power, allowing the Emperor to maintain his superior position. Corruption and evildoing would lead to his downfall. The scholar's role was to aid the Emperor in interpreting and doing what was correct and proper.[25] These philosophical concepts fit into the peasant's pattern of society as they understood it. They believed that the man who was good and was moral improved his lot in this life and in the hereafter. Such a man merited the respect of his family and society. This concept was alien to much of Western thought regarding the use of power and the means of achieving it.

The Western concept of law and order was not easy for Chinese immigrants to understand. China's system of government, based on morality, had no need for such a legal system. There was no private law to adjudicate internal differences. No Chinese official would think of listening to a complaint lodged by a family member against another. This was a matter to be settled by the clan leader. Morality and law were one and the same. The penal code, created and administered by the Emperor, punished only the uncivilized and the barbarians. There was an extensive set of administrative codes covering the operation of the complex Chinese bureaucracy, reaching from Peking all the way down into the villages.[26]

Chinese emigrants to California also came into contact

with what Western countries called national consciousness. The very concept of nation was missing in the Chinese mind. China's philosophical, social, and political ideas were integrated into a oneness which substituted culture for nationalism. The Son of Heaven, the Chinese Emperor, saw himself operating on a universal level striving to perfect the relationship between man and cosmic force. He believed that he ruled over all of mankind, regardless of race or language.[27]

In 222 B.C., Chêng created the first empire and assumed the title of First Emperor. He established a unified imperial government, a pattern which lasted 2,000 years.[28] Succeeding dynasties were in time overthrown, but all kept intact the concept of a centralized imperial government.

On June 6, 1644, the Manchus captured Peking and founded the Ch'ing Dynasty which lasted until the creation of the Republic in 1912. The Manchus introduced no major economic or social changes, but some of their customs had lasting impact. They dictated that men shave the front part of their heads and wear their hair in a queue. The Ming robe, similar to the Japanese kimono, was forbidden and was replaced with the Manchu costume of a skullcap and a Tartar gown with high collar and side fastenings. Although loud protests against these decrees were heard, particularly from Kwangtung Province, the queue and the new dress style became a part of Chinese life. Reformers in the nineteenth and twentieth centuries encountered great opposition when they tried to abolish the queue.[29] The Tartar robe has remained a part of the fashionable dress of Chinese women.

Pearl River Delta residents were reminded of the Manchu overlordship through continual contact with civil servants. Tax collection, government regulations, and flood control projects were carried on constantly. The villages were administered as part of a district, or a "hsien," the lowest administrative level. Two prefectures with twelve districts

encompassed the Pearl River Delta. Overseeing these prefectures was the Governor of the Province of Kwangtung,
who resided in the provincial capital, Canton.[30]

The Chinese bureaucracy had arbitrarily divided the
land into administrative units without regard to existing
patterns of culture and language. The city of Canton, for
example, was divided into two districts. These, along with
a third, were known collectively by the Delta Chinese as
Sam Yup, the Three Districts.[31] The Three Districts spoke
a purer Cantonese dialect, hardly understood by residents
from the two adjacent districts. These two culturally were
more closely tied to two districts of a neighboring prefecture. The Delta Chinese referred to these as Sze Yup, the
Four Districts.[32] The urban Cantonese felt a contempt for
those Chinese from the Four Districts which was recipro-
cated by these rural residents.[33]

The Cantonese felt themselves superior to other Chinese
of the region, for they belonged to the group known as the
Punti, the indigenous Delta people. In the thirteenth
century, a wave of newcomers, the Hakka, had moved
into South China from the northeastern provinces. By the
seventeenth century, they had arrived in the mountain areas
of Kwangtung. In time, they acquired land of their own,
lived in separate villages, and established a culture apart
from the Punti. Haaka men and women worked hard in
the fields.[34]

A third group held in contempt by the Cantonese were
the Tanka, or boat people—century-old outcasts who lived
on the rivers as ferry operators and smugglers. They were
forbidden to marry the Cantonese or compete in the civil-
service examinations, the one remote hope of the peasant
class to escape its environment.[35]

While contact had been open and frequent through the
centuries between China and the West, commercial routes
to China became commonly traveled by the English and
Dutch in the eighteenth and nineteenth centuries. The

United States made its first contact with China on August 23, 1784, when the *Empress of China* arrived at Macao and proceeded upriver to Canton, the only port open to foreigners.[36] As the China Trade developed, American ships bypassed Macao and Hong Kong and moved directly to Whampoa on the Pearl River, the anchorage for all foreign ships trading with Canton. At Whampoa the Chinese Superintendent of Maritime Customs collected the tribute owed the Emperor and his own "cumshaw," a gratuity or gift. The cargo then was lightered by barge twelve miles to one of the *hongs*, known collectively as the Thirteen Factories, at Canton. These warehouses, monopolies of Chinese merchants, served as a buffer between Chinese society and the foreign devils.[37]

Major Samuel Shaw of Boston was in charge of the cargo on the *Empress of China*. His account of this early voyage and his willingness to talk to all upon his return to the United States led many to send ships to China. The treasures sought were tea, silk, china, and unbleached cotton nankeens.[38] Shaw returned to Canton in 1786 to establish the shipping firm of Shaw & Randall and to serve as honorary American Consul.[39]

During the nineteenth century, Great Britain engaged in a widespread opium trade. When Chinese officials attempted to repress this trade, the Opium War broke out in 1839. At the war's conclusion, the British wrung concessions from the defeated Chinese, embodied in a treaty which included the most favored nation clause. The ports of Shanghai, Ningpo, Foochow, and Amoy were opened to foreign trade.[40]

As a consequence of the treaties granted to Great Britain, American merchants demanded similar concessions. In 1844, the Treaty of Wanghia gave them fixed tariff duties, the most favored nation clause, and extraterritorial rights in civil and criminal matters. This official recognition by China gave impetus to American missionary efforts.[41]

Relations between the United States and China changed with Chinese immigration. The high point in diplomatic relations between the two nations occurred in 1868 with the signing of the Burlingame Treaty reaffirming American rights, disavowing American intentions to intervene, and giving to the Chinese the most favored nation privileges of travel and residence in the United States.[42] The treaty became operative at a time when American agitation for Chinese exclusion was beginning to build.

With the announcement of James Marshall's discovery of gold on the American River in California, Chinese from Kwangtung Province immediately made plans to embark upon the long uncertain voyage to the "Golden Mountain,"[43] the name given California by the Chinese. Several factors converged at approximately the same time to impel people to break ties with family and country. Too many people on the land, coupled with the dangers of flood or frequent crop failure, brought millions of Chinese face to face with famine. The recent war with European powers in the Pearl River Delta area created additional economic hardships. Taxes had been increased to pay for the war and the indemnities levied by European powers.[44]

More crushing was the T'ai-P'ing rebellion which started upriver in the neighboring province of Kwangsi in 1851. The revolt against the weak Manchu Emperor, lasting thirteen years, had swept down through Kwangtung to the sea and north along the coast into Fukien Province. In the Pearl River Delta local uprisings caused constant turmoil. Over the years the Punti, the local people, and the Hakka, the guest people, had warred extensively. During the T'ai-P'ing war the Hakka had sided with the Manchus. In 1856, the Punti allied with regional bandits and rebels to drive the Hakka from their villages. Many Hakka, now landless, emigrated overseas to start life anew.[45]

The Chinese who went overseas during the nineteenth century violated imperial decree. The Manchus had long ago imposed the order to prohibit sympathizers of the Ming Dynasty from fleeing the country. Anyone caught emigrating could be beheaded. The imperial government refused to recognize the fact that anyone had migrated. But in 1859, Kwangtung provincial authorities allowed recruitment for the coolie trade. When the Burlingame Treaty affirmed the right of the Chinese to travel, the Chinese government demanded protection for its citizens in foreign countries.[46]

At mid-century, the Chinese of Kwangtung Province, confronted by unsettling changes, were ready when opportunity came. The dream and the lure were the same, whether men went to Southeast Asia or to California. After making their fortunes, they expected to return to the arms of their families, whom they planned to support in the interim by sending money home. These Chinese peasants bound for California were no different than the French immigrant or the New York farmer heading for California. None planned to make his ultimate home in the land by the Pacific—the age-old dream of getting rich quickly and returning home a conquering hero remained universal. The hope of turning dream into reality caused the trickle of Chinese migration to grow into a substantial flow.

CHAPTER 2

Forward to the "Golden Mountain": The Trans-Pacific Crossing, 1849-1882

THE CHINESE HAVE BEEN MIGRATING BEYOND THEIR BORDERS for centuries. During the Tan Dynasty (618-906), they migrated into Southeast Asia. However, large-scale migration did not occur until the time of the T'ai-P'ing Rebellion in the 1850's.[1]

With the abolition of slavery in the British Empire in 1833, West Indies plantation owners had, by the 1840's, become desperate for field labor. They had been impressed with the use of Chinese in the Malay Peninsula and Strait Settlements plantations. Starting in 1845, Chinese went as coolies under a contract labor system to the West Indies and Latin America where they were held in virtual slavery. Plantation owners contacted British merchants in Hong Kong to procure coolies through a system widely known as the "buying and selling of pigs." The Hong Kong firms in turn retained Chinese brokers who were paid for each coolie delivered to the barracoons or "pig-pens." Men, ensnared by the brokers, were frequently gamblers pushed into debt which forced them to offer their labor as payment, prisoners taken in clan fights, or kidnap victims. The Pacific coolie trade, as nefarious as the African slave trade, had a shockingly high mortality rate. The vessels carrying coolies were small, lacking proper passenger space, and were provisioned with bad food and water.[2]

The seaports of Amoy, Hong Kong, and Macao flourished as supply centers for coolie labor. The transportation of these unfortunate wretches in ships of all nations continued for about twenty years. In 1862 the United States Congress prohibited American citizens in American vessels from engaging in such business.[3]

During the nineteenth century, anti-Chinese forces in the United States generated much heat over the transportation of coolies to California. Most came, however, not under the coolie system, but by a credit-ticket system. Coolie became a color word used in discriminatory declamations by opponents of the Chinese. Roswell P. Flower, a member of the House of Representatives from New York City, during the 1882 exclusion debate made use of a standard labor argument against the Chinese:

The cooly [sic] system is a system of slavery; Chinese labor is brought here by companies for a certain sum per capita. It comes to perform certain work, to secure certain pay, and finally to return home so much the richer. It comes in the interests of those who are obliged to employ labor. It comes to aid those who have mines to work or railroads to build, or factories to be manned, or labor of any sort to be done. It is bought and brought by capital to increase the profits of capital; it is a wage-saving, labor-robbing, wage-reducing machine, bought and worked in the interest of capital. The tool itself—the Chinaman—is the passive instrument in the hands of masters.[4]

Representative Flower's refrain was well known to Californians. In 1859, the *Sacramento Union* had editorialized about the dangers of Chinese labor:

The Chinese coolie is forcing white labor to leave the state. Slave labor always displaces free labor—so it is with slavery of the Chinese. . . . to maintain the Caucasian race of this continent in its purity, this tide of Mongolian immigrants should be turned back on its source. . . .

Socially and morally, the Chinese are a canker, a nuisance upon the body politic. They form a class by themselves and set at defiance all our moral and many of our civil laws.[5]

United States Department of State immigration records, generally regarded to be sketchy and unreliable, show that between 1820 and 1849 forty-three Chinese entered the country. Three of this number sailed from Canton on January 4, 1847, for New York to enroll in Monson Academy at Monson, Massachusetts. Two boys completed the course at the academy in 1849. One, Yung Wing, graduated from Yale University in 1844, the first Chinese graduate of an American college. In 1852, he became a naturalized American citizen, but the Department of State repudiated his status in 1898.[6] Yung Wing was an exception, for most Chinese, particularly those on the West Coast, were denied outright the right of naturalization. From 1851 to 1860, 41,397 Chinese immigrated to the United States while another 64,301 arrived during the next decade. The frenzy of anti-Chinese agitation in the 1870's coincided with the peak period of Chinese immigration—123,201.[7]

Much of what constitutes the early record of Chinese immigration was written by hostile whites convinced that a system of coolie trade and slavery existed. Little is known about the real people, the Chinese pioneers who settled in California. The actual date of the first Chinese arrival in San Francisco cannot be determined. Hubert H. Bancroft, the California historian, asserts that the American ship *Eagle* was the first ship to sail from Canton to San Francisco, arriving in February, 1848. Bancroft reports that two men and one woman of Chinese ancestry were on board.[8] The *San Francisco Star* noted in April, 1848, that "two or three Celestials . . . have found ready employment in the city."[9]

During the winter of 1847-1848, James Marshall was building a sawmill for John Sutter on the American River in the lower reaches of California's Sierra Nevada. On January 24, 1848, Marshall discovered gold in the mill's tailrace. Word spread like wildfire and the rush was on. In the next several years, pastoral California was transformed into a polyglot society as men from the world over rushed to the goldfields. The impact upon the United States as well as upon other nations, including China, was almost beyond comprehension. The miners, interested in getting rich quickly, did not keep records, but the California State Mining Bureau has estimated that gold equal to a value of about ten million dollars was mined in 1848. In the peak year, 1852, gold valued at about eighty million dollars was mined. From 1850 to the outbreak of the Civil War, gold production annually exceeded fifty million dollars.[10]

James O'Meara, an observer of nineteenth-century California, has presented a picture of early Chinese settlement. He, too, subscribed to the view that "they are not qualified for citizenship as a race." O'Meara stated that of several hundred Chinese in San Francisco by the fall of 1849, most had paid their own fare and had started mercantile enterprises; some others worked as mechanics. O'Meara felt that because the Chinese could not compete with Europeans and Americans they moved to other kinds of employment. He claimed that in these first years no Chinese worked as common laborers nor had he seen any in the goldfields.[11]

As long as the Chinese remained in the restricted area of "Little China" in San Francisco, they were accepted as worthy people and their "quaint customs" were tolerated with amusement by white American society. This view of the Chinese quickly changed as their numbers increased. More and more of the newer arrivals were not able to finance the ocean crossing. Hence they entered into financial arrangements as contract laborers or through credit-ticketing.

Attempts to launch a contract labor system between the Pearl River Delta and California were short-lived.[12] An early California political issue revolved around contract labor. At the 1849 California Constitutional Convention when the question of Negro slavery was debated at length, several delegates held that slaves would give Southerners an unfair advantage in the goldfields. John McDougal, California's first lieutenant governor, proposed that the first legislature should also prohibit the ingress of former slaves under possible indentures.[13] California joined the Union in 1850 with slavery outlawed.

Since most new arrivals to California were gold seekers,

the new state suffered labor shortages. San Francisco Bay Area employers turned to China as a source of workers. Early in March, 1852, Senator George B. Tingley, a Whig from Santa Clara County, concerned about the employers' problems, introduced in the California Senate a measure to enforce through the courts the binding of the Chinese to prior commitments.[14] His bill would remedy such complaints as one made by Edward Lucatt that Chinese under contract just disappeared and local authorities had no interest in helping the contractor find them.[15]

Tingley's bill divided Californians on the Chinese issue. His efforts to solve the state's labor problem launched the anti-Chinese movement which gained in momentum and acrimony over the years. Governor John Bigler, a Democrat, sent a special message regarding Chinese immigration to the legislature on April 23, 1852. He submitted two propositions —to use the state's taxing power to check indiscriminate and unlimited Asiatic immigration and to petition Congress for prompt action prohibiting the importation of coolies as laborers in the mines.[16]

The California Senate committee, reporting out the Tingley bill, also called for Chinese exclusion.[17] The 1852 Democratic State Convention unanimously adopted a resolution "that we do not approve of the bill offered by Tingley, in the legislature, providing for the introduction of serfs or coolies into California to compete with white laborers, who at the same time constitute the democracy and aristocracy of this state."[18]

Opposition from the public and the fact that contract labor was unprofitable soon ended this phase of financing immigration to California. In 1853, members of Chinese mercantile companies admitted that they had tried to develop a contract system but had abandoned it because they were losing money.[19]

Apart from those Chinese who paid their own way, or the few who entered into labor contracts, the vast majority utilized the credit-ticket system. Even so, the anti-Chinese argument that was continuously advanced from the 1850's into the 1880's held that the Chinese were brought here as servile labor. In 1882, Senator Thomas F. Baynard of Delaware (later United States Secretary of State, 1885-1889) maintained that "they are not coming here of their own volition; they are brought here for human greed, and their labor is sold in advance."[20]

The period of heavy Chinese immigration coincided with the emergence of the United States as a great power, with the benefits of an industrial society becoming available to more and more Americans as their standard of living improved. Some of the costs were the despoiling of natural resources and the degradation of the laborer as a pawn in a spreading industrial complex. Inexpensive Chinese labor was an important factor.[21]

In the years following the Civil War, workers organized to protect themselves from the free run of big business. Labor saw the immigration of Chinese as another weapon of the big companies. By 1900, the American Federation of Labor, opposed to child labor and Asian labor as unfair competition, was one of the national leaders in the fight to restrict immigration. Alexander Saxton has cogently demonstrated why Chinese labor was treated differently than were other recently arrived immigrant laborers. Saxton's views, reinforced by Heizer and Almquist in *The Other Californians*, hold that the Chinese inherited the long-standing hostility of whites against people of color, particularly blacks. White Californians, conditioned to the notion that blacks were inferior persons and servile workers, easily transferred these perceptions to the Chinese.[22]

In 1876, a joint Congressional committee, under the nominal chairmanship of Senator Oliver P. Morton of Indiana, met in San Francisco to investigate Chinese immigration.[23] Frank M. Pixley, editor of the San Francisco *Argonaut* and a prominent California Republican, joined

Mayor Andrew J. Bryant in indicating to the committee the fears of San Francisco. Pixley, while hostile to the Chinese, nonetheless gave a favorable picture of these immigrants. He lamented that the Chinese were so successful as workers that they were driving away white labor. Pixley claimed that the Chinese came to the United States "under labor contracts . . . voluntarily entered into, and they are, therefore, in that sense, free immigrants to our coast." It cost $40 for the Pacific crossing. Members of the San Francisco Chinese business community who entered into the ticket-crediting enterprise were making, Pixley claimed, large profits as agents or as middle-men.[24] Friends and enemies of the Chinese commonly agreed that the system was based upon debt-bondage rather than upon service-contract.

Ezekial B. Vreeland, United States Deputy Commissioner of Immigration in San Francisco, 1873-1876, testified to the committee that 80 percent of the Chinese entering through the port of San Francisco during his tenure came under the auspices of one of the Chinese Six Companies and remained attached to that company until the debt was liquidated. Each company found employment for its debtors.[25] Colonel Frederick A. Bee, attorney for the Chinese Six Companies, also testified that the Chinese in California labored to repay money debts. He claimed that "there is not a Chinaman here who comes under a service contract."[26]

The credit-ticket system started in Hong Kong in 1850-51 when two portrait painters, Wo Hang and Hing Wa, sent men to California for hire. Thomas H. King, a San Francisco merchant and a sea captain in the China Trade who was attached for a time to the United States Consulate in Hong Kong, outlined the beginnings of the traffic to the joint Congressional committee. He noted that as other Hong Kong merchants joined, California agents were required to look after their interests. King held that these agents in time became the wealthy Chinese merchants of

San Francisco. He asserted that mercantile affairs remained only one part of their activities as they also kept track of the Chinese immigrants throughout the West. William Olmstead, another San Francisco merchant who had resided in China from 1862 to 1870, verified much of King's testimony. Chinese merchants, he claimed, advanced ticket money in return for a high interest rate. Olmstead outlined the financial gains. The ships were chartered at a fixed sum with profits derived from the transportation of workers. The charter group sold to ticket financiers blocks of passage tickets at a discount—their first source of profit. The tickets were then sold to other Hong Kong merchants and to the workers at the regular passage rate plus interest of 4 to 8 percent.[27]

Continuous supervision of Chinese debtors in California until they had repaid their debts was essential to the Hong Kong brokers. Persia Campbell, leading authority on Chinese coolie emigration, confirms Commissioner Vreeland's view that the San Francisco Six Companies maintained strict control.[28] Those Chinese utilizing the credit-ticket system were obliged, upon arrival in San·Francisco, to register with the company representative of their home district. Campbell and others claim in addition that the Six Companies had an agreement with the Pacific Mail Steamship Company that it would not accept returning Chinese without first clearing with the companies.[29]

The Chinese dispersed throughout the West to labor under this credit-ticket arrangement. Relationships with the company remained tranquil as long as an individual made his monthly payment.[30] The Chinese existed at a poverty level, receiving low wages for their work. Even so, they gained materially a bit more than they had in China.[31] The dream of coming to the Golden Mountain to make a fortune and return home still seemed possible to most. For many, however, this was the impossible dream. The Chinese themselves told the joint Congressional committee:

The United States has been open to Chinese emigration for more than twenty years. Many Chinamen have come; few have returned. . . . They have expected to come here for one or two years and make a little fortune and return. Who among them ever thought of all these difficulties? Expensive rents, expensive living . . . yet they are compelled to labor and live in daily poverty, quite unable to return to their native land.[32]

The vast number of Chinese who came to the United States from 1850 through 1880 came under a debt obligation. The lure was so strong that about 229,000 made the Pacific crossing. The ocean passage was carried out largely in American or British bottoms. During the heyday of the clipper ships, the advertised crossing time was forty-five days. The record was thirty days but fifty-five to sixty days was closer to the average. In 1866, the Pacific Mail Steamship Company entered the China Trade and gained a virtual monopoly of the transportation of Chinese. Its first steamer, the *Colorado,* crossed from San Francisco to Hong Kong in thirty-one days.[33]

On April 25, 1861, the American clipper ship *Bald Eagle* passed through the Golden Gate after a passage of forty-one days from Hong Kong. One of the passengers was Andrew Wilson, a British journalist returning to London. Four hundred Chinese were also on board. Wilson noted that the first-class passengers seldom saw the Chinese for only their cooks were given freedom on deck to prepare meals. He felt that the Chinese were not being transported as coolies but were going to California of their own free will. He reported that the Chinese broker who had chartered space on the *Bald Eagle* set up cooking places and bunks and provided provisions of pork and rice which turned out to be spoiled. The bunks continually broke down and when the weather was bad, there was no cooking on deck and therefore no food for the Chinese.[34]

The arrival of a Pacific Mail steamship at the San Francisco dock was a major sight in the 1860's-70's. When the *Great Republic* arrived in 1869, an observer recorded:

her main deck is packed with Chinamen,—every foot of space being occupied by them,—who are gazing in silent wonder at the new land whose fame had reached them beyond the seas, and whose riches these swart representatives of the toiling millions of Asia have come to develop.

. . . .

The custom-house officers have done their work here quickly, and perhaps effectually, and now all is ready at the forward gangway. A living stream of the blue-coated men of Asia, bending long bamboo poles across their shoulders, from which depend packages of bedding, matting, clothing, and things of which we know neither the names or the uses, pours down the plank the moment that the word is given, "All ready!" They appear to be of an average age of twenty-five years,—very few being under fifteen, and none apparently over forty years,—and, though somewhat less in stature than Caucasians, healthy, active, and able-bodied to a man. As they come down unto the wharf, they separate into messes or gangs of ten, twenty or thirty each, and, being recognized through some to us incomprehensible free-masonry system of signs by agents of the Six Companies as they come, are assigned places on the . . .wharf. Each man carries his entire earthly possessions, and few are overloaded. . . . They are all dressed in coarse but clean and new cotton blouses and loose baggy breeches, blue cotton cloth stockings which reach to the knees, and slippers or shoes with heavy wooden soles . . .; and most of them carry one or two broad-brimmed hats of split bamboo and huge palm-leaf fans. . . . For two mortal hours the blue stream pours down from the steamer upon the wharf; a regiment has landed already, and still they come.

. . . .

As fast as the groups of coolies have been successively searched, they are turned out of the gates, and hurried away towards the Chinese quarter of the city by agents of the Six Companies.[35]

The United States Custom Station in San Francisco reported processing 43,841 Chinese from 1849 through 1854. From 1855 through 1867, arrivals fluctuated from a high of 8,434 in 1860 to a low of 2,242 in 1866.

An examination of these annual entry rates explodes one of the persistent Chinese immigration myths—that the construction of the Central Pacific Railroad signaled the even wider opening of the gates of China. Records show, however, that by the time of the Civil War, immigration had leveled off and then declined. Actual construction of the railroad began in 1863 and the rails joined at Promontory Point in 1869. From 1865 to 1867 the annual average immigration was 2,166 while at the same time departures averaged 3,470.[36] Not until after 1869 did the number of Chinese arrivals increase, in part due to refinements in the credit-ticket system and because the railroad had secured a contractor to furnish most of its new workers from China.

✻ ✻ ✻ ✻

During this same period, the Kingdom of Hawaii, in the midst of agricultural expansion, sought field hands for its sugar plantations. The Chinese, one of the first immigrant groups to arrive, served a key role in the development of the islands' economy. As early as the 1790's, the Hawaiian Islands attracted foreigners to its shores. Edward Bell, a sea captain, wrote in his log of early 1794 that eleven foreigners resided with King Kamehameha on the Kona Coast on the big island of Hawaii.[37]

With the California gold discovery, labor was soon at a premium on the islands. The Royal Hawaiian Agricultural Society in August, 1850, agreed that foreign labor was needed for the plantations. While the society hoped to secure Europeans, the Chinese were considered an excellent source for immediate use. Although there was some opposition, a committee of the society completed negotiations the next month with a Honolulu merchant to bring 200 Chinese to the islands under a five-year labor contract. This contract was never consummated and in 1851 the society engaged a British ship captain who imported 200 Chinese from Amoy on January 3, 1852. Later that year, he brought another 100 or so. Each Chinese was committed to five years' labor for $3.00 a month plus food, clothing, and housing. The employer also paid all transportation costs from China.[38]

In 1855 about 180 more Chinese arrived. King Kamehameha IV stated that those Chinese who had been brought to Hawaii to solve the labor problem had not lived up to expectations. He indicated further that they presented assimilation problems. The King desired that immigrants from other Pacific islands be induced to migrate to rebuild the depleted native Hawaiian population. Others joined in opposition to the Chinese. The president of the agricultural society declared that the Chinese had recently been dismissed from the plantations because they were unmanageable. Yet the Chinese had already become familiar figures in the islands as agriculturalists, bankers, house servants, mechanics, and merchants. They had intermarried with the Hawaiians and Chinese-Hawaiian children were held in high regard. In 1857, when coolie contracts expired, many Chinese moved into the towns amid some resistance. As in the United States, the adjustment to their new environment was not easy since the Hawaiian Chinese were expected to conform to standards set by the dominant society.[39]

Many Hawaiian residents became alarmed during the 1860's as population continued to decline wth resulting labor shortages. Agriculture kept expanding and its need for field hands increased.

TABLE I

POPULATION CHARACTERISTICS, HAWAIIAN ISLANDS,
1860-1900[a]

Year	Hawaiian & Part-Hawaiian	Chinese	Caucasian	Other	Total
1860	66,984	700	1,600	516	69,800
1866	58,795	1,200	2,000	794	62,959
1872	51,531	2,038	2,944	384	56,897
1876	49,500	2,500	3,500	250*	55,750
1900	40,000	26,000	27,000	79,000**	172,000

[a] Ralph S. Kuykendall, *The Hawaiian Kingdom*, II, 177 and III, 116.
* This figure represents 250 Portuguese who have been considered as a separate ethnic group in the islands.
** This encompasses 18,000 Portuguese and 61,000 Japanese.

In 1864, a committee of the Planters' Society recommended that the government consult with planters about labor needs and develop plans to send an agent to China or to India to recruit 300 to 500 laborers. The King appointed a committee which thought the "right kind" of Chinese would make good immigrants. In October, the Bureau of Immigration was created to oversee the importation of laborers. Dr. William Hillebrand was sent to China to locate workers. He sent two shiploads of 522 Chinese, including ninety-five women and three children. They were bound to a five-year term and received lodging and food and a $4 monthly wage plus a $2 bonus at Chinese New Year. During the reign of Kamehameha V (1865-1872), about 1,700 Chinese were transported to Hawaii to work on the sugar plantations.[40]

With the influx of Chinese, the same fears as expressed by Californians increased among whites and hostile newspaper articles appeared. Native Hawaiians also opposed Chinese immigration. This led the Honolulu Chinese merchants on October 29, 1870, to send a letter to a public meeting concerned with contract labor. The merchants pointed out the evils of such labor which, they said, attracted the poorest types from China. They felt a system of free immigration would be more successful in attracting the more desirable kinds of people.[41]

Over the next two decades, the population of the islands almost doubled. By 1896, the total had reached 109,000. The city of Honolulu grew from 15,000 in 1872 to 30,000 in 1896. Most of the Chinese were crowded into the older section of the city. Chinatown in 1872 had an estimated population of 632; this was judged to be 7,693 in 1896.

As the labor contracts expired in 1874, the Hawaiian government arranged for two firms each to bring 100 workers from China. The government paid an advance of $25 per person. One firm met its quota while the second could only import twenty people. Two years later, the government called for 1,400 Chinese. Most of the immigrants of the 1870's came directly from China, although many were fleeing the persecutions of the western United States.[42]

Faced with a supposed flood of immigrants, authorities proposed a plan of restriction. In July, 1883, the King's cabinet council resolved that only a limited number of Chinese could enter Hawaii and developed regulations of enforcement. Only the Pacific Mail Steamship Company and the Occidental and Oriental Steamship Company were authorized carriers. The total number of Chinese in any three-month period could not exceed 600. Emigration from China slackened but numbers from the mainland increased. To meet agriculture's continual needs, labor contractors turned to Germans, Pacific Islanders, Portuguese, and Japanese.[43]

The Hawaiian Chinese never suffered the indignities heaped upon the Chinese on the United States mainland. While there was some heated opposition to the Chinese in Hawaii, this resistance always collapsed in the face of economic necessity for field labor.

CHAPTER III

Closed Arms, Cold Hearts:
Years of Discrimination

DISLIKE AND SUSPICION OF THE CHINESE REMAINED SO POTENT that the next one hundred years could not dissipate it. For instance, in 1943 the Citizens Committee to Repeal Chinese Exclusion asked Congress to admit Chinese immigrants once more. In the midst of World War II, even with China an acknowledged ally, the old arguments against Chinese immigration resurfaced. Racism, based upon cultural and economic fears, still motivated large numbers of Americans. Deviation from the Caucasian standard regarding color and appearance has been the predominant basis for segregation and discrimination in the United States. The Chinese, Japanese, and other Asian groups also suffered because they preferred their own cultural heritage to that of the dominant group. Thus, conflict was inevitable, for white America disdained all immigrants who did not merge with the dominant culture.

Prejudice in the United States has been supported by a nineteenth-century value structure which holds that rural, white, Protestant America is the norm to which all must conform. Many Protestants believed their religion to be superior; the white man's burden is basically an extension of Calvinism. American education has continued to place a preponderant emphasis upon Western civilization. And in day-to-day life, Americans have accepted the idea of the middle-class white as the measure against which success and failure is judged. Against such a scale, Asian civilizations were bound to fail.[1]

The 1943 Citizens Committee received letters reiterating long-standing fears of prejudiced white Americans:

> What you advocate . . . is to the detriment of all American citizens of the white race, and, while I do not question the sincerity of your motives, I think you and your associates who are seeking to repeal the Chinese exclusion act are actually enemies of the American people as we exist today.
>
> If you want a polyglot, mongrel race, then repeal the Chinese Exclusion Act, and amalgamate with the negroes and the Chinese and we will have what I am sure you, in my opinion, are unwittingly working for.[2]

In the 1940's, no less than in the decades of the nineteenth century, the Chinese represented an unknown group for most Americans. Frank Pixley, speaking for San Francisco in 1876, summed up the Pacific Coast prejudice, a view still held in the mid-twentieth century:

> The burden of our accusation against them is that they come in conflict with our labor interests; that they can never assimilate with us; that they are a perpetual, unchanging, and unchangeable alien element that can never become homogeneous; that their civilization is demoralizing and degrading to our people; that they degrade and dishonor labor; that they can never become citizens, and that an alien, degraded labor class, without desire of citizenship, without education, and without interest in the country it inhabits, is an element both demoralizing and dangerous to the community within which it exists.[3]

In January, 1852, outgoing Governor John McDougal of California suggested that the Chinese could contribute in developing the Sacramento and San Joaquin Rivers' delta lands. He called them "one of the most worthy classes of our newly adopted citizens—to whom the climate and character of these lands are peculiarly suited."[4] This initial official friendship disappeared immediately during the debate over the Tingley Coolie Bill and Governor John Bigler's leadership against the Chinese.[5]

The *Daily Alta California* in 1852 noted that growing repression of Chinese miners brought two different motives into conflict. The state government, seeking revenue through taxes and licenses, allowed the Chinese to mine while American miners' resolutions sought to deny this right.[6] The California legislature launched the first of many bills aimed specifically at the Chinese when the Foreign Miners' Tax was set at $3.00 a month. Those arrested could not sue or defend themselves in court. Later modifications restricted the Chinese even more. In 1855, the tax was set at $4.00 a month for foreigners eligible for citizenship; for those not eligible for citizenship, the $4.00 tax increased another $2.00 a month each succeeding year.[7] The Chinese were easy victims of this kind of hostile legislation because in 1790, the First Congress of the United States had declared that only free white persons were eligible for citizenship.[8]

Throughout the 1850's Chinese miners financed, with their taxes, California state and county governments. El Dorado County derived $102,000 from these taxes between 1853 and 1855. Nevada County collected $16,909 from the Chinese in December, 1854, but only $7,142 from property and poll taxes.[9] When increased taxes and violence drove many Chinese out of the mines, California faced a financial crisis for several years.

On January 18, 1855, a convention of Shasta County miners passed resolutions against the Chinese as did many other mining communities during the next few years. As the miners ran out of places to pan for gold, they released their frustrations against the Chinese who eked out their living picking over abandoned claims. The Shasta convention resolved:

That the immense number of Chinamen flocking into this country has become an evil too great to be borne. That it becomes the American miners to take prompt and decisive measures to stop an evil that threatens to overwhelm us;

That it is our opinion that no measures short of prohibition and total expulsion of all Chinamen thence will remedy the evil from which we suffer;

That we, the miners of Shasta County, forbid Chinamen from working in the mines of this county after the 25th of February, 1855;

That we earnestly request the cooperation of the miners of Trinity, Siskiyou, and all other mining counties throughout the State;

That all persons who have Chinamen in their employ working the mines of Shasta County, be requested to notify and dismiss the same on or before the 25th of February.[10]

From 1855 until the end of the decade, Chinese were expelled from one mining camp after another.[11] Their supposed threat to American labor became an early issue in the developing hostility.

The enduring theme of Chinese cultural inferiority was launched in the 1850's. White Americans were equally vocal about the assimilation issue. The *Daily Alta* editorialized in 1853 that it opposed citizenship for

The Chinese are morally a far worse class to have among us than the negro. . . . They do not mix with our people, and it is undesirable that they should, for nothing but degradation can result to us from the contact.[12]

The next year the paper requested that the San Francisco Board of Health establish itself as an instrument of exclusion. The *Daily Alta* declaimed that the Chinese were "generally filthy beyond description."[13] For several months, the paper crusaded against Chinatown. On September 4, 1854, a letter to the editor protested the location of the Chinese in the midst of white people:

They wash in the nude in open air near white men's houses. This is intolerable to our female population.

Mexican dancehalls have been suppressed but the Chinese with their filth, carelessness and outrages of common decency remain. Each day they threaten us with scourge and fire.[14]

When Horace Greeley traveled through California in the late 1850's, he observed that the Chinese were hardly utilized as a part of California's labor force. He reported that the Chinese were confined to exhausted mining areas which, if productive, led the whites to drive them out. Greeley claimed that " 'John' does not seem to be a very bad fellow but he is treated worse than though he were." In his opinion the Chinese were sensual and interested in self-gratification; however, he added that, unlike the whites, Chinese were never seen drunk in public. Greeley concluded that the Chinese would compare well with any other people.[15]

The admitted long-range goal of Westerners was to exclude Chinese from the United States. To accomplish this, Congressional support had to be secured for only that body could enact legislation regulating immigration. Until the 1882 exclusion act, Western state and territorial legislatures tried driving out the Chinese by harassment. They enacted discriminatory measures with limiting clauses of aliens "eligible for citizenship" or "ineligible for citizenship."[16] California, the recipient of most Chinese immigrants, led the way. In 1855, the state taxed each ship a $50.00 head tax on each passenger ineligible for citizenship who was transported to one of its ports. The state courts quickly declared the law unconstitutional.[17]

The California Supreme Court delivered the Chinese to white aggressors during the first decade of anti-Chinese persecution. A white man, convicted of murder, appealed to the Supreme Court in 1854. Chief Justice Hugh Murray delivered the opinion, based on an 1850 statute which provided that "No black, or Mulatto person, or Indian shall be allowed to give evidence in favor of, or against a white man."[18] Murray held that the Chinese came from Asia, earlier known to the Western world as the Indies and therefore were considered to be Indians. He also maintained that the word "white" automatically excluded all but Caucasians from the right of testimony. Even if these points were not valid, he stated, he would rule against the right of Chinese testimony, for not to do so would lead them to demand and receive "all the equal rights of citizenship, and we might soon see them at the polls, in the jury box, upon the bench and in our legislative halls."[19] Following Murray's decision, cases brought to court by the Chinese were usually dismissed when no white witnesses appeared.[20] The guaranteed right of trial by jury was thus generally denied to the Chinese.

The Civil War brought a temporary cessation to the discriminations of the 1850's. About 1867, Western white laborers reopened the anti-coolie movement. Their activities which attracted national attention were sustained for the next decade.

So strong was the hostility towards the Chinese that California refused to ratify the Fourteenth and Fifteenth Amendments for fear the Chinese would thus acquire equal civil rights.[21] Henry H. Haight, successful Democratic candidate, stated at his 1868 gubernatorial inauguration that California opposed Negro and Chinese suffrage. He elaborated, saying that Congress had made no distinction between the two racial groups. He opposed giving the ballot to any "inferior" race. He then declared:

What we desire for the permanent benefit of California is a population of white men, who will make this State their home, bringing up families here, and meet the responsibilities and discharge the duties of freemen. We ought not to desire an effete population of Asiatics for a free State like ours.[22]

Haight and others opposed the Burlingame Treaty of 1868. Californians continued to agitate for modification of the treaty, after its signing, to prevent continued immigration of large numbers of Chinese.[23]

American cultural arguments have long supported the supremacy of the Western world over the Eastern world of China, Japan, and other Asian nations. Americans observed that Chinese living in the United States were not Christians, did not contribute to Western society, lived in crowded areas, and were dangerous health hazards. These "facts" were signs of their inferiority. Even though many Christian churches opened missions in California to save Chinese souls, it was obvious to most whites that salvation was doubtful. The views of William Slocum, a spokesman opposed to business monopoly in 1878, reflect the apprehensions of white society:

> The idea of Christianizing the Chinese is an absurdity. They are more likely to make buddhists of us than we are to make Christians of them. They belong to a dead civilization and they offer nothing to us but the threat of destruction.[24]

In considering educational opportunities for the Chinese, white attitudes reinforced the cult of superiority. California Superintendent of Public Instruction Andrew Moulder expressed this view in his 1859 report:

> Had it been intended by the framers of the law that the children of inferior races should be educated side by side with the whites, it is manifest the annual school census would have included children of all colors.
>
> If this attempt to force Africans, Chinese, and Diggers [Indians] into our white schools is persisted in, it must result in the ruin of our Schools.

Moulder then asked the legislature to create separate schools and to empower him to withhold money from any school district which permitted "inferior children in the common school."[25]

California in 1863-64 made provisions for separate schools with black, Chinese and Indian children excluded from the regular public schools. Local districts had to erect separate facilities; but schools for the minority children were not built and they were denied an education. This was modified in 1866, the children being allowed to attend white schools if the majority of the white parents raised no objections.[26]

During the 1870's, voices of both Chinese and whites occasionally called for educational equality but nothing came of these demands.[27] However, on January 9, 1885, a San Francisco judge ruled that under the Fourteenth Amendment a ten-year-old Chinese girl, Mamie Tape, had the right to attend public school. The judge noted that the California legislature required equal educational facilities for all children and to deny the Chinese this right violated the law and the Constitution. Conscious of potential public wrath, he added that if evil results followed his decision, the fault was not that of the judiciary.[28]

The California State Supreme Court upheld the decision but the legislature had heard the lower court judge. State law was amended to read that school trustees:

> have power to exclude children of filthy or vicious habits, or children suffering from contagious or infectious diseases, and also to establish separate schools for children of Mongolian or Chinese descent. When such separate schools are established, Chinese or Mongolian children must not be admitted into any other school....[29]

Armed with this law, the San Francisco Board of Education created the Oriental School in Chinatown which all Chinese were required to attend. This school later became the center of an international crisis between Japan and the United States.

During the period of intense harassment (1867-1882), various California municipalities, yielding to public pressure, enacted discriminatory measures. It was not by accident that San Francisco led in such legislation for it was here that the largest Chinese community was located. Its Chinatown was the political, economic, and social center of Chinese life in the United States during these years and for a long time after.[30]

The San Francisco Board of Supervisors' Cubic Air Ordinance of July 2, 1870, required 500 cubic feet of air space per occupant in rooming houses. Both landlord and occupant could be charged for violations. At first enforcement was spotty but in 1873, several newspapers started an anti-Chinese agitation. The police chief made 152 arrests in July and 95 in August which led to 177 convictions. No more arrests were made until April, 1876. From April through June, 918 arrests were made. On April 3, 1876, the California legislature made the ordinance state law.[31]

The San Francisco Board of Supervisors in December, 1870, enacted the "basket ordinance" which made it a misdemeanor for any person to carry, while using the sidewalks, baskets suspended from a pole. Arrests were made, Chinese fined the lowest amount—$5.00—and a test case was begun. The state supreme court held that basket-carrying might be a nuisance and the board had the right to protect citizens from such hazards.[32]

On May 26, 1873, San Francisco supervisors enacted three ordinances which were blatantly discriminatory—regarding queues, shipment of human bones, and laundry. The famous Queue Ordinance called for the cutting of the hair of all male prisoners in the county jail to within one inch of the scalp. As indicated earlier, the Mongols had enforced the wearing of queues upon all Chinese males. By the 1870's, Chinese took great pride in their queues and to lose them led to great personal embarrassment. The ordinance was vetoed by the mayor and the board could not muster enough votes to override.[33]

The second ordinance forbade the removal of bodies and bones without the consent of the county coroner. This law was directed at the Chinese custom of sending the bones of the dead back to China for burial with family ancestors.[34]

Also amended was the existing Laundry Ordinance. One amendment required each laundry to pay a $15.00 fee per quarter for each employee. Perhaps the most ingenious piece of discrimination was a second amendment which required each laundry employing one horse-drawn wagon to pay a $2.00 per quarter fee; for those with two wagons, the fee was $4.00 per quarter while those using no wagons paid $15.00 per quarter. The Chinese were the only laundrymen who picked up and delivered by foot. The mayor vetoed this measure too, but the board overrode his veto. When the city tried to enforce the ordinance, the superior court found it unconstitutional.[35]

Following state enactment of the 1876 cubic air law, the

Chinese determined to risk arrest and jail. With the jail overcrowded, in itself an interesting civic violation of the law, the Board of Supervisors pushed through the Queue Ordinance which was vigorously enforced by Sheriff Matthew Nunan. This had the desired effect of keeping the Chinese from wanting to be jailed. When Sheriff Nunan was sued by a Chinese, Ho Ah Kow, Supreme Court Justice Stephen Field, sitting with the U. S. Circuit Court, delivered the opinion in favor of the Chinese. He held that a legislature did not have the authority to cut anyone's hair and that the measure was avowedly discriminatory.[36]

California's legal attacks against the Chinese climaxed with its Second Constitutional Convention in 1879. The convention responded to major economic and social issues of the 1870's. Suffering workers and farmers tried to make scapegoats of the railroads, absentee owners, bankers, and the Chinese. Article XIX of the new constitution entitled "Aliens" was clearly aimed at the Chinese. This hostile article had four sections. The first directed the legislature to protect the state from certain aliens or remove them from the state. Section 2 made it impossible for any corporation to employ directly or indirectly any Chinese or Mongolian. This provision was soon declared unconstitutional for it violated the Burlingame Treaty. Section 3 held that Chinese could not be employed on any California public work except as punishment for crime. The last section discouraged the immigration of foreigners ineligible for citizenship.[37] The constitutional convention was California's last all-out effort to use legal devices to expel the Chinese. Four years later, Congress adopted exclusion as national policy. Westerners then agitated in the halls of Congress rather than in state capitols to keep the Chinese from American shores.

Legal discrimination did not produce quick results. Laborers who feared economic competition and racists who wanted a white America often resorted to violence. Gold brought out the best and worst in men who, in times of stress, rose to a state of high idealism or reverted to savagery. The need for justice in mining camps caused vigilante action to replace absent, or distant, law. San Francisco resorted to vigilance committees three times from 1851 to 1877 because local and state governments seemed corrupt or were not operating in a manner acceptable to certain factions. Californians were not averse to taking the law into their own hands when occasion demanded.[38]

Following the Civil War, raids upon the Chinese occurred with sickening frequency. In January, 1867, contractors building a wharf in San Francisco employed twenty-five to thirty Chinese at one dollar and 12½ cents a day. Fellow white workers threatened violence unless the Chinese were dismissed. When the demands were not met, the white workers stoned the Chinese, driving them away. The rioters prepared to assault the ropewalk at Hunter's Point and the Mission Woolen Mills to run off the Chinese working at those two establishments. The police arrested the rioters who were found guilty and sentenced to jail.[39]

In Los Angeles on October 23, 1871, two Chinese companies allegedly fought over the ownership of a Chinese woman. Arrests were made and the participants released on bail the next day. Fighting broke out again and the police intervened once more. Two officers were wounded and a civilian killed. Within minutes, a mob of some 500 men stormed the Chinese quarter, looted the property, and killed perhaps eighteen people. Fifteen Chinese were hanged from quickly erected gallows. The other deaths occurred when the buildings were burned.[40]

With California state leaders of both major parties espousing strong anti-Chinese positions, violence continued. In May, 1876, citizens of Antioch burned the Chinese quarter.[41] In June, whites burned a Chinese house in Truckee and then shot the Chinese as they tried to escape. Although the town was reported to have been outraged, those arrested were acquitted at the trial. The newspaper correspondent wrote that the "public sanctions the verdict." The *Sacramento Union* wondered what the verdict would have been if the Chinese had burned out the whites.[42]

Those responsible for the Truckee massacre were reported to have been members of the Order of Caucasians, an organization founded in Gilroy, California, for the purpose of aiding "all white men and women in securing work at living prices when such work is needed and the persons are competent in place of employment of Chinese."[43] The Order of Caucasians in 1877 was accused of violence at Chico, California, where there had been several attempts to burn both the old and new Chinatowns. On March 15, three Chinese were shot, two others fatally wounded and their cabins set on fire. Two days later, Chico's leading citizens received notices: "Get rid of your Chinese help within fifteen days or suffer the consequences." Eleven men were arrested and found guilty of these crimes and for making threats against the white establishment.[44]

The formation of the Workingmen's Party was the capstone of the efforts of California laborers to safeguard their economic interests. On July 23, 1877, a mass meeting on sand lots in front of the San Francisco city hall extended sympathy to Eastern railroad workers. During the course of the meeting, anti-coolie agitators called for action against the Chinese. Part of the crowd left to burn Chinese wash houses. The next day San Francisco merchants formed a Committee of Public Safety and a "pick handle brigade" to protect the Pacific Mail Steamship Company docks and other private property. On the night of July 25 there was some incendiarism but the "pick handle brigade" held fast and mob action quickly dissipated.[45]

One of the brigade members, Dennis Kearney, joined the newly formed Workingmen's Party of California and soon emerged as its leader. He was a spellbinding speaker with but few themes—corrupt politicians, criminal capitalists, and alien Chinese. From the streets of San Francisco, Kearney, a demagogue feared greatly by the establishment, exhorted that "the Chinese must go."[46] During a sand-lot speech in December, 1877, his listeners cheered when he exclaimed, "We will drive out the Chinese if we have to destroy the whole state of California."[47]

The 1877-78 state legislature approved a referendum on the Chinese immigration question. The vote, part of the regular 1879 state election, was 883 in favor of immigration and 154,658 against. Only 5,884 people voting in the general election chose not to express an opinion on immigration.[48] What state officials did not say, while commenting on the overwhelming opposition, was that every state ballot had only the words "Against Chinese Immigration" and a place to vote. If a voter wished to vote for the Chinese, he had to scratch out the word "Against" and add "For."[49]

In the face of such antagonism and confronted with the same economic conditions as white workers, the Chinese moved throughout the West. But they did not escape the white man's wrath. In November, 1880, the Chinese minister protested to Secretary of State William Evarts about the outrage visited upon the Chinese in Denver, Colorado, where property was destroyed and one person killed. Subsequent investigation showed that the Chinese had been placed in jail for their protection and while they were locked up, a mob destroyed the property of 400 Chinese at an estimated loss of over $50,000.[50]

On September 2, 1885, a tragic end to an unsuccessful strike by white miners in Rock Springs, Wyoming, occurred. A group of some 150 armed miners attacked the Chinese workers in a barrage that lasted ten hours. Twenty-eight Chinese were killed and another fifteen were wounded. Property loss was estimated to be about $150,000. Since Wyoming was federal territory, Congress had to consider the issue of compensation. Many Congressmen claimed that if the Chinese had not been there the tragedy would not have occurred. This was, in their eyes, further reason for extending exclusion. Other Congressmen, expressing genuine sorrow, attempted to pass legislation providing compensation. Even with these attempts, coupled with the protestations from the Chinese Legation, there was no remuneration.[51]

On September 5, 1885, a band of whites killed two Chinese hop pickers in Squk Valley, Washington Territory. General unemployment in the territory led to demands for complete expulsion of the Chinese. At Tacoma, in November, the Knights of Labor, supported by Mayor R. Jacob Weisback, a German immigrant and a member of the Knights, led in shipping the Chinese out of town. A few days later, the empty Chinese buildings were burned.

In Seattle in February, 1886, the Chinese were driven from their homes and taken to the docks for transportation to San Francisco. The anti-Chinese committee provided tickets and 193 Chinese sailed. When the sheriff's forces arrived a fight ensued; one member of the mob was killed and two were wounded.[52]

Trouble also broke out the same year at Douglas Island near Juneau, Alaska, where about 100 Chinese were attacked and set drift in the ocean.[53] Chang Yen Hoon, China's Minister to the United States, in his protests to the State Department summed up the attitude of his government. He was quite pointed in his observations that not a single murderer of his compatriots had been punished. In the 1885-86 riots, the Chinese had suffered the loss of fifty lives and $250,000,000.[54]

Grover Cleveland in a message to Congress protested the cruel treatment of the Chinese, but the President used the situation to suggest that immigration should be curtailed since they could not be assured protection here.

Much of this violence can be traced to race prejudice and competition of labor, which can not, however, justify the opposition of strangers whose safety is guaranteed by our treaty with China equally with the most favored nations.

In opening our vast domain to alien elements the purpose of our law givers was to invite assimilation and not to provide an arena for endless antagonism. The paramount duty of maintaining public order and defending the interests of our own people may require the adoption of measures of restrictions, but they should not tolerate the oppression of individuals of a friendly race. . . .[55]

The Chinese made official protests and were usually informed that if an injustice happened in a state it was a local matter over which the federal government had no control. If the incident took place in federal territory, the response was that the matter must be settled in the courts. A typical response from California came after a protest was lodged against the driving of the Chinese from a small Sutter County community. The Chinese Consul in reporting to the legation in Washington noted that he had requested help from Governor George Stoneman: "His reply is same in all cases like this: the sheriff of Sutter County has not notified me of his inability to enforce the law in his county."[56]

American labor through the years opposed Chinese immigration because it posed a threat to union members. Samuel Gompers, leader of the American Federation of Labor, accepted without question the view of Chinese inferiority. His 1901 presidential report stated that "there cannot be any honest division of opinion on Chinese exclusion." Gompers opposed the Chinese, and later the Japanese, on both racist and economic grounds. He held, in accepting the melting-pot theory of immigration, that Asians were unfit and that obstacles between white and yellow were too great to surmount. He knew that the yellow race naturally lied, cheated, and murdered. He maintained that Chinatowns were centers of passion and evils such as opium smoking, gambling, and prostitution. He accepted unquestioningly the view that Chinese "love to prey upon American girls." He found evidence of this in the fact that the Chinese left their own women in China. Gompers expressed for American labor and for many East Coast racists what had been traditional West Coast arguments against the Chinese and Japanese. Economically, he feared them because they offered competition.[57]

According to one interpretation, Gompers's views gained widespread acceptance because he described in simplistic terms what had gone wrong in America. It became reasonable to blame the foreigner for the ills of society. People from all walks of life also believed that races inherited certain moral and intellectual characteristics.[58]

From almost the first moment the Chinese landed in San Francisco in the 1850's, they were subjected to harsh treatment. The aim was to exclude them from the United States because of basically racist fears and beliefs. Economic and social problems from time to time led whites to give vent to their hatred through vocal or physical acts. It was not until the United States Congress enacted legislation leading to the complete exclusion of Chinese immigrants that tensions on the West Coast decreased. Tragically, one important reason for the decrease of hostility was the increased antagonism against the Japanese who had become the new hate objects.

CHAPTER IV

The Chinese and the Marketplace

THE CHINESE CAME IN THE 1850's, AS DID OTHER ARGONAUTS, in search of gold. Arriving late in the Mother Lode, they were few in numbers compared to miners from the United States or Europe. The Chinese adapted easily to the difficult conditions of working in cold rivers under a boiling sun. Contemporary observers claimed they were not adept at using the pick and shovel or mechanical mining devices needed for larger claims.[1] J. D. Borthwick, one of the more competent chroniclers, noted that they worked in gangs rather than individually or in small groups. He reported the building of wing dams—one of which was "two or three hundred yards in length . . . of large pine trees laid one on the top of the other."[2] These dams diverted the river from the gravel bar which then lay exposed to the hands and tools of the miners who grubbed for the gold. During the years of gold fever, the Chinese did not fight over claims or join other miners in the rush to a new field. They worked abandoned claims or poor "$2 a day" claims. If they made a big strike, chances were they would be driven off.[3]

The Chinese found area after area closed to them by the frustrated white miners. Their seeming backwardness was the consequence of white discrimination. They had to be prepared to abandon their claims quickly or risk being killed. High-cost mining equipment required a fairly permanent installation. The Chinese therefore relied primarily upon the portable rocker which could be transported easily.[4]

In 1850, only about 500 Chinese were listed among the

57,787 miners. Most preferred to work in San Francisco.[5] By 1852 this situation had changed. Their influx coincided with the beginning of company mining and of difficult times for the independent American miner.

By 1860, quartz and hydraulic mining companies dominated gold production. In 1860 there were 82,573 miners, of whom 24,282 were Chinese.[6] Ten years later there were only 30,330 miners. The Chinese numbered 17,363; some still struggled over worked-out placer claims while others turned to hard-rock mining and the construction and maintenance of ditches for hydraulic operations. During the heyday of quartz mining the Chinese did most of the construction work. They began leaving the mines for other occupations just as the Civil War was ending and California's economy was expanding in new directions.

The Chinese miners, as did their white counterparts, moved throughout the western territories. A large number left California for the southern Oregon gold fields. Discriminatory patterns were developing there when gold was discovered on British Columbia's Fraser River. Most white miners rushed to Canada, leaving the Oregon claims for the Chinese. A sizeable number of Chinese followed to Canada; others went to the Rocky Mountain strikes in Colorado, Idaho, and Montana. As in California, they picked over abandoned claims in these areas for many years.[7] They also worked in quicksilver mines, particularly in the Lake County area of California (1875-1900) and in the coal mines at Rock Springs, Wyoming, where the 1885 violence occurred, and in other coal areas in Wyoming and Utah.[8]

During the Civil War, Congress approved the central transcontinental railroad route. The Union Pacific won the construction contract westward from Omaha while the Central Pacific was to build from California. The Central Pacific's search for a sufficient labor force and the Chinese response is one of the familiar stories about their contribution to the United States.

In 1858, the California Central Pacific Railroad employed Chinese to replace white workers who had gone to the Fraser River goldfields. The *Sacramento Union* reported that the company had

some fifty Chinamen employed, and they find them very good working hands. They do not work as rapidly as the white men, but they keep constantly at it from sunrise until sunset. The experiment bids fair to demonstrate that Chinese laborers can be profitably employed in grading railroads in California....[9]

Chinese also helped build the San Jose to San Francisco railroad.[10]

On January 8, 1863, Leland Stanford, Governor of California and President of the Central Pacific Railroad Company, turned over the first shovelful of dirt at the foot of K Street in Sacramento, California. The company's experiment to have various sections of track constructed by subcontract proved uneconomical and inefficient since each subcontractor competed for the same supplies and laborers. Soon, Charles Crocker & Co. became the prime construction contractor. After two years, the Central Pacific had less than fifty miles of operating track. J. H. Strobridge, the construction superintendent for Charles Crocker, demanded 5,000 more workers. Advertisements, circulated throughout every post office in California, offered premium wages for laborers. Only about 800 men answered the call.[11] Former Governor Frederick Low, United States Commissioner charged with overseeing the construction, revealed that Crocker had told him that he had several times suggested to Strobridge that they "must come to Chinese." Strobridge had replied, "I will not boss Chinese. I will not be responsible for the work done on the road by Chinese labor." Low recollected that the railroad was paying $45 a month and board to white labor and even so, construction had come to a standstill. In February, 1865, Strobridge hired fifty Chinese to fill dump carts, but said they could not drive horses or strike the drills. Within six months, the Chinese were doing all jobs on the road. They were at that time paid $31 a month without board.[12] The standard wage then for common labor in California was about $25 a month.[13]

The Central Pacific's need for a large labor supply coincided with the Chinese exodus from the mines. The February experiment and subsequent trials were so successful that by early fall in 1865 the railroad had employed 3,000 Chinese. Agents of Sisson, Wallace & Co., a San Francisco mercantile firm, went through the Mother Lode hiring Chinese. Estimates vary as to the total number employed on the road, ranging from 8,000 to 10,000.[14] The railroad, experiencing labor shortages before and racing with the Union Pacific to reap high federal subsidies for every mile of track laid, also engaged merchants to import labor from China. Charles Crocker testified to the Joint Committee that he had contracted with Cornelius Koopmanschap for as many as 2,000 workers from China but that he had secured only 500.[15] Crocker then turned to Sisson, Wallace & Co. to handle overseas recruitment.[16] The labor this firm brought from China came too late to be of value in the construction of the transcontinental railroad, but played a significant role as the Central Pacific and its successor, the Southern Pacific, expanded its network of tracks throughout the Far West.

Sisson, Wallace & Co., after locating Chinese workers, formed work gangs of twenty-five to thirty men. Each gang had its own head man who worked with a white foreman who oversaw several gangs. Each payday, the head man divided the gang's earnings among its members.[17] The Central Pacific first paid Chinese workers $26 a month—a $1.00 a day, the "standard wage for Chinese at that time."[18] The pay was raised to $30 and then to $35. Even so, on June 24, 1867, in the High Sierras, the Chinese struck for $40 a month and an eight-hour day. Crocker cut off their food supply and the strike ended.[19]

At the end of the line, Chinese gangs worked hard. Each

gang had a cook who prepared meals and kept bath water hot. The gang's head man, in addition to keeping accounts, bought provisions and other supplies, the cost of which was deducted from each individual's monthly earnings. The Chinese labored from sunrise to sunset six days a week. After expenses, each man cleared from $25 to $30 a month.

The diet was strictly Chinese: "dried oysters, dried cuttle fish, dried fish, sweet rice, crackers, dried bamboo, salted cabbage, Chinese sugar, dried fruits and vegetables, vermicelli, dried seaweed, Chinese bacon, dried abalone, dried mushrooms, peanut oil, tea, rice, pork, and poultry."[20] Dried foods, prior to refrigeration, were commonly used the world over. The Chinese also drank gallons of lukewarm tea. The Crocker company provided low cloth tents but many Chinese preferred to live in dugouts or to burrow into the earth.[21]

About the time the Chinese gangs demonstrated their worth, construction crews reached Cape Horn, a perpendicular rocky promontory in the Sierra Nevada, 1,400 feet above the American River. Chinese drillers were lowered over the side of the wall in baskets to drill holes for black gunpowder explosives. Once the charge was set and lit, they were hauled quickly to the top as the charge exploded below.[22] The road inched on through hard granite. A year more was spent hacking the roadbed through the mountains and still the summit was not reached.

In December, 1866, during one of the worst recorded winters, Crocker ordered an attack on the Donner Summit. The Chinese built a settlement beneath the many feet of snow. They extended chimneys and air shafts as the snow piled up, but other than that, remained buried, living by lantern light. Tunnels extended from the camps to the rock portal of the railroad tunnel. Crews continued drilling, blasting, and hauling rock through the winter.[23]

The following spring, the assault continued unabated.

Recalling this event before the joint Congressional committee several years later, Crocker testified that the Chinese

... are equal to the best white men. We tested that in the Summit tunnel, which is in the very hardest granite. We had a shaft down in the center. We were cutting both ways from the bottom of that shaft. The company were in a very great hurry for that tunnel, as it was the key to the position across the mountains, and they urged me to get the very best Cornish miners and put them in the tunnel so as to hurry it, and we did so. We went to Virginia City and got some Cornish miners out of those mines and paid them extra wages. We put them into one side of the shaft, the heading leading from one side, and we had Chinamen on the other side. We measured the work every Sunday morning; and the Chinamen without fail always outmeasured the Cornish miners; that is to say, they would cut more rock in a week than the Cornish miners did, and there it was hard work, steady pounding on the rock, bone-labor. The Chinese were skilled in using the hammer and drill; and they proved themselves equal to the very best Cornish miners in that work. They are very trusty, they are very intelligent, and they live up to their contracts.[24]

In the summer of 1868, the railroad broke through the Sierra Nevada Mountains, surprising those who predicted that the Union Pacific would meet the Central Pacific at the California-Nevada line. The relatively flat terrain of Nevada then lay before the Big Four crews. The subjugation of the California mountains had been possible only because of Chinese labor. As the two railroads approached each other in Utah, any final doubts of their ability were ended when Central Pacific crews laid ten miles and fifty-six feet of track in one twelve-hour period, beating the best Union Pacific had been able to do by two miles.[25]

With the driving of the Golden Spike at Promontory Point, the Big Four, Charles Crocker, Mark Hopkins, Henry Huntington, and Leland Stanford, turned to other rail construction projects. During the next nine years "Crocker's Pets" built slightly more than 1,800 miles of track in California alone.[26] Throughout the West, the Chinese railroad worker proved invaluable.

California farmers also turned to former Chinese miners

to provide needed labor. From Spanish and Mexican days, California agriculture was a large-scale operation. Unlike China's small-plot, hand-to-mouth-existence farming, the California Chinese were generally engaged in enterprises producing goods for sale. Carey McWilliams's term, "Factories in the Field," is most descriptive of the situation. Agoston Haraszthy, the father of California viticulture, introduced Chinese workers to northern California vineyards in the 1860's employing about 100 at $1.00 a day. When they were not needed by his Buena Vista Vinicultural Society, they were hired out to other vineyards or as harvest laborers.[27]

During the 1870's and long after, California farmers primarily needed casual harvest labor and not permanent workers. Seasonal employment, a pattern which has continued to the present, has led Western agriculture to rely upon cheap, unattached workers. In the 1870's, the Chinese met the need; later it was the Japanese, Filipinos, "Okies," and Mexicans. By 1880, seasonal farm work was the third largest Chinese occupation in California, surpassed only by mining and domestic service.[28]

During the 1870's, wheat was a major California commodity grown in the Great Central Valley. The abundant harvest needed seasonal workers. George D. Robert of the Tidewater Reclamation Company told the joint Congressional committee that his company placed great reliance upon the Chinese:

I will state one instance where we gave white labor a very fair test a few years ago. We had a very large wheatfield. It was harvesttime, and the superintendent wrote down to send him up a couple of hundred white men. I went to all the labor institutions here and employed men of all kind, of all nations. We gave them the usual country wages whatever it was, $35 or $40 a month, I think. We had to abandon it after trying a couple of weeks, and losing a great deal of wheat by the experiment. Those men would not work more than two or three days, or a week, and then they would quit. I kept the steamer here almost loaded sending up white men, but they would leave as fast as I sent them. I then went to a Chinaman and told him that I wanted to contract for binding and shocking wheat. We did the reaping by machine. I made the contract at so much per acre. The weather was warm. They went up there. Several hundred of them came. We had one or two hundred acres that had been reaped, and needed putting up very badly; and the next morning it was all in shock. The Chinamen did the work that night. They did the work well and faithfully, and of course we abandoned white labor. Since then we have done all machine-work with white men, but field-work of the kind we would contract with Chinamen to do.[29]

Another contemporary account by a friend of the Chinese paid tribute to their value as farmhands:

On many ranches all the laborers are people whose muscles were hardened on the little farms in China. . . . We find that the dairy men are largely employing this class of help. . . . Visit a hop plantation in the picking season, and count its 50, 60, or 70 pickers in the garb of the eastern Asiatics, working steadily and noiselessly on from morning till night, gathering, curing and sacking the crop. . . . Go through the fields of strawberries and other small fruits, . . . the vineyards and orchards, and you will learn most of these fruits are gathered or boxed for market by this same people. . . .[30]

The railroad made it possible for horticulturists to ship fruit from the West Coast to Eastern markets. The actual contribution of the Chinese, acknowledged experts in fruit growing, is almost impossible to assess. The *Pacific Rural Press* on two occasions in 1893 reported:

The availability of Chinese labor gave the fruit growers hope. They extended their operations and the Chinese proved equal to all that had been expected of them. They became especially clever in the packing of fruit; in fact, the Chinese have become the only considerable body of people who understand how to pick fruit for Eastern shipment.

. . . .

The Chinese are the mainstay of the orchardist and thus far it must be said the only supply of labor which he can depend upon. They are expert pickers and packers of fruit and may be relied upon to work steadily through the season. It is difficult to see how our annual fruit crop could be harvested and prepared for market without the Chinamen.[31]

Ironically, in 1893, the year following the passage of the Geary Act excluding Chinese laborers, California orchardists acknowledged their complete reliance upon Chinese help for survival.

In addition to the Chinese contribution to agriculture, tribute is due them for their reclamation work. America's great food basket of today, the California Delta of the Sacramento and San Joaquin Rivers, as well as many other areas of the Great Valley, was made productive by Chinese labor which built levees, drainage ditches, and irrigation systems.[32]

Near most California cities in the nineteenth century, Chinese truck gardeners and flower growers operated tiny but efficient plots. Henryk Sienkiewicz, a Polish writer, has left a description of the San Francisco truck gardens, where the Chinese lived in little huts in the midst of their crops. Every morning their fresh vegetables were peddled door to door in the city. The gardeners tilled the soil with care, endlessly. Sienkiewicz wrote:

. . . whoever goes to the outskirts of the city will perceive at the ends of the unfinished streets, on the hills, valleys, and slopes, on the roadsides, in fact, everywhere, small vegetable gardens encircling the city with one belt of greenness. The ant-like labor of the Chinese has transformed the sterile sand into the most fertile black earth. . . . The fruits and vegetables, raspberries, and strawberries under the care of Chinese gardeners grow to a fabulous size. I have seen strawberries as large as small pears and heads of cabbage four times the size of European heads, and pumpkins the size of our wash tubs. . . .[33]

South of San Francisco along the peninsula, the Chinese started the flower industry, specializing in asters and chrysanthemums. As late as the 1960's, the Chinese were the prime growers of asters; earlier the Japanese had become the major producers of chrysanthemums.[34] The *San Francisco Chronicle* described a 1902 scene at the Southern Pacific railroad station:

Chinese with great baskets like lidless trunks came ambling from the station, 8 or 10 of them, each with his offering of fresh flowers wherewith to pile high the light burden to be borne up Third Street by the express wagons.[35]

The San Francisco Bay Area Chinese turned to surrounding waters as another source of livelihood. In the days before man killed off most of the marine life in the bay, Chinese fishing villages dotted the shoreline. An interesting description of such a village appeared in *Chambers's Journal* in 1854:

Many of our readers may not be aware that on the south side of Rincon Point San Francisco, near the mouth of Mission Creek, there is a settlement of Chinese well worth a visit. It consists of about one hundred and fifty inhabitants, who are chiefly engaged in fishing. They have twenty-five boats, some of which may be seen at all hours moving over the waters—some going to, others returning from the fishing-grounds. The houses are placed in a line on each side of the one street of the village, and look neat and comfortable. Here and there, a group is seen making fish-lines, and with their rude machines, stacking in heaps the quantities of fish which, lying on all sides around, dry in the sun, and emit an ancient and fish-like odour. The fish which they catch consist of sturgeon, rates, and shark, and large quantities of herring. The latter are dried whole, while the larger are cut into thin pieces. When they are sufficiently dry, they are packed in barrels, boxes, or sacks, and sent into town to be disposed of to those of their countrymen who are going to the mines or are bound upon long voyages. An intelligent Chinaman told us that the average yield of their fishing a day was about three thousand pounds, and that they found ready sale for them at five dollars the hundred pounds . . .[36]

By 1880, the Chinese, fairly well excluded from salmon fishing, were active in fishing for sturgeon. The San Francisco dealers who handled the dried-fish market for the Chinese communities in the West processed halibut, bluefish, redfish, yellowtail, rockfish, rock cod, flounder, squid, and the like.[37]

The Chinese also fished for shrimp and abalone. By 1897 there were twenty-six Chinese shrimp camps on San Francisco Bay. In 1930 there were still fourteen. After being cooked, the shrimp was dried. In 1882, the price for fresh shrimp was 4¢ a pound while dried meat sold for 5¢ to

8¢. The amount caught exceeded local demands and consequently there grew a good export business to the Far East and the Hawaiian Islands.[38] Abalones were prized both for meat and shells. The catch was dried and shipped to China. In 1879 the meat brought $38,880 while the shells, used as inlay in Chinese lacquer work, earned $88,825.[39]

Local industries, which met Pacific Coast market needs, prospered until national producers reached California markets by railroad. Many Pacific Coast operators attempted to meet the influx of competition by using inexpensive labor. Once more, the Chinese proved to be the dependable workers.

The cigar industry also turned early to the use of Chinese.[40] They were also essential in the woolen mills. Chinese firms and laborers dominated the manufacture of ready-made clothes. As the clothing industry moved from home work to a routinized factory system, the Chinese proved they could readily adapt to such a change.[41] They also provided essential labor for the San Francisco boot, shoe, and slipper industries.[42] Wherever there was a labor need—construction, agricultural, or industrial—the Chinese demonstrated their competence. Employer after employer indicated his preference for white labor if it were available. However, white workers did not want to engage in menial tasks and those who had to do so proved unreliable.

Any person, when asked what kind of work the Chinese do in the United States, is likely to name one of three stereotypes—domestic servant, laundryman, or restaurateur. Nineteenth-century Chinese turned to these jobs, in part because of exclusion from certain occupations and in part because they gravitated to jobs where they would not be subject to competition and discrimination.

The West used Chinese extensively as domestic servants. There were few women on the frontier but their traditional chores—cleaning, washing, ironing, and cooking—still remained. George F. Seward estimated that there must have been about 5,000 Chinese house servants in San Francisco in 1876.[43] He concluded that this work, when compared to the economic importance of railroads, mines, and fields, appeared to have little effect on the community, but thought if the Chinese were suddenly removed as servants most whites would become more aware of their contribution.[44]

As miners poured into California, they discovered they had to wash their own clothes or find someone else to do it. They first hired Mexican and Indian women and even sent laundry to Hawaii and China.[45] Bancroft reports that Wah Lee set up the first "wash-house establishment" in 1851. Others quickly followed.[46] The *New York Illustrated News* in 1853 described a California Chinese laundry:

What a truly industrious people they are! At work, cheerfully and briskly at ten o'clock at night. Huge piles of linens and underclothing, disposed in baskets about the room, near the different ironers. Those at work dampening and ironing—peculiar processes both. A bowl of water is standing by the ironer's side, as in ordinary laundries, but used very differently. Instead of dipping the fingers in the water and then snapping them over dry clothes, the operator puts his head in the bowl, fills his mouth with water, and then blows so the water comes from his mouth in a *mist*, resembling the emission of steam from an escapepipe, at the same time so directing his head that the mist is scattered all over the place he is about to iron. He then seizes his flat iron. It is a vessel resembling a small deep metallic washbasin having a highly polished flat bottom and a fire kept burning continually in it. Thus, they keep the iron hot without running to the fire every five minutes and spitting on the iron to ascertain whether it is still hot.[47]

The laundry, a visible and tangible sign of Chinese in a community, was subject to attack when whites went on racist rampages. This was the one occupation that first escaped the geographical limits of the Far West. By the 1870's there were Chinese laundries in Chicago, St. Louis, Baltimore, and New York.[48] As the Chinese moved east, they set up businesses which did not need excessive capital. Sung describes the motivations driving Chinese laundry owners:

They were independent and self-sufficient. They were free from the insecurity of unemployment, cutbacks, layoffs, and business cycles. They answered only to themselves and their customers, and when these were satisfied, they did not suffer the pangs of hunger. Their fortunes depended upon their own initiative and efforts, and the Chinese were resourceful and hard-working.[49]

At the turn of this century the Chinese hand laundries were a familiar sight in most American cities with the workers toiling long hours into the night. New arrivals found in laundering one way to begin life here. In 1950 Chicago had 430 Chinese laundries as well as 167 restaurants, 21 grocery stores, 30 general merchandise stores, 10 food manufacturing concerns and 11 gift shops, all run by Chinese.[50] Recently the small Chinese laundry has been disappearing, as have many other small businesses in the United States. Profits have diminished because of steam laundries operating on a large scale, the home automatic washer and dryer units, and commercial laundromats.

Most American cities have at least one Chinese restaurant. From the days of their first migration to this country, the Chinese have cooked for others in homes, ranch houses, mess halls, or in their own restaurants. In many early California mining communities, the Chinese restaurant was the only place to eat where the food was plentiful and good. The Chinese had a reputation as gourmet cooks and the banquets of San Francisco's Chinatown, duplicated now by excellent Chinese restaurants throughout the nation, were noted as delights not to be missed.[51] A San Francisco banquet of the imperial style would consist of at least three different phases:

with a half hour recess to an ante-room to smoke and talk, and to listen to music. Each phase of the dinner consisted of from a dozen to twenty different courses. Included in the menu were such items as sharks fin, stewed pigeon with bamboo soup, fish sinews with ham, stewed chicken with watercress, seaweed, stewed ducks, bamboo soup, birds-nest soup, and tea.

There were also Chinese teahouses serving luncheon and a Sunday brunch. Tea and dim sum were mainstays on the menu. Dim sum is a steamed pasty dough stuffed with meat, shrimp, or a steamed bun with pork, mashed lotus seed, or brown sugar.[52]

The two most familiar dishes are chop suey and chow mein. Like the martini, the origin of these two dishes is unknown. The Chinese of San Francisco, Chicago, and New York all claim that chop suey originated in their city. The basic story is that Li Hung Chang, China's viceroy and foreign minister in 1896, returned from a good-will mission to Russia via the United States. It was discovered that he preferred simple assorted vegetable dishes with bits of meat. It became known as chop suey, Cantonese for miscellaneous mixture.[53] Regardless of origin, the popularity of the dish spread throughout the nation. Chow mein is reported to have been discovered when a Chinese cook dropped some noodles into deep fat by mistake. Chow mein consists of meat or fish, bean sprouts, onion, and celery served over the deep-fat fried noodles.[54]

Chinese restaurants, scattered through the cities of America, have provided economic success and security for Chinese of the second and third generation. They have also furnished a financial base for the younger Chinese to move into other professions and occupations.

In the years since World War II, the Chinese have escaped the occupational stereotypes and have proven their competencies in many areas of this country's economic life. Their abilities have been such as to overcome previous discrimination. Positions in Caucasian firms, formerly closed, have now become available. The racism experienced by Pardee Lowe, second-generation California Chinese, is disappearing, but there are unfortunately still some instances. Lowe wanted to find summer employment instead of going to Chinese school. He approached a San Francisco bank in reply to classified ads for boys between the ages of 12 and

16. At his first interview, he was told that all the jobs had been taken. He checked the papers and saw that the advertisements continued to appear. The impact of color and being Chinese surfaced into awareness:

The feeling was intensified as I made the round of the other nine firms. Everywhere I was greeted with perturbation, amusement, pity or irritation—and always with identically the same answer. "Sorry," they invariably said, "the position has just been filled." My jaunty self-confidence soon wilted. I sensed something was radically, fundamentally wrong. It just didn't seem possible that overnight all of the positions could have been occupied, particularly not when everybody spoke of a labor shortage. Suspicion began to dawn. What had Father said? "American firms do not customarily employ Chinese."[55]

The Chinese still have difficulty with some color-sensitive labor unions, particularly on the Pacific Coast. Hawaiian unions have led the way in being blind to color and race, providing apprentice training to those who qualify. The Chinese have been successful in the business and professional world. In addition to a thriving restaurant enterprise, the import and export business, retail stores, some maritime enterprises and Chinese-American banks demonstrate the new avenues open to Chinese. In the professional fields, Chinese physicians, dentists, engineers, and scientists have established successful careers.[56]

The Chinese, members of the American pluralistic society, have made outstanding contributions to economic enterprises, particularly in the development of the Western states and Hawaii. In more recent times, their economic contributions have followed patterns similar to other well-established immigrant groups.

CHAPTER V

Chinese Immigration, 1880's-1960's
From Exclusion to Parity

ON MAY 6, 1882, PRESIDENT CHESTER ARTHUR SIGNED THE Chinese Exclusion Act, the goal long sought by the Pacific Coast. The law excluded both skilled and unskilled laborers for ten years. All other Chinese entering the United States had to have identification certificates, issued by the Chinese government.[1] This Congressional act was the first departure from the American tradition of keeping the country a haven for the oppressed of all nations. The legislation of 1882 excluding the immigration of people possessing particular racial characteristics led directly to the immigration quota system in the 1920's.[2]

Confusion quickly developed as to what the act meant and how its attending penalties were to be enforced. Western exclusionists felt the law was full of loopholes since West Coast ports still admitted many Chinese into this country. Among these were merchants, scholars, and ministers who retained the right of entry. Suspicious minds believed the Chinese were thwarting the law. In 1884, President Arthur signed a measure providing for further restrictions. It became more difficult for resident Chinese of the United States to return after visits to the homeland; additionally, the definition of merchant was more tightly drawn.[3] The 1884 act was the first of many refinements. In 1888, President Grover Cleveland signed the Scott Act, a measure of outright persecution. This law prohibited resident Chinese laborers from returning to this country after a visit to China unless they possessed lawful wives, children, or parents in the United States, or owned property valued at $1,000.[4]

The restrictions proved effective. During the 1880's, 61,711 Chinese arrived at American ports, a 50 percent reduction from the previous decade. The United States Census showed the Chinese population had increased by 42,256 during the 1870's. The total increase in the next decade was only 2,023.[5]

With the continuation of restriction, the total number admitted between 1890 and 1900 dropped to 14,799, 76 percent less than the previous decade and 88 percent less than in the 1870's. Those still admitted included Chinese government officials, scholars, merchants, travelers, and persons in transit across the United States to Europe. The total Chinese population in 1900 was 89,863; this was 17,625 fewer than in 1890.[6]

Faced with the expiration of the 1882 act, Congress enacted in 1892 the Geary Act which continued existing regulatory laws for another ten years. The burden of proof as to right of residence belonged to the Chinese. Those illegally in the United States were subject to imprisonment and deportation. All Chinese laborers in the United States had one year to apply for a certificate of residence. Failure to do so resulted in deportation.[7] The Chinese protested the Geary Act in the courts. They lost a test case in 1893 when the United States Supreme Court held that Congress could exclude or expel aliens and could require registration. Deportation was a valid consequence, said the court.[8]

When the Hawaiian Islands, with their growing Chinese population, were annexed to the United States in 1898, Congress prohibited further Chinese immigration to the islands except as permitted under existing United States law. Chinese laborers of Hawaii were prohibited from moving to the mainland. In 1900, the Geary Act provisions of registration and deportation were extended to the islands.[9]

As the expiration of the Geary Act approached, the Chinese exclusion issue reclaimed national attention. The A. F. of L. in 1900, under the leadership of Samuel Gompers, an immigrant himself, called for stronger Chinese exclusion laws. James D. Phelan, Democratic mayor of San Francisco, a progressive in domestic political reform, commenced his long career of hostility toward Asians. The immigration matter assumed such national importance that President Theodore Roosevelt stated in his first annual message in December, 1901:

> Not only must our labor be protected by the tariff, but it should also be protected so far as it is possible from the presence in this country of any laborers brought over by contract, or of those who, coming freely, yet represent a standard of living so depressed that they can undersell our men in the labor market and drag them to a lower level. I regard it as necessary, with this end in view, to re-enact immediately the law excluding Chinese laborers, and to strengthen it wherever necessary in order to make its enforcement entirely effective.[10]

Congress passed legislation in 1902 continuing existing legislation.[11]

In January, 1904, China gave formal notice that it planned to terminate the 1894 treaty the following December. Since by this treaty China had accepted exclusion legislation, this announcement placed in doubt all immigration regulations. To overcome this problem, Congress amended the 1902 act to continue all laws "regulating, suspending, or prohibiting the coming of Chinese persons or persons of Chinese descent into the United States, and the residence of such persons therein," and to include sections of the Scott Act of 1888. The amendment extended these provisions to

> the island territory under the jurisdiction of the United States, and prohibit the immigration of Chinese laborers, not citizens of the United States, from such island territory to the mainland territory of the United States, whether in such island territory at the time of cession or not, and from one portion of the island territory of the

United States to another portion of said island territory: Provided, however, That said laws shall not apply to the transit of Chinese laborers from one island to another island of the same group; and any islands within the jurisdiction of any State or the district of Alaska shall be considered a part of the mainland under this section.[12]

With this enactment, exclusion was completed.

✤　＊　＊　✤

The treatment of Chinese immigrants by immigration officials during these years was criticized in many quarters. The fairly complex Chinese identification certificate and registration procedures made harassment easy. Returning Chinese residents were subjected to long periods of questioning on the premise that they were seeking illegal entry. In the hands of hostile officials the laws became punitive weapons. All Chinese passing through immigration stations, whether returning laborers, rich merchants, or students, were subjected to this treatment.[13]

The tragedy of Fu Chi Hao illustrates the treatment to which the Chinese were subjected. Hao arrived in San Francisco in the fall of 1901 in the company of an American missionary who was taking him to Oberlin College. After á delay of several days on board ship in San Francisco Bay, he learned that his passport and those of other Chinese students were not in proper form. The passports had been issued by the wrong person in China and the American consul in Tientsin had made some recording errors. The students, denied the right to land, were ordered back to China.

American friends intervened with the Secretary of the Treasury while the Chinese minister protested to the State Department. The students were then transferred to the Angel Island Detention Shed. Hao described it as about 100 feet square with whitewashed windows covered with wire mesh. As many as 200 people were crowded into this confinement which had no chairs or tables. They slept and ate on the floor like animals. Hao reported that kicking and swearing by the officials was not uncommon. The internees could neither send nor receive letters. Friends could visit them only with permission of the authorities. The efforts of friends and of the Chinese consul in San Francisco led to their release after a week's confinement. The consul had to post a $2,000 bond before the release was completed. Hao and the other students remained in San Francisco for about six months awaiting new passports.

Later they moved to Tacoma to stay at the home of their missionary sponsor. In August, 1902, a year after arrival, they started for Oberlin with considerable energy and money expended. The San Francisco bondsman consented to their move and immigration officials indicated they could go on the condition that the new passports, when received, would be acceptable.

The group chose to travel east on the Canadian Pacific railroad. Too late they learned that this railroad traveled mostly through Canada. United States border officials let them leave. Three days later, they reached the boundary at Portal, North Dakota, where another set of American officials detained them for six weeks. Telegrams flowed back and forth between Portal and Washington, D.C. The decision was that they had no right of reentry. Denied admittance, they moved to Toronto to seek refuge in Canada. There they found telegrams from the desperate consul urging their immediate return to San Francisco via Vancouver, British Columbia, for American officials were demanding forfeiture of the bond.

The students prepared to obey, but found that United States law prohibited the selling of tickets to any Chinese who did not have proper entry certificates. Immigration law demanded their return but the same law prevented them from securing transportation. The United States Attorney General ruled that they could remain in Canada for three months without forfeiting bond while a third set of passports was secured. In January, 1903, the students reached Oberlin College, sixteen months after arrival in San Francisco.[14] These Chinese students survived the treatment of the immigration bureaucracy because they had friends and money. Other Chinese, not so fortunate, were defeated and sent back to China.

In 1917, moving further down the exclusionist road, Congress created the "barred zone" and declared that natives of most of Asia and the Southeastern Pacific were inadmissible. Only Japan was exempted. In truth the 1917 act was aimed specifically at the growing influx of immigrants from India.[15]

Following World War I, segments of American society continued to fear open immigration. Restrictive legislation aimed at reducing the number of "undesirable" immigrants was enacted. Quota systems and national origins became the basis for European immigration. Asians were excluded by the 1924 immigration act which barred aliens ineligible for citizenship. The net then ensnared the Japanese.[16]

A long-standing problem facing immigrant families was the status of wives and children. In the nineteenth century, a wife assumed the citizenship of her husband. But in 1921, Congress enacted legislation denying to an alien-born woman her husband's citizenship.[17] For American-born Chinese males, these restrictive changes imposed tragic hardships. Because of the unbalanced sex ratio, they had been forced to seek wives in China. The 1924 immigration act denied the right of entry to alien-born wives. Their wives, aliens ineligible for citizenship, were excluded and compelled to remain in China. The children of these marriages were admissible.[18] Congress attempted in 1930 some changes which had bizarre results. The law allowed admission of wives of those marriages made prior to 1924. However, no provisions were made concerning marriages consummated after 1924 nor was there any concern for Chinese-born husbands of American citizens.[19]

American law provided that children of American-born fathers inherited the father's citizenship. When American-born Chinese husbands visited their families in China, an unusual phenomenon occurred. They seemed to sire only boy babies. The sons could claim United States citizenship and emigrate to the United States. Sojourners began to report "sons" even when none were born. Thus, "slots" in a sojourner's family were created by nonexistent sons or by vacancies if his own flesh and blood died. These slots became available for sale to other boys, known as "paper sons."[20]

The racket required only money and patience. A Chinese in the United States would revisit the home country, say for a year, perhaps longer. Upon his return, he would inform immigration officials that his wife (in China) had born him a child, maybe two or three.... Since the self-styled father could claim that he was a citizen, his child, accordingly, was a citizen and so registered.

Years later, having established a slot or two—or more—on his family tree, the man then arranged with Chinese brokers in Hong Kong and other places to sell his slot . . . for prices ranging from $2,500-$6,000.[21]

The Refugee Escape Act of September 11, 1957, protected the "paper sons" for the deportation requirement was waived under certain conditions. The San Francisco District Office of the Immigration and Naturalization Service received some 8,000 confessions of illegal entry for the ten-year period 1959-1969, as "paper sons" sought to legitimize their entry.[22]

In 1942, concerned citizens pushed for repeal of the Chinese exclusion laws. In the closing days of May, 1943, the Citizens Committee to Repeal Chinese Exclusion was formed and a lobbyist placed in Washington to push for legislation.[23] The A. F. of L. and the national conventions of the American Legion and the Veterans of Foreign Wars opposed any removal of barriers. The California Joint Immigration Committee and the Native Sons of the Golden West also remained adamant in their fear of the Yellow Peril.[24]

The alliance of China and the United States in the war against Japan perhaps did the most in ending the exclusion laws. The Citizens Committee based its reasoning on the fact that repeal would remove a major propaganda weapon from Japan who claimed to be fighting for an Asia for Asians. Equally important was the moral issue of racial discrimination.[25] In rebuttal the exclusionists of 1943 dusted off timeworn arguments about the Yellow Peril and the inundation of white America. Westerners opposed to repeal sought an alliance with Southerners, a ploy successful in the past. As the blacks were beginning to assert their right to their place in American life, the *Grizzly Bear,* the official organ of the Native Sons of the Golden West, editorialized:

These bills should be defeated! Their passage will but add fuel to the race-fire smouldering now in this country but likely to break forth at any time. If you let in Chinese, others will follow. We have one race problem that is not solved.[26]

Representative Ed Gosset of Texas agreed in part as he stated that he "and the rest of the boys down below the Mason-Dixon Line do not like the idea of tying this thing up with social equality and racial equality." Gosset, one of the leading Congressional supporters for repeal, carefully differentiated between the war effort and racism.[27] Joseph R. Farrington, delegate from Hawaii to Congress, countered racial arguments when he stated: "The record of Hawaii is proof that the Chinese can be accepted in the life of this country without injurious or disastrous results, and on the contrary, can become a great asset to us."[28]

President Franklin Roosevelt urged Congress to repeal exclusion. His October 11, 1943, message centered upon the war effort: "I regard this legislation as important in the cause of winning the war and of establishing a secure peace. By the repeal of the Chinese exclusion laws we can correct a historic mistake and silence the distorted Japanese propaganda."[29] On December 13, 1943, President Roosevelt signed the act "to Repeal the Chinese Exclusion Acts, to Establish Quotas, and for Other Purposes." Unlike other immigration laws based on national origin, this new law still retained racial characteristics. On the positive side, the law made it possible for Chinese aliens to become American citizens, providing an annual quota of 105 a year. To prevent a flood of people from areas other than China, 75 percent of the quota was set for Chinese emigrating from China. The discriminatory phrase "ineligible for citizenship" was removed.[30]

The quota figure was never filled during the years the law was in operation, for there was a further set of barriers: 50 percent of the quota was reserved for skilled workers; 30 percent was reserved for parents of Chinese American citizens over twenty-one years of age, and 20 percent went to spouses and children of permanent resident Chinese aliens. Twenty-five percent of any portion of a quota not utilized by one of the first three groups could be designated for brothers and sisters of American citizens and sons and daughters if they could not qualify under one of the other quotas.[31]

Both the 1943 law and the later McCarran-Walter Act of 1952 changed exclusion to restriction. The McCarran-Walter Act codified numerous immigration and naturalization laws. This law did not liberalize immigration opportunities for the Chinese. Their quota remained at 105. Regardless of where they lived in the world, any alien with at least 50 percent Chinese ancestry was charged against China's total. An additional quota of 100 was chargeable against the Asia-Pacific Triangle to accommodate people of mixed Asian ancestry and European colonies such as Hong Kong.[32] Fifty percent of the quota was reserved for skilled workers which for Chinese included professors, doctors, dentists, nurses, engineers, and other professionals. These did not always receive first preference if there was a need somewhere for a fine cook or some other specific occupation.[33]

During the turmoil of the 1950's and with the spread of Communism in Asia and Europe, Congressional legislation provided for displaced persons and refugees.[34] As the Communist wave crossed China, refugees flooded Hong Kong. John F. Kennedy signed a presidential directive on May 23, 1962, permitting Hong Kong refugees to enter the United States immediately as parolees and until December, 1965. By June 30, 1966, 15,111 Chinese entered the United States from Hong Kong—most had been on waiting lists for years for visas. By June, 1967, 9,126 of these had gained permanent resident status.[35]

On October 3, 1965, President Lyndon B. Johnson, at the base of the Statue of Liberty, signed into law the abolition of the national origins system. Restrictions for the Asia-Pacific Triangle ended at once. The 1965 act placed all unused national quotas into a common pool which qualified aliens from oversubscribed countries could utilize during the interim period, July 1, 1965-June 30, 1968.[36] After July 1, 1968, each nation outside the Western Hemisphere had a quota not to exceed 20,000 a year. Quotas were based upon the country of birth, not upon nationality or race. Persons born in Hong Kong, however, were charged to Great Britain's quota, but these emigrants could not exceed 1 percent of the number of British visas issued per year.

The Chinese quickly availed themselves of their new right to enter the United States. The *San Francisco Chronicle* reported toward the end of October, 1966, that 6,000 Hong Kong Chinese had utilized the special $350 airfare to leave the China coast for the Golden Mountain.[37] For the fiscal year 1966, 13,736 Chinese entered the United States with a highpoint of 19,741 reached in 1967. From June 30, 1966, through June 30, 1970, 75,748 Chinese have entered the United States.[38] In 1970, 3,064 settled in California; 2,819 in the state of New York. New York City had replaced San Francisco as the major point of new urban settlement with 2,699 settling in that eastern city and 1,605 in the latter.[39] Like their ancestors in the nineteenth century and all immigrants in general, the new arrivals came primarily to improve their economic condition.

CHAPTER VI

Becoming Members of a Pluralistic Society

THE CHINESE FIRST CONGREGATED IN DISTINCT DISTRICTS WITH-
in American cities where they recreated a culture similar to
that of China. Major cities still count Chinatowns as one
of their ethnic neighborhoods. America's Chinatowns range
from San Francisco's highly complex organism to towns
with a few Chinese shops on a block or two along a street.
These smaller centers provide the same needed contact, as
in large Chinatowns, where recent news of home, Chinese
food, and gambling can be found.[1]

The first immigrants built San Francisco's Chinatown,
which has always had the largest number of Chinese. In
1960, one of every ten Chinese in the United States lived
in this city by the bay. America's first Chinatown started
on Sacramento Street between Kearny and Dupont (now
Grant Avenue) Streets. By the time of the 1906 San Francisco earthquake, Chinatown remained confined to an
area slightly in excess of twelve city blocks.

In the mid 1850's, the San Francisco *Daily Alta* described
Chinatown:

. . . The majority of the houses were of Chinese importation, and
were stores, stocked with hams, tea, dried fish, dried ducks, and
other . . . Chinese eatables, besides copper pots and kettles, fans,
shawls, chessmen, and all sorts of curiosities. Suspended over the
doors were brilliantly-colored boards, about the size and shape of a
headboard over a grave, covered with Chinese characters, and with
several yards of red ribbon streaming from them; while the streets
were thronged with . . . Celestials, chattering vociferously as they

rushed about from store to store, or standing in groups studying the Chinese bills posted up in the shop windows, which may have been play-bills—for there was a Chinese theatre—or perhaps advertisements informing the public. . . .[2]

Unfortunately, white settlers in San Francisco could not translate the signboards which provided insights to Chinese character. Store signs had special significance and were prepared only after consulting a scholar. Restaurants proclaimed themselves as "the chamber of the odors of distant lands" or "garden of the golden valley" while one cigar maker sported the sign "fountain of the most excellent." Apothecary shops noted that they were the "hall of joyful relief" or "hall of harmony and apricot forests."[3]

San Francisco's Chinatown became a city within the larger city, cut off from the encircling economic and social activities. Here Chinese residents lived following the traditions of old China. In fact, the San Franciscans lived more in the past than did their relatives in China as they became cut off from the homeland and lived with memories, not the realities, of the old life.

Visitors today to a large American Chinatown pass curio and antique stores designed to lure them inside. There are also establishments serving Chinese food and drinks catering to Western tastes. But once a person leaves these attractions, he encounters stores stocked for the Chinese community. Here are the open-air vegetable stalls, butcher shops, live poultry shops, and herb stores. Here too are restaurants which the Chinese patronize. Chinatown offers to the Chinese several options—complete insularity, a refuge from daily contact with the dominant white world, or a place to refresh one's ties with the past even though he has abandoned Chinatown for the suburbs.[4]

The Chinese duplicated this first experience of urban living throughout the United States.[5] In 1970 the second largest Chinatown was in New York City. Beginning 100 years ago along Doyers Street, it became an eight-block area bounded by Baxter and Canal Streets and the Bowery.[6] In New York's Chinatown, as elsewhere, the Chinese have blended into the patterns of the dominant American society. Chinese language schools there have been relatively unsuccessful. Marriage has followed the American values, not Chinese.

Chinese sojourners, cut off from China, developed organizations to substitute for home and family. Historically, all Chinese who have resided away from their hometowns have banded together:

> The uses and the regulations of these societies are . . . very much the same in Chinese cities as they are in San Francisco, Sacramento, and Stockton. In Shanghae and Ningpo, where Canton and Fukeen people resided for trade, there were the guild halls, the Ui Kuns of the People from each of those provinces. So in Canton, there were the society-rooms or clubhouses of the Chinamen from other portions of the empire who were sojourning in that city.[7]

District organizations played a significant role for San Francisco Chinese whose only contact with home were fellow immigrants from the same region of the Pearl River Delta.

In 1851 the Cantonese from the Kwangtung Three Districts of Namhoi, Punyu, and Shuntak organized the Sam Yup Company. By year's end, men from the Four Districts of Sunwui, Sunning, Yanping, and Hoiping organized the Sze Yap (sometimes See Yup) Company. In 1852 the Chungshan men, also important in Hawaiian settlements, organized the Yeong Wo Company. The fourth association, not based upon geographical origin, was comprised of the Pearl River Hakka, the Hip Kat Association, later known as the Yan Wo Company. The most powerful of these associations was established in 1854 when most of the Sunning District men withdrew from the Sze Yap Company to form the Ning Yeung Company. In 1862, the sixth company was formed when more members of the old Sze Yap Company withdrew under the leadership of the Yee clan from Sunning and the Ong clan of Hoiping to form Hop Wo. These two fam-

ilies, small in numbers, felt their interests were not well
served in the larger organization. The remnants of the Sze
Yap Company reformed as Kong Chow. A seventh company,
Shew Hing Association, was created in the 1880's.[8]

TABLE II

THE CHINESE SIX COMPANIES IN CALIFORNIA

Company	Date Organized	1853[a]	1877[b]	1940[c]
Sam Yup	1851	4,000	11,000	1,500
Sze Yap	1851	9,500	15,000	2,500
(Kong Chow)	(1863)			
Yeong Wo	1852	7,500	12,000	2,500
Yan Wo	1852	1,000	4,300	500
(Hip Kat)				
Ning Yeung	1854	-----	75,000	13,500
Hop Wo	1862	-----	34,000	3,000
Shew Hing	1880's	-----	-----	4,000
		22,000	151,300	27,500

[a]California, *Assembly Journal Appendix*, 4th Sess. (1854), pp. 7-12.

[b]Otis Gibson, *The Chinese in America* (Cincinnati: Hitchcock and
Walden, 1877), p. 21.

[c]William Hoy, *The Chinese Six Companies* (San Francisco: Chinese
Consolidated Benevolent Association, c. 1942), p. 17.

These district associations, or companies, all constructed
during the 1850's large establishments in San Francisco
which compared favorably with existing public buildings.[9]
The San Francisco Chinese merchants controlled and utilized the companies to enforce the credit-ticket system.
Company representatives met arrivals at dockside and took
them to the *Ui Kun,* or company house, where they spread
their mats and prepared meals. These houses had rooms in
which to honor the spirits of deceased members and for
religious purposes. The companies also cared for the indi-
gent sick, disabled, and unemployed. Each company for a
time assumed the responsibility of returning the bones of

the deceased to his family in China. In short, the associations provided needed social services.[10]

Augustus W. Loomis, an advocate of the Chinese in the late 1860's, acknowledged that the Six Companies controlled the exodus to China: "A person proposing to return to China has been required, a certain number of days previous to sailing, to report his name to the company to which he belongs, whereupon the books are searched to see whether all his dues are paid; also to see whether a person bearing his name has been reported to the company as indebted to other parties."[11]

The companies also arbitrated cases of misunderstanding or quarrels between countrymen, giving rise to the anti-Chinese claim that a secret government operated within Chinatown. Given the early injustice meted out by California's judicial system, it seemed necessary to the Chinese to settle differences their own way.

Following a time of discord in the early 1860's, the district companies formed the Chung Wah Kung Saw, Assembly Hall of Chinese, to coordinate common efforts. This organization has been commonly known as the Chinese Six Companies. The presidency of this board rotated among the companies. Only the Yan Wo Company, the Hakka group, was excluded from this office, a reminder of the long-standing hatred between the two groups.[12] In 1901, the Six Companies incorporated as the Chinese Benevolent Association.[13]

The Six Companies for many years exerted powerful control over the destinies of Chinese in this country:

As to power and influence, in its early days, it was practically the Supreme Court of the Chinese in California. By general agreement it was empowered to speak and act for all the California Chinese in problems and affairs which affected the majority of them. It also became the official board of arbitration for disputes which arose between the various district groups, as well as other social groups. It was given the power to initiate and promote programs for the general welfare of the California Chinese. Then, too, before the establishment of any Chinese Consular or other diplomatic agency in America, the Chinese Six Companies acted as spokesman for the Imperial Manchu government in its relations with the Chinese in America.[14]

The Chinese Benevolent Association format was utilized in other American cities. Each association has asserted its role as supreme arbitrator for its community, maintaining that all other local organizations such as family associations, district associations, chambers of commerce, and others were all subordinate. For example, forty groups held membership and paid dues in the New York Chinese Consolidated Benevolent Association by virtue of being a Chinese organization. Individuals could not belong.[15]

In the United States, as in China, the family has been the primary social unit. Immigrants were able to identify other family members quickly for there are only 438 surnames in China.[16] In this country, the importance of family associations varies with their locality. These, like district associations, have become less meaningful to long-time Chinese residents and the American Chinese. Family associations in San Francisco and New York recently have regained some prestige as new immigrants have entered these two cities.

The early Chinese in the West congregated at the store of a fellow family member, the forerunner of family associations. The date of the first such organization is not known but large families have long been organized. The Wongs, with a membership in California alone of over 5,000, is the largest single family. It is estimated that there are more than 15,000 Wongs in the United States.[17] The Lau, Quan, Cheung, and Chew families in San Francisco created the Four Families to offset their small numbers and to confront the larger associations on more equal terms.[18] In New York City there were about sixty family associations in 1970.[19] As in China, family matters are ruled by the elders who have the responsibility to guide younger members, to protect the family name, and to take care of the many assorted problems. Pardee Lowe related the powerful pull of the family association when his father was honored by their clan:

> Stepmother's first move was to summon relatives and kinsmen from near and far. For these latter she dispatched imperious telegrams. They came in a hurry. Two kinsmen, one at Portland and the other at Los Angeles, hopped planes and flew. All in order to fulfill properly their duties as members of the Greater Family.
>
> This display of clan solidarity amazed me. Upon inquiring of Cousin Brightness the Third as to the reasons, I received this humorour reply:—
>
> "In American slang, your father is the 'Big Shot' of the Greater Family. According to Chinese custom, he is the Senior Elder Uncle of the Clan in America because he is closest to 'Original Ancestor' who founded the mighty Han Dynasty."[20]

Most Americans are unfamiliar with life in American Chinatowns. Stereotyping, based on ignorance and prejudice, has resulted. The sensational has been utilized by tour guides of San Francisco and New York to titillate audiences. The Chinese stereotype has been reinforced by American journalism and movies. The time-worn concept of "Chinks" as coolies and the seeming lack of concern for human life has been commonly accepted. The wise Chinese has been depicted as a pidgin-speaking disciple of Confucius. He has been caricatured as wearing the Manchu costume and the pigtail, both products of bygone days.

Movies portrayed the Chinese as hatchetmen, sing-song girls, or Fu Manchus. The one exception was the brilliant Chinese counterpart to Sherlock Holmes—Charlie Chan. Fu Manchu became the classic Hollywood villain prototype —the view known by many Americans:

a Chinese wearing a long, silk-brocaded gown, reaching to his ankles, and soft-soled slippers of black cloth. His ankles were wound with white tape-like material, binding his pants legs. Fu Manchu's hands and mien compelled attention. His long, graceful hands had claw-like finger nails several inches long. He inevitably walked with his hands folded in front of him and hidden in long sleeves of his brocaded robe. When angered or in danger—as was frequent—a sharp dagger flew out of his sleeve. . . . Fu Manchu's almond-shaped eyes pierced his victims', hypnotizing them and rendering them helpless, while he imposed his will upon them. He hissed when he was angry, or stroked his thin, long beard and moustachios when he was conniving revenge.[21]

News stories, in the past, based upon Chinese prostitution, opium users, and tong warfare, stressed the sinister. These devoted considerable detail to the dark, dank alleys of Chinatowns onto which open the doors of the assorted dens of iniquity.

District and family associations perpetuated tradition and adherence to Chinese ways. However, in the nineteenth century a group of supposedly fraternal brotherhoods challenged the Six Companies for control of San Francisco's Chinatown. These organizations, the tongs, soon monopolized the control of vice—prostitution, gambling, and opium. The Hip Yee Tong in 1852 was founded for the sole purpose of importing sing-song girls (prostitutes). The members enriched themselves at the expense of the girls and their customers.[22]

Unlike Hip Yee Tong, which restricted its activities to one enterprise, Chee Kung Tong was a forerunner of the gangster organizations of later America. It controlled crime wherever there was a Chinatown. Its eastern branch was called Yee Hing Oey—the Society of Righteous Brethren. Chee Kung ironically meant "The Chamber of High Justice." The Tongs originally had idealistic ties with China and with the Triad Society, one of the revolutionary groups opposed to the Manchus.[23]

Criminal tongs such as Hip Shing, the Hall of Victorious Union, controlled gambling in San Francisco. The Wa Ting Shan Tong, the Flowery Arbor Mountain Booth, taxed the houses of prostitution for protection, while the On Leong Society, the Chamber of Tranquil Conscientiousness, trafficked in slave girls. The hatchetmen, or highbinders, forerunners of Murder, Incorporated, killed on contract. Some of these societies were named the Hall of Realized Repose, Hall of Auspicious Victory, and Hall of Associated Conquerors. Newspapers, finding tong wars good copy, described in lurid details street fights in San Francisco and New York. The San Francisco tongs reached the pinnacle of their power in the 1890's but their success was their undoing. Their open flaunting of the San Francisco police department brought strong reaction and repression. The earthquake and fire of 1906 destroyed the tongs' establishments and allowed the reorganized Chinese Benevolent Association to regain control.[24]

The Chinese, as other immigrants, brought their religious beliefs of Buddhism and Taoism with them. When the need arose for the construction of a Chinese temple for the benefit of a family member, white people immediately saw evidence of an imported religious system which threatened them. These temples were under the jurisdiction of priests or caretakers who held a high position in Chinese American society. To qualify, one had to read and write, something most peasants could not do. In addition to maintaining the temple, the priest wrote and read letters for the community, providing him with his income.[25]

Throughout the West, these temples were built in much the same style as other frontier structures. The Weaverville Temple, a California State Historical Park, was built with rough unfinished lumber. The temple's one large room housed the altar and the statue of the temple god. A lean-to was built against it to provide a room for the caretaker. An interesting account of Chinese temples has been prepared from a series of interviews with Chingwah Lee, former custodian of San Francisco's T'ien Hou Temple.

The structures varied greatly in size and stateliness but all were colorful and presented an exotic sight to the local inhabitants. Some, in fact, were mere lean-tos or sheds. When I was a seven-year-old refugee from the Earthquake of 1906 and my parents were taking the family about the Bay region, I recall being exposed to a tiny chapel hardly more than four feet square, just big enough for a single person to kneel, bow and pray before a ruddy-faced image in a colorful garment. This sanctuary was visited by shrimp fishermen near Richmond.

Sometimes the highest floor of an organization was reserved as a sanctuary—to be as near the gods as possible. Such is the case with the Shew Hing District Association, one of the two oldest temples in San Francisco. Located on Waverly Place, this street has always been called by the Chinese *T'ien Hou Miao* or the Street of the T'ien Hou Temple. Some associations had a specially-built penthouse for the shrine. Such is the case with the Chin Family Association on Washington Street in San Francisco.

The well known Kong Chow Temple, probably the oldest in San Francisco, was rebuilt on Pine Street about five years after the fire, and is still in existence. The building has the place of worship on the top floor, the administrative offices for the Kong Chow Association and quarters for the temple keepers on the second floor and a classroom was located on the ground floor. Behind the old school were storage areas for lanterns and banners used in parades; also a kitchen for the cooking of *tsai* (monks' meals) for festive occasions in the old days. It also has a relatively spacious courtyard and fountain.[26]

Each temple was a shrine to a particular deity. The following account describes some of the more important deities of the American Chinese:

The enshrined deities reflect the needs of the early Chinese pioneers. Perhaps the most popular god is *Kuan Kung*, often called the God of Literature and Valor or the God of Peace and War. In life he was always fighting for justice and he is described as having a ruddy complexion or his image has him with an orange-red face, one hand holding an open book, the other an ever-ready halbert. He is also depicted seated, flanked by his son holding the Seal of Office with an old companion at arms holding his weapon.

Equally popular is the worship of Pei Ti or the God of the North. His full title is *Hsuan T'ien Shang Ti* or True Lord of the Black Pavilion of Heaven. With his four-edged magic sword he conquered the Demon King and his horde who were ravishing the universe. He is represented in imperial garments, one foot over a tortoise and entwining serpent. These represent two evil marshals of the Demon King whom he has vanquished.

. . . .

Perhaps the most popular deity of all time and throughout the Far East is *Kuan Yin* or "One who hears prayers." In the West, *Kuan Yin* is called the Goddess of Mercy and is often mistaken for a madonna by some. The images one finds of her reveal a serene lady with a gentle mien, but *Kuan Yin* is actually the offspring of Amitabha Buddha, resolved to serve this world till every living creature has received salvation.[27]

Through observing traditional festivals, present-day Chinese continue to contribute to the plurality of American life. Perhaps the best known holiday is the Chinese New Year. In preparation for the new year, houses are thoroughly cleaned. Once the holiday begins, no cleaning is permitted for to sweep floors might symbolically brush out the good luck which has just arrived. Red paper, denoting good luck, is replaced throughout the house and by the front door for the occasion.[28] As the new year approaches, firecrackers explode and as midnight arrives, the noise rolling through the streets and city resembles the sound of rifles being discharged by an army. One of the more recent controversies between the Mayor of San Francisco and Chinatown was his ban on firecrackers. Parades and celebrations mark the festival. At the time of Chinese New Year, the dragon dances and chases away evil spirits. In Honolulu, the dragon, propelled by boys, parades through the streets pausing at store fronts to dance. The store owner then lights a string of several hundred firecrackers to scare away evil spirits. He also throws lighted firecrackers at the dragon's feet to frighten other spirits. The dragon and the firecrackers allow good luck to prevail. Suspended over the door of the store is an offering wrapped in red paper which the dragon devours as it leaves. Inside is money which keeps the many feet of the dragon happy.

Another important festival is that of Pure Brightness, also known as Chinese Memorial Day. In China visits to family tombs honoring the clan ancestors were a traditional observance. Such a ceremony is observed still in many American Chinese centers. The elder member of the family sweeps the graves with willow branches. The family engages in cleaning the grave site and leaving favorite cooked Chinese foods. Tombstones are painted red, or decorated with red paper while red candles, incense, and paper money are burned. Firecrackers are exploded to frighten away lurking evil spirits.[29]

Other important festivals are the Spirits' Festival (honoring departed family members), Moon Festival (an agricultural celebration), and Festival of the Winter Solstice (another period of placing offerings on family ancestral altars).[30]

Immigrants to the United States have hoped that their children would remember and cherish the culture of the mother country. The establishment of language schools was one way that the Chinese, and later the Japanese, attempted to transmit the culture. Scholars first established Chinese language schools in San Francisco. In 1884 the first community Chinese School in the Bay city was the Ch'ing School in which some sixty students attended two classes. Instruction was along classic lines, with students memorizing their lessons to recite to the instructor until perfect.[31]

The Chinese Central High School, located on the upper story of the Six Companies' building, carried on this civic tradition. In the mid-1960's the school enrolled about 650. Classes were held two hours a day, five days a week, an overload beyond the student's day in regular school.[32] Pardee Lowe's experiences in Chinese School confirms the attitudes of more recent reluctant scholars:

The teacher devoted one hour each evening to our beginners' class, during which we were expected to grasp firmly the fundamentals of the language as well as rudimentary ideas of Chinese history, geography, and philosophy. For the remaining two hours we were left alone. We spent them memorizing our lessons aloud, drawing Chinese characters with smelly black ink and pencil-like bamboo paintbrushes, or, more frequently, reading Western novels and magazines borrowed from East Belleville's Public Library behind our Chinese textbooks.

Pardee concluded that he and his classmates did not understand, nor did they care to, the Chinese curriculum.[33]

*   *   *   *

Chinatowns still stand as visible signs of the fallacy of

the melting-pot theory but remain proud symbols of a pluralistic society. In recent years the population in these racial
ghettos has declined although San Francisco's and New
York's residential problems have become complicated by
the influx of Hong Kong Chinese. There are several studies
about the sociological problems connected with the various
Chinatowns. The communities were created predominantly
by a male population. When normal family life was possible, those who could escaped the ghetto. Throughout the
country, many Chinatowns have developed under the aegis
of a particular clan. For a time a close-knit tie was maintained, but American born Chinese have withdrawn when
possible from Chinese patterns. Linked with this repudiation by the youth has been the lack of acceptable social life
in many small Chinatowns. Better educated than their parents, they have also looked with disfavor upon long hours
of work at low pay. In the 1960's, conflict has grown between
American Chinese youth and Hong Kong immigrants, an
interesting parallel to the centuries-old Punti-Hakka feud.[34]

But while many American Chinese have escaped the
ghetto, still they rely upon these centers for special goods
and services.[35] As they realize their own cultural heritage,
these traditional Chinese communities remain important as
the custodians of the past. Chinese families which have in
essence become "Americanized" still retain cultural affilia-
tions—food, a bilingual approach to language, Chinese organizations, and some pressure against mixed marriages.[36]

In 1904, a group of native-born San Francisco Chinese
Americans felt it was time to assert control over their own
destinies and not be governed by China or by immigrants
brought over to manage one of the Six Companies. Walter
U. Lum, Joseph K. Lum, and Ng Gunn formed the Native
Sons of the Golden State to protect citizenship rights of
native-born Chinese. When the organization spread from
San Francisco to other California cities and then to other
states, it became known as the Chinese American Citizens

Alliance. With headquarters in San Francisco, it has fought discrimination against Chinese Americans.[37]

The influx of new immigrants from Hong Kong has caused internal problems in San Francisco's Chinatown in particular. Many of the recent arrivals are youths with language problems. The addition of 33,000 people behind the tourist façade of Chinatown has led to the open surfacing of long-standing ghetto problems confronting urban America everywhere. Housing, welfare, health, drugs, juvenile delinquency are common problems regardless of skin color. But Chinatown, overcrowded, showed signs in 1970 of the growing tension. One-third of the families earned less than the Federal poverty level. In 1970, the unemployment rate was 12.8 percent compared with 6.7 percent for San Francisco and 3.9 percent for the country. Substandard housing was 67 percent compared with 19 percent for the rest of San Francisco.[38]

In Chinatown, the youth have challenged the authority of the establishment, the Six Companies. They have called themselves the new Yellow Peril and have organized to attack the problems that confront and disturb them. In 1968, San Francisco State College Chinese activists led in the organization of the Free University of Chinatown Kids, Unincorporated. Some three hundred Hong Kong youth formed the largest and toughest street gang in the area. In Berkeley, Chinese and Japanese intellectuals who had disregarded Chinatown because of its backwardness, joined forces to combat problems of the Chinese people. Out of this came the Asian-American Political Alliance.

At San Francisco State College, the Asians, emulating the Black Panthers' demand for Black Studies, launched the Third World movement. In Chinatown, many of the Chinese youth adopted the Black Panthers' protest style. Mouthing Maoist statements, they formed the Red Guard. By 1970, many Chinese youth were no longer satisfied with yesterday's answers to today's and tomorrow's problems.[39]

Part II

The Japanese Americans

CHAPTER VII

Japan, The Island Empire

IN THE 1880's THE EXCLUSIONISTS SUCCESSFULLY LOCKED THE door against Chinese immigration, but Western agriculturalists still needed cheap farm labor. They turned to the Japanese to provide this manpower; the cycle of immigration and perseverance in the face of discrimination, prejudice, and exclusion began to repeat itself.

Japan, separated from the Asian land mass by the Sea of Japan, remained closed to the outside world from the 1630's until the 1850's. Japan, through self-enforced isolation, had had time to instill cultural traditions. The Japanese remained secure while China was being forced by Europeans to open her doors, and the Chinese had taken to the high seas to seek their fortune. Change came to Japan on July 8, 1853, about the time the flood of immigrants from the Pearl River Delta was attracted to California. On that day, Commodore Matthew C. Perry of the United States Navy, sailed into Tokyo Bay. He returned in February, 1854, to sign a treaty ending Japanese isolation.[1]

The Island Kingdom, brought suddenly into contact with nineteenth-century imperialism and industrialism, consists of some 4,000 islands, strung along an arc of about 1,000 miles. The empire's landmass is less than 150,000 square miles.[2] Four large islands constitute the major centers of Japanese life. In the north is the cold, underpopulated Hokkaido, where one of Japan's ethnic minorities, the Ainu, live. The Ainu have certain physical characteristics which resemble early Caucasian types.[3]

[85]

The largest, and most populous, island is Honshu, the hub of culture and civilization. Honshu, with Tokyo and other large cities, became the area of intense industrialization. Along its southern shore lies the lovely Inland Sea. Across this sea is the smaller island of Shikoku. To the southwest lies the island of Kyushu, the point of contact with Chinese and early European commerce.[4]

The terrain is accentuated by extensive mountain chains with marked characteristics of volcanism. Mt. Fuji, over 12,000 feet high, is the most famous extinct volcano. An accompanying aspect of volcanism is the common occurrence of earthquakes and the threat of *tsunami*, mistakenly called tidal waves.[5]

Food production utilizes the islands' level land—only 20 percent of the total landmass. The most extensive level area is the Kwanto plain on Honshu, about 2,700 square miles. Situated near Tokyo, it slopes eastward to the Pacific. Other "flat" areas are the plains of Nobi and Kansai, also on Honshu.[6]

From earliest times, the influence of China upon language, art, and religion has been apparent. The Confucian concept of family and Emperor has also had major impact. The Yamoto state emerged in the fourth century. This feudal society, based upon a closed and hereditary aristocracy, began as a conglomeration of clans, headed by an emperor. Shinto was its religion. The Taika Reform (645-650), building upon the social and economic ideas flowing from China, attempted to create a centralized state modeled after China's T'ang Dynasty. Private ownership of land disappeared with title vested in the Emperor who initiated a redistribution of the land. While there were some changes following the surge of reform, in actuality the occupancy of estates remained virtually in the hands of the same large landlords, known as daimyo.[7]

The Taika Reform led to Japan's classical age, a span of about 350 years. The Emperor's personal land surrounded the town of Kyoto which by 795 became the imperial residence. All rulers lived there until 1868. The Emperor, a weak figurehead, was manipulated by clans, or families, such as the Fujiwara. From the thirteenth to the nineteenth century, regents were chosen from one of the branches of the Fujiwara family. Politically, the classical age divides into two periods, Nara (710-794) and Heian (795-1185). The basic characteristics of Japanese social and religious thinking were developed in the Nara period.[8]

In 1185, the Minamoto family, an emerging powerful force, devised a style of administration which, with few minor changes, persisted until the Meiji Restoration. In 1192, the Emperor appointed Yoritomo of the Minamoto family as Shogun—the supreme general in charge of all imperial troops. Yoritomo set up headquarters at the town of Kamakura, south of Tokyo. Here was the first de facto capital, located at other than the Emperor's residence in Kyoto.[9]

Yoritomo imposed upon the existing imperial administrative structure his own successful family organizational plan, which in turn was duplicated by his military retainers at their own holdings. A centralized shogunal rule was created, supported by vassal allegiance to the Shogun. Yoritomo appointed personal retainers to be self-supporting estate managers of the Emperor's lands. He maintained power over the Emperor through control of the military forces.[10]

Milton W. Meyers summarizes the impact of shogunal control:

This emerging dominance of the military over the civilian authority had continuing significance in Japanese national life. Japan turned its back upon the Chinese example of the educated civilian bureaucrat in political affairs.[11]

Japan's political life underwent a major change in 1603 following a struggle for control. Tokugawa Ieyasu emerged as Shogun and the Tokugawa reign lasted until 1868. The

Tokugawa Shoguns ruled from their stronghold, Edo, present-day Tokyo. This Shogunate maintained rigid control over the Emperor through a system of court officials who screened all business and appointments.[12]

By the late 1630's, the Tokugawas virtually closed Japan's contact with the rest of the world. The Dutch retained one port at Deshima, which was carefully guarded and regulated. After 1637 Japanese were forbidden to leave from or return to the empire. The Tokugawa aim to attain political stability was achieved. For over two hundred years, a calm settled over the land and cultural patterns of quiet seclusion and conformity were attained.[13]

Around 1850, the Tokugawa Shogunate was subjected to internal stress and external pressures. Into this chaos sailed Perry and his four ships. From the time of Perry's arrival until 1868, the Shogunate struggled to survive. The Tokugawas had based their rule upon loyalty to, and protection of, the Emperor. After 1853 they were unable to continue this stance as concessions were made to foreigners. European navies began bombarding Japanese cities in retaliation for supposed treaty violations. By 1866, internal conditions had deteriorated and civil war resulted. The daimyo, the great feudal lords, of the Choshu clan from the southwestern tip of Honshu joined with the daimyo of the Satsuma and other clans from the neighbor island of Kyushu in defense of the Emperor.[14] The samurai, the warrior class, from those areas joined the daimyo in the struggle to topple the Tokugawa clan from supremacy. The rebels successfully repulsed the Tokugawan invasion of their homeland. Taking the offensive, the samurai rebels marched to the walls of Edo. With his stronghold threatened, the Tokugawa Shogun capitulated without a fight.[15]

The new Emperor, Meiji, succeeded to the throne in 1867 at Kyoto. He announced in January, 1868, the restoration of imperial rule. He then moved his capital to Tokyo, and modern Japan began. The reign was designated Meiji;

for the first time in centuries, the Emperor was a political force. His reassumption of imperial power has been called the Meiji Restoration.[16] For the next twenty years, Meiji leaders pressed for a modern political state with a parliamentary form of government. In the industrial world, the zaibatsu, or cartels, achieved success through hard work and governmental encouragement. Mitsui, Mitsubishi, and Sumitomo were the family names of the leaders of some of these industrial complexes. In a sense, they became the daimyo of the new Japan.[17]

In the short space of fifty years following the Meiji Restoration, Japan changed more dramatically than at any time in that country's long history. By 1900 Japan had become a world power. Economically, the nation started its shift from an almost complete agricultural base, centered on rice production, to an ever increasing industrialization. Socially, Japan's cultural isolation weakened in the face of Western inroads. The nation's population, which had stabilized during the Tokugawa era, began to increase rapidly. Industrialization accommodated much of this increased population but for some, overpopulation meant starvation or emigration.[18]

The popular saying that dukes do not emigrate also applied to Meiji Japan. The country's political, social, and economic leaders had no reason to leave. Those hardest hit by Japan's move from isolation and agriculture to internationalism and industrialism were rural, conservative, tradition-bound farmers.[19] This change in Japan's internal structure coincided with the demand for agricultural labor in Hawaii and California. The Hawaiian sugar plantations moving into full production, needed field hands.[20] Californians, successful in the national Chinese exclusion fight, found they still needed unskilled agricultural labor.[21]

In neat, compact houses located in tiny villages in southwestern Japan, decisions were reached which sent a father or a son to the sugar fields of Hawaii or the farms of California. Village families received the news impassively. This moment of apparent impassiveness epitomized an apex in Japanese culture. Over the centuries the people had developed a high sense of social conformity which restricted the display of emotions. Behind their masked faces was the hope that the emigrant would meet with success and that he would return soon to his family. The belief that his moment of personal triumph would redound to the glory of the family in the eyes of the village was another significant aspect of Japanese society.[22]

Increasing numbers of such decisions were reached throughout southern Japan from about 1885 to 1910. Hiroshima Prefecture and its southern prefectural neighbor, Yamaguchi, provided most of the Japanese sons who migrated from the island of Honshu during these years. The prefecture of Kumamoto, across the inland sea on the island of Kyushu, was a third major contributor. This section of Japan remained rural during the Meiji Restoration and suffered heavily from overpopulation. After 1868 the old-time caste system broke down; for the peasants, about the only difference was political—a change of tax collectors. Tied closely to the soil, they had little awareness of the restoration. They knew that their children were now provided an education and that the new nation was disrupting the serenity of their lives.[23]

Those emigrating had learned their value system largely from their families. They had worked hard on family farms which averaged slightly more than an acre in southern Japan. The peasants of Hiroshima and their neighbors cultivated rice. The climate, verging between temperate and subtropical, allowed for two plantings a year. As in China, agriculture was the key to life. Existence was difficult, stripped to the bare essentials of eking out a livelihood against the forces of nature. It had been thus in Japan for centuries until change came with the Meiji Restoration.[24]

Japanese peasant families were at the bottom of the economic and social ladder while the Emperor and his family resided at the top. During the Tokugawa Shogunate, the samurai, or warrior class, had ranked next in importance.[25] After the Emperor returned to power in 1868, he divested the samurai of their feudal positions, though many managed to secure political and economic leadership positions. In the new era, members of the lower classes now found advancement possible through service in the army, navy, and civil service. With the evolution of the zaibatsu, the cartels, into economic dominance, other new opportunities allowed the peasant to escape his environment.[26]

Even as Japan underwent vast changes and Westernization made inroads into the culture, peasant families clung to the old ways. They had long accepted the force of external authority where rules and obligations set the behavior and conduct of an individual within the larger society. Each person was expected to accept these rules without question. Society, whether family, town, or nation, was the important element to which the individual owed a debt and to which he must conform.[27]

The Japanese as well as Western societies developed a view of right and wrong which was translated into a moral code. The Japanese understood the Western view which frowned upon sinners who transgressed. Right and wrong in the Japanese family was related to the group demands. A young Japanese was instructed that when others frowned, or laughed, at his actions, he brought shame not only to himself, but even worse, to his family. Such pressures upon people led naturally to impassive conformity. Individuals earned respect through success. Competition in all phases of life within established norms was one certain road to success.[28]

In this societal plan, balanced between the possibility of personal embarrassment and triumph, Japanese culture developed a complex, yet very humane, method of easing those moments of embarrassment when success was not possible.

When a person was guilty of error, observers allowed him to save "face" by seeming to ignore the transgression. Proper form called for the observer to remain impassive.[29]

Japanese society demanded then an intense conformity. With society playing such a major role in the shaping of life, one could not easily escape scrutiny. To succeed demanded a high degree of self-discipline. The power of mind over material things was important. A sense of confidence, developed over the centuries, had induced a belief in their own superiority. Failure seemed to manifest a character flaw in the person—a concept which could be appreciated by Western-world Calvinists.[30]

The emphasis on conformity and self-control reflected an agricultural society dependent upon natural forces. Where many people lived crowded closely together, Japanese culture emphasized the small and the uncluttered. Neatness truly counted in crowded homes and small gardens. Japanese gardens were manicured immaculately; floral arrangements stressed the simple beauty in a singleness of concept rather than a demonstration of profusion. Japanese art was a true expression of the philosophical concept of character.

The Japanese have been greatly influenced by the art and culture of China, which they adapted for their own use. The appreciation of beauty in nature has found expression through the centuries in literature and art. Instead of attempting to flee nature, the Japanese have enjoyed it as a source of beauty and acknowledged it as the life-giver.[31]

Shinto, a nature cult whose *kami*, or deities, were natural phenomena, was the foundation of Japanese religious experience. *Kami* filled the observer with a feeling of awe. Sprinkled throughout Japan are Shinto shrines, standing amidst beautiful surroundings, ranging from majestic Fuji to an old empress tree in the center of some village.[32] The ultimate Shinto *kami* was the Sun Goddess, the ancestor of the Emperor. In its early form, Shinto was a simple appreciation of nature. A basic aspect of primitive Shinto was ritual purity. Thus, bathing, a love for cleanliness, has become coupled with love for beauty.[33]

Shinto provided a needed emotional release in the face of societal pressures. Through the centuries, Shinto remained largely unchanged and formed the basis for religious beliefs concerning birth, marriage, and death. The Emperor had an important role in Shinto through his direct relationship with the Sun Goddess.[34]

Following the Meiji Restoration, Shinto moved toward becoming a state religion. Those nationalists who wished to espouse the cause of centralism used Shinto and emperor worship as helpful tools. Young Japanese were taught to associate religion and patriotism. In the 1870's State Shinto more and more emphasized the divinity of the Emperor. Official ceremonies connecting his central role in the state and in religion were created. Sect Shinto carried on the traditional common age-old beliefs.[35]

Missing in the Shinto framework was any thought of life after death. The Japanese, as the Chinese, became attracted to Buddhism because of its concerns with an afterlife. Buddhism filtered into Japan through China. Much of the mysticism of India, unattractive to both Chinese and Japanese thought, was changed. The Japanese, too, avoided adopting any rigid form, allowing for an accommodation with Shinto and for additional borrowings from Confucianism and Taoism.[36]

In Japan, a Zen sect developed which drew upon Taoist teachings of China and the Japanese love of nature. Zen held that through meditation, an intuitive understanding of a oneness with nature could develop and a clear knowledge of the basic principles of the universe would occur.[37]

Buddhism, combined with Confucian concepts of social order and filial respect for authority, blended easily with Shinto to provide religious experiences. Christianity, which came with the Dutch and Portuguese and later with Protestant missionaries, failed as a major religion in Japan. Its contribution was the input of Western ideas which had the greatest impact upon Japanese thinking during the Meiji period.[38]

As Japan approached 1900, her society, culture, rising industrial power, and new military might all projected her far beyond any other Asian nation into the international sphere. In the early twentieth century, she competed on even terms with Western countries, except for Great Britain and the United States, the two major naval powers in the Pacific.

Japan's industrial development moved her in two directions. One led into international competition as she sought colonies beyond her borders in the Western tradition as sources of raw materials and possible markets for manufactured goods. The other saw peasants immigrating to other lands to escape the grinding poverty of Japanese agriculture. These people joined the mainstream of mankind as they sought new homes for economic gain. During the first two decades of the twentieth century, the Japanese government remained sensitive to the treatment of its nationals. Thus the two movements of internationalism and emigration were entwined during much of the first half of the twentieth century.

CHAPTER VIII

Search for Success: Immigration to Hawaii and the United States, 1868-1907

IN 1960, 464,468 PERSONS OF JAPANESE DESCENT RESIDED IN the United States. Like the immigrants from China, the Japanese congregated mostly in Pacific Coast states and Hawaii. The island state has always had the largest number of Japanese. Most Japanese immigrants to mainland United States arrived between 1890 and 1924.

In the 1860's, the Kingdom of Hawaii's Bureau of Immigration sought alternatives to importing Chinese labor. Polynesians from other islands were therefore recruited and a group of 126 arrived in 1869. On June 19, 1868, 148 Japanese arrived in Honolulu to become contract laborers. Although Japan forbade emigration, Eugene M. Van Reed, Hawaiian consul general in Japan, carried out his immigration plan during a period of confusion and civil war. The proposal received financial support from the Bureau of Immigration; its board members hoped that the Japanese might be the answer to their problem:

. . . Japanese were more like the natives of these islands, than any others we could get to immigrate here. The Japanese considered themselves of the same origin with these Natives; they certainly resembled our native race very much, and there was not the slightest doubt that they would readily amalgamate.[1]

These first laborers were contracted to work for three years for $4.00 a month plus food, lodging, and medical care. When difficulties arose between contractors and employees, Japan sent investigators who demanded that any dissatisfied worker be returned to Japan. The Hawaiian government agreed to pay his passage. However, most of these first immigrants preferred to remain. Hawaiians found they met the bureau's expectations. Although the Japanese government allowed them to stay, migration was restricted for the next fifteen years.[2]

Communications between the two governments in the 1880's led to hopes of reopening immigration. In 1880 Robert W. Irwin became the Hawaiian consul general in Japan; in 1882 Walter M. Gibson emerged as head of King Kalakaua's new cabinet. These two men, one in Tokyo and the other in Honolulu, worked diligently to promote Japanese immigration.[3] In 1883 Irwin received appointment as special commissioner to encourage Japanese immigration. Colonel Curtis P. Iaukea, a Hawaiian, was sent to Japan to assist him. Gibson instructed Iaukea in December, 1883 to the effect that:

this Government is prepared to provide free passage for Japanese agricultural laborers or domestic servants, with their wives, if married, and a certain number of their children. The only equivalent that the Government will ask for this will be the selection by their own agents of the persons who are to be thus the recipients of this bounty. The emigrants shall not be required to contract for service beforehand, neither shall they be under any obligation to enter into service on arrival here, but the Government will on their part undertake to find them employment on one or other of our plantations at rates not less than a reasonable minimum to be fixed before the emigrant leaves Japan. The Government will also undertake to provide food and lodging for the emigrants on their arrival here until they have had a reasonable opportunity to find employment or until they intimate that they prefer to take care of themselves rather than take service.[4]

Early in 1884, the Japanese government informed Iaukea that an agreement seemed possible. Japan's internal social changes and its growing economic depression led that government to consider emigration as one solution. Hawaii's offer seemed most inviting.

Commissioner Irwin sought out possible immigrants, but he determined to avoid the 1868 mistake of recruiting urban Japanese. He deliberately went to the rural prefectures of Hiroshima, Yamaguchi, and to neighboring prefectures on the island of Kyushu to find laborers. The inhabitants of these areas were among the poorest in the Island Empire.[5]

Irwin's efforts bore fruit on February 8, 1885, when 943 Japanese—676 men, 159 women, and 108 children—arrived in Honolulu. Before leaving Japan, the men signed a three-year contract with the Hawaiian government. The government furnished free steerage passage to Honolulu for the worker and, if married, for his wife. It agreed to find work for both as agricultural laborers with monthly wages of $9 for men and $6 for wives. Food allowances were $6 and $4 respectively. The government additionally promised free housing, medical care, and fuel and agreed to sell them rice at no more than 5¢ a pound. The laborers were to work a twenty-six-day month. Field hands worked a ten-hour day while twelve hours were required in the sugar mills. Every month the Japanese consul in Honolulu received 25 percent of each worker's wages to be deposited in the worker's account in the Hawaiian Government Postal Savings Bank.[6]

Unlike most European countries, Japan showed great concern about the welfare of her emigrants. Improper treatment, she believed, would injure her national prestige. The Japanese government sent with the 1885 contract laborers a foreign service officer to serve as its consul in Honolulu. On the same ship was G. O. Nakayama who was appointed by the Hawaiian Bureau of Immigration as inspector of Japanese immigrants. He provided a vital liaison between laborers, contractors, and the Bureau.[7]

On June 17, 1885, Commissioner Irwin escorted his second group of 930 men, 34 women, and 14 children. The Japanese government received word of ill treatment of the immigrants. An investigation found the complaints to be true. The Hawaiian government agreed to protect the Japanese from plantation owners. From this developed the emigration convention of January 28, 1886, setting terms of emigration from Japan for the next five years. All emigration was by contract, not to exceed three years, signed by the emigrant and an agent of the Hawaiian Bureau of Immigration. The Hawaiian government assumed the responsibility of overseeing the performance of the planters and other users of contract labor. Additionally, the Hawaiian government furnished free steerage passage on first-class steamers and employed inspectors, interpreters, and Japanese physicians.[8]

From the time of the 1885 arrivals to the end of the island kingdom in 1894, Hawaii's Bureau of Immigration arranged twenty-six emigrations. The total was 28,691—23,071 men, 5,487 women, and 133 children. By the end of 1894, after subtracting returnees and deaths, 20,271 Japanese lived in Hawaii. They comprised about 20 percent of the kingdom's total population and about 64 percent of the plantation labor force.[9]

✿   ✿   ✿   ✿

About a year after the first Japanese laborers arrived in Honolulu, the S.S. *China* berthed at the San Francisco docks on May 27, 1869. On board were Japanese refugees from the recent overthrow of the Tokugawa Shogunate who were the vanguard of the projected Wakamatsu Tea and Silk Farm Colony. They were the first Japanese colonizers on the mainland United States, although there is evidence that there were some Japanese engaged in horticulture and agriculture in Alameda County in 1868.[10]

The Wakamatsu Colony, guided by John H. Schnell, who was married to a Japanese, brought mulberry trees for silk farming, bamboo shoots, tea seeds, and grape seedlings.

In early 1870, almost too late, sixty boxes of tea plants and eighteen packages of fruit trees arrived.[11] By late October, 1869, Schnell and other members of the company had fallen ill. When thirteen new Japanese arrived, there was no one to welcome them.[12] Schnell left Gold Hill with his wife and children, promising to return but never did. The Wakamatsu Colony lasted for about two years but did not flourish due in large part to the hostility of the climate and their neighbors. Soon there were only three colonists remaining. One was the Schnell nursemaid, Okei Ito, who died at Gold Hill in 1871 at the age of nineteen. The other two, both men, lived in the area for several years.[13] On June 7, 1969, Governor Ronald Reagan led Americans of Japanese ancestry and others in the dedication of a plaque in memory of the colony at Gold Hill in the Sierra Nevada foothills, near the very spot where James Marshall had discovered gold.[14]

The *Sacramento Union* compared the new Japanese immigrants with the undesired Chinese:

> These group of Japanese are of the "better" class, talk English, and are very anxious to find a permanent home in this State. . . . It is in the interest of California to welcome and encourage these immigrants. . . . As the Indians learned much from the whites that was useful to them so there is probably much knowledge in the possession of these Asiatics that we could profit from, to compensate us in some measure from the very enlightened prejudice against their coppery color. They will at all events teach us how to produce teas and silk, some useful lessons in frugality, industry, and possibly in politeness.[15]

Other Japanese followed the Wakamatsu colonists to the United States. One such was Matsudair Tadaatsu who became a mining engineer in Colorado. One report maintains that about half of the 1,300 Japanese in the United States in 1887 were students.[16] In 1880, the emigration still restricted, the Japanese in the United States numbered only 148. In 1886, responding to its internal problems, the government legalized emigration. Wages of 14¢ a day in Japan made many young people willing to risk an ocean crossing for the riches which surely accompanied the commonly reported wage of $2 a day. Actually, most Japanese in California agriculture started for less than $1 a day.[17] Like the Hawaiian immigrants, large numbers of West Coast immigrants came from those rural prefectures where agricultural conditions were at their worst.

Japan maintained its paternalistic attitude towards its emigrants, screening those who left and supervising them once they reached their destination. While this had drawbacks, it gave young persons leaving home for the unknown a sense of security. In 1896 the Japanese Parliament enacted an immigrants' protection law which compelled each laborer leaving the country to offer evidence that someone would provide funds to care for him if he became ill overseas and would arrange for his eventual return to Japan. Such requirements were too stringent for individuals to meet and gave impetus to emigration companies who could post the necessary bond.[18]

An interesting commentary on the background of these early Japanese immigrants is provided by Hisaakira Kano in his 1919 book, *Tunnels under the Pacific*. The author felt it was desirable to apologize for the people some considered inferior. Kano cited the fact that most of the Japanese immigrants came from prefectures such as Yamaguchi, Hiroshima, Wakayama, and Okayama. They were, he felt, unware of the new intellectual life of Japan. These immigrants remembered their prefectures where customs and traditions of feudal Japan remained strong. Having lived in isolation in their provinces until their migration, they believed such was true for all Japan. Kano reported that he and his fellow educated Japanese were both sorry and surprised at the lack of culture among Japanese agricultural workers. He resented the fact that Americans classified all Japanese as being lower than uneducated and vulgar Italian and Russian laborers.[19]

Kano's views were contested by Harry Kitano who notes that by the end of the nineteenth century, Japan required four years of education and that another four years was optional. Most immigrants from Japan, he contended, were literate and had a deep appreciation for education.[20]

Japanese emigration companies capitalized upon the needs of Hawaii and California agricultural interests and other industries in the Western states and Alaska. The transpacific shipment of agricultural laborers paralleled the movement of Chinese in earlier decades. Profit was high for those Japanese who operated emigration companies. Companies received service fees from the emigrant, commissions for selling tickets, and remunerations from potential employers.[21]

Those Japanese who entered into debt bondage had experiences similar to the Chinese. One company agent recruiting workers for the Northern Pacific railroad collected the fare of 45 yen ($22.50). If one did not have the money, the agent arranged for a down payment of 25 yen with the balance plus interest to be deducted from wages earned in the United States.[22]

After emigration became possible, Japanese laborers started arriving in the United States in greater numbers. From 1886 to 1890 the influx was about 200 immigrants a year. The 1890 census showed 2,039 Japanese residing in continental United States. The decade of the nineties saw large numbers of young unmarried males venture forth to make their fortunes in the United States. Dissatisfied Japanese in Hawaii also made their way to Pacific Coast states. The beginning of the twentieth century saw the number of Japanese residents in the United States increase tenfold to 24,326. Like the Chinese and other immigrant groups, at first they dreamed of the time they would return to their homes. For most, this dream grew more hazy each passing day.

The Superintendent of Immigration reported in 1892 that "Japan guards the emigration of her people with jealous care." If the receiving country looked with disfavor upon immigration, the empire severely restricted emigration. In 1897 the Superintendent found "these immigrants were intelligent, thrifty, possessed of small sums of money and most of them desired to engage in agricultural pursuits."[23] The Japanese emigration companies provided Western clothing, rehearsed answers to be given Customs officials and saw that each immigrant had a small amount of money upon arrival in the United States.[24] This appeared to some Americans as a well conceived plot to gain control of Western states.

When in 1886 the government of Japan allowed emigration, white supremacists were prepared. They had vocabulary and tools set to meet any new challenge. After gaining victory over the Chinese, they had remained mobilized.

In May, 1892, the *San Francisco Call* headlined a news story: "Japs Pouring In; 'Put up Bars' Says our Working People." While the newspaper found them to be pleasant people, the rhetorical question was asked: " 'Have we not enough of them now?' The answer of all the working girls and boys of California is 'Yes; not only enough, but too many. Keep the rest of the crowd out.' "[25] The *Call* revealed that the Japanese were in nearly every business and worked very cheaply. The newspaper claimed an important discovery—a Japanese agent was in San Francisco to encourage immigration.[26]

On May 30, 1892, Dennis Kearney, responding to the alarm sounded by the newspaper, delivered an address at the San Francisco City Hall. He held that the city was threatened with a new evil—the Japanese who were being brought in as cheap contract laborers as the Chinese had been. Kearney lashed out at those Japanese attending public school at the expense of the taxpayer and mingling with American girls. Soon these same people, he claimed, would be taking bread from the mouths of working men.[27] In this one speech, Kearney managed to reiterate all the touchstones of white prejudice against the Asian.

The Japanese minister in Washington protested to the Secretary of State about the 1897 boycott in Idaho against Japanese and Chinese business by the Knights of Labor. In addition the State of Idaho had made it illegal for any state agency or private corporation to give employment to aliens ineligible for citizenship.[28]

By 1899, the temper of the annual immigration reports was changing. The Immigration Service, using the same vocabulary once used against the Chinese, discovered a coolie class of Japanese entering Pacific ports. The report found something sinister in that:

Evidence is in the possession of the bureau of the existence of an elaborate and ingenious system by means of which this class whose apparent skill in the arts of evasion coupled with the difficulty of securing interpreters, other than such as are themselves natives of Japan, renders their examination by U. S. officials peculiarly difficult, are brought over under contract made through agents of principal cities of the Pacific Coast to work under contractors for various kinds of construction in which cheap and unskilled labor can be utilized. Present indications point to a steadily increasing immigration of this character and means should be provided to follow it to its final destination for the purpose of ascertaining if possible whether it is in violation of the law.[29]

When the Chinese arrived, representatives of the Six Companies took them in tow and placed them in jobs. In the 1890's and the first decade of the twentieth century, Japanese boarding houses and hotels served a similar purpose. These Japanese, under obligation to a particular emigrant company, were investments to be protected. Immigration officials attempted to prove the substance of the 1899 charge that contract labor was being sent to Japanese agents on the West Coast for assignment. Japanese hotel operators maintained this was not so; they usually went to dockside at the request of a friend in Japan who wished that the emigrants be provided with temporary housing.

In 1900, Seattle, a major port of entry, had six Japanese hotels similar to the Chinese dormitories in San Francisco. But here the similarity ended, for the Japanese had to pay cash for room and board. Five years later, as the number of immigrants increased, about sixty-five concerns were doing business. Since the new arrivals congregated at these hotels, labor recruiters kept close contact with the owners. Some recruiters had contracted with white employers to provide gangs of workers—a situation similar to Chinese work gangs.

The number of Japanese immigrants to the West Coast for most of the 1890's averaged about 1,500 a year. In 1898 and 1899 the number exceeded 2,000. But with the new century, the number skyrocketed. The years 1901-1910 were those of peak immigration from Japan when 129,797 people arrived. Immigration officials processed 12,635 in 1900. The next year, the number dropped to 5,269 and then accelerated again to over 10,000. The peak year of 1907 saw 30,226 Japanese—27,240 males and 2,986 females—come through American ports.[30]

In the first years of the 1900's, color-conscious Californians became aware of this new Asian influx. Having just solved in 1902 the Chinese immigration issue, they were menaced by a new yellow peril. As some 90,000 Japanese arrived on the West Coast during the first five years, racial prejudice and fear vented hostility upon them.

A mass labor meeting was held in San Francisco on May 7, 1900, to which representatives from throughout California were sent to urge Congress to extend the Chinese exclusion laws. An adjunct of this meeting was a resolution asking that the Japanese be included in exclusion legislation.[31] San Francisco Mayor James D. Phelan stated his opposition:

> The Japanese are starting the same tide of immigration which we thought we had checked twenty years ago. . . . The Chinese and Japanese are not bona fide citizens. They are not the stuff of which American citizens can be made. . . . Personally we have nothing

against Japanese but as they will not assimilate with us and their social life is so different from ours, let them keep at a respectful distance.[32]

Shortly after the convention, Congressman Julius Kahn of San Francisco reported that Commissioner General of Immigration Terence V. Powderly claimed the Japanese were a problem. Kahn told his constituents that "I will leave no stone unturned during the remaining days of the session to start the machinery for the exclusion of the Japanese."[33] The following year, both the Montana and Idaho legislatures memorialized Congress calling for exclusion of Japanese laborers and those of Japanese descent.[34]

On February 23, 1905, the *San Francisco Chronicle* struck out at the Japanese with a series of inflammatory headlines. The first read: "Japanese Invasion the Problem of the Hour for the United States: More than One Hundred Thousand of the Little Brown Men Now in the United States—One-Third in California." Other headlines claimed that: "Crime and Poverty Go Hand in Hand with Asiatic Labor"; "Japanese Sweat Shops Are A Blot on the City"; "Japanese a Menace to American Women"; "Brown Men An Evil in the Public Schools: Adult Japanese Crowd Out Children."[35] The California State Legislature following the newspaper attack passed a resolution asking Congress to "limit and diminish the further immigration of Japanese."[36] This resolution started the cycle of anti-Japanese legislation which paralleled the legal discrimination against the Chinese.

The early anti-Japanese agitation was centered in San Francisco with leadership coming from labor unions. San Francisco labor had captured control of City Hall when its candidate Eugene Schmitz was elected mayor. In May, 1905, a mass labor meeting was held to organize the Japanese and Korean Exclusion League. Four West Coast labor leaders were prominent in the anti-Japanese movement. Patrick Henry McCarthy, an Irish immigrant, headed the San Francisco Building Trades Council and was later mayor of the city. Andrew Furuseth, a Norwegian, instrumental in seamen's reform during the Wilson administration, was also hostile to Asians. Furuseth and Walter MacArthur of Scotland were leaders in the Sailors' Union. Another member, Olaf Tveitmoe, of Swedish origin, was named president of the new league.[37] The league reasserted charges made against the Chinese years before: assimilation would only injure American citizens; Japanese should neither marry Americans nor become citizens. The standard-of-living argument in opposition to the Japanese was also advanced.[38]

President Theodore Roosevelt, this same month, wrote George Kennan that he thought the California legislature was right in its recent protest against Japanese immigration "for their very frugality, abstemiousness, and clannishness make them formidable to our laboring class, and you may not know they have begun to offer a serious problem in Hawaii—all the more serious because they keep an entirely distinct and alien mass."[39] But the President made it clear that California's actions affronted the nation's well-being and such irresponsibility could easily plunge the United States into war.[40] Western Congressmen introduced bills to restrict the immigration of Japanese and Koreans although Roosevelt's 1905 annual message called for a nondiscriminatory immigration policy.[41]

On October 11, 1906, the San Francisco Board of Education issued its famous order which excluded all Chinese, Japanese, and Korean children from neighborhood schools and sent them to that city's Oriental school.[42] However, no Japanese child ever attended the Oriental school. When the San Francisco Chinese had in 1902 sought writs of mandate to allow a Chinese girl to attend a neighborhood school, both state and federal courts upheld existing state law. The federal judge stated: "It is well settled that the State has the right to provide separate schools for the children of different races, and such action is not forbidden by the Fourteenth Amendment to the Constitution, provided the schools so established make no discrimination in the educational facilities which they afford."[43]

California's discriminatory school measures endured for several decades, although there was no statewide pattern. Los Angeles, for example, never established separate schools for Asians. Under the California Education Code, created in 1929, some Sacramento River Delta districts continued to operate separate schools. The Japanese American Citizens League of Florin, California, persuaded that local board to close its Oriental school in 1940. At the time of the 1942 Japanese evacuation, one segregated school still existed at Courtland, Sacramento County.[44] In 1945, the parents of Takao Aratani, an eight-year-old American Japanese, challenged the constitutionality of California's separate school provision. A Los Angeles County Superior Court agreed that segregation on the basis of race or ancestry violated the Fourteenth Amendment. The California legislature repealed the provisions in 1946.[45]

The Federal Government in 1906 supported Japan's opposition to California's school law. In response to Japan's official protest, Roosevelt pointed out the lack of constitutional federal power in the face of the sovereignty of individual states. He informed the Japanese ambassador that the Department of Justice was preparing court action and that Secretary of Commerce and Labor Victor H. Metcalf, a Californian, was trying to resolve the situation.[46]

Internationally Japan was much stronger than China had ever been. Her rapid industrialization and strong military machine made her a power in the western Pacific. Her need for men for the military and the imposition of a universal conscription law were factors in hastening the decision of many young men to migrate eastward.

Japan's easy military victories over China in 1894 and Russia in 1905 had sobering effect upon the United States. In 1906, when the crisis created by the San Francisco Board of Education appeared to violate the treaty with Japan,

President Roosevelt manifested great apprehension over the activities of Western exclusionists in sharp contast to his lack of concern for the Chinese. Secretary of State Elihu Root confided in a secret memorandum to Metcalf the new-born but long-lasting fears which motivated the Federal Government's actions:

1. The Japanese are a proud and sensitive warlike people. They are particularly sensitive about anything which questions that equality. One-tenth of the insults which have been visited upon China by the people of the United States would lead to immediate war.

2. Japan is ready for war. It probably has the most effective equipment and personnel now existing in the world.

3. We are not ready for war and we could not be ready to meet Japan on anything like equal terms for a long period. The loss of the Philippines, Hawaii, and probably the Pacific Coast with the complete destruction of our commerce on the Pacific would occur before we were ready for a real fight.

4. It is difficult to estimate the national humiliation and loss which would result. While we would ultimately drive them out of our own country, there is little or no prospect of our ever being able to inflict any effective reprisals upon Japan. The loss suffered by us would be probably permanent and irreparable.

5. The Japanese tendency to war is greatly increased by the fact that the mass of the Japanese people were filled with rage at being checked in what they consider a clear and certain conquest of Russia.

6. The Japanese government always conducts its affairs like a military commander planning a campaign and it has extraordinary capacity for prompt and sudden action. If they see that the tendency of events is going to lead to war, they will not hesitate for an instant to bring it on at a time most favorable to them and that will be first, before we can have made adequate preparations, and second, before the Panama Canal is finished.

7. The position of Japan in China and Manchuria is commanding. Any hostile action against the Japanese would injure our trade in China.

8. In any controversy that arises, we shall not only be in an attitude absolutely without justification as between us and Japan but without justification in the eyes of the world because of the things done in San Francisco. The exclusion of the children and the boy-cotting of the restaurants—this constitutes a clear violation of our treaty with Japan. We will then be in a controversy in which Japan is justified. Even if there were no violation of the treaty, the attitude taken toward the Japanese is intrinsically unfair and indefensible. The Japanese are far superior to a very large part of the immigrants

who are coming into our Atlantic ports from Eastern Europe. They rank high among people of the world in civilization and the qualities of good citizenship. They associate and always will associate upon equal terms with the best and most highly cultivated and the ablest of mankind. The San Francisco attitude toward them is an exhibition of the same provincial and unrestricted narrowness and prejudice which the Japanese abandoned when Commodore Perry convinced them of its folly and which made Korea the Hermit Kingdom.

9. The government of the United States cannot and will not submit to being forced into an unjust quarrel and subject it to a national humiliation and disaster by the action of a few ignorant narrowminded and prejudiced men who wish to monopolize for themselves the labor market of San Francisco. The entire power of the federal government within the limits of the Constitution will be used and used promptly and vigorously to enforce observance of treaties which under the Constitution are the supreme law of the land and to secure decent treatment for a people of a great and friendly power within the territory of the United States.[47]

When Metcalf arrived in San Francisco he informed the commercial interests what might happen if they allowed labor elements to pursue dangerous tactics. After talking to state and city leaders, Metcalf informed Roosevelt that "while the Supreme Court of California and other thinking minds are alive to the significance and consequence of this matter, many of the people of this state are with a narrow provincialism, fomented and fostered by the newspapers, practically as hostile to the Japanese as to the Chinese."[48] No doubt the pessimism of the Secretary was influenced by expressions such as this statement of the *San Francisco Chronicle*:

A federal official who should attempt to enforce a contrary doctrine would find no one to obey him. Even if it were thinkable—which it is not—that the Supreme Court of the United States should assert Federal authority over the schools of a state, under any pretense, or upon any theory, the decision could never be enforced even by an army of the United States for there would be no army for that purpose. . . . It is doubtless true that California would not obey a mandate of the Supreme Court to admit Asiatics to our public schools but it would not be rebellion, for we should have behind us nine-tenths of the American people.[49]

Metcalf submitted his report to the President on November 26, 1906. He had examined the Cooks and Waiters Union's October boycotts against Japanese restaurants and assaults upon the Japanese. He concluded that if the city's police demonstrated further inability, it would be necessary for the Federal Government to protect Japan's treaty rights.[50]

His investigation focused mostly upon the school board's decision. He uncovered an amazing furor over very little and assessed properly that the issue was but a symptom of the city's major concern, the exclusion of Japanese labor. When the city schools had reopened in July, 1906, following the fire and earthquake of April, San Francisco citizens found ninety-three Japanese students enrolled in twenty-three different schools. George Kennan, in a separate investigation, found that on December 8, 1906, the total school population was 28,736. Sixty-eight of these were Japanese subjects and another twenty-five Japanese were United States citizens by birth. Kennan indicated their ages ranged from seven to twenty-six years; six in the primary grades were more than fifteen years old.[51] Metcalf found that objections of San Franciscans to young men attending primary grades were valid. His report emphasized labor's fear of being replaced by the Japanese.[52]

In his 1906 annual message, Roosevelt paid a glowing tribute to Japan and its people and castigated the action of San Francisco. Calling the school order a wicked absurdity, he demanded fair treatment for the Japanese.[53] He then displayed the Big Stick to California, much to the disgust of Western exclusionists:

Even as the law now is something can be done by the Federal Government toward this end, and in the matter now before me affecting the Japanese everything that it is in my power to do will be done, and all of the forces, military and civil of the United States which I may lawfully employ will be so employed. There should, however, be no particle of doubt as to the power of the National Government completely to perform and enforce its own obligations to other nations. The mob of a single city may at any time perform acts of lawless violence against some class of foreigners which would plunge us into war. That city by itself would be powerless to make defense against the foreign power thus assaulted, and if independent of this Government it would never venture to perform or permit the performance of the acts complained of. The entire power and the whole duty to protect the offending city or the offending community lies in the hands of the United States Government. It is unthinkable that we should continue a policy under which a given locality may be allowed to commit a crime against a friendly nation, and the United States limited, not to preventing the commission of the crime, but in the last resort, to defending the people who have committed it against the consequence of their own wrongdoing.[54]

The year's turbulence closed with battlelines firmly drawn. The school board based its position on states' rights while the President emphasized the supremacy of the treaty over state law. But both sides agreed that the matter was tied to the growing demand for exclusion of Japanese labor.

San Francisco's Board of Education and its mayor, Eugene Schmitz, traveled to Washington to meet with Roosevelt. As the San Francisco delegates entered the White House on February 9, 1907, Schmitz insisted that:

After the fire we found that the Japanese were crowding the white children out of the schools and the only course to pursue was to take advantage of the State law and establish separate schools. This was done. The white children took the places of the Japanese in the white schools and the Oriental schools were established for the Japanese.[55]

This he asserted in the face of the acknowledged fact that only ninety-three pupils were involved.

During the growing crisis over Japanese immigration, Root cabled Ambassador Luke E. Wright in Tokyo that the Federal Government could not maintain control over the Western state governments and that Congress might pass an exclusion bill. Root thought it would be much better if the Japanese themselves proposed a program of self-exclusion or regulation. Thus the plan known as the Gentlemen's Agreement was suggested to the Japanese government.[56]

On March 13, 1907, the board rescinded its October order and adopted three new resolutions which had Roosevelt's blessings: school principals would examine the educational qualifications of all alien children; age levels were set for admittance; and if any child had an English-language deficiency or did not qualify because of age, he was placed in a special school or class.[57] Federal pressures forced the board and the California legislature to yield.

Roosevelt was successful in having the San Francisco school officials abandon their discriminatory rules. The President and Root negotiated with the Japanese government the implementation of the Gentlemen's Agreement. During late 1907 and early 1908 the State Department completed arrangements. The Japanese government agreed not to issue passports to skilled or unskilled laborers to the mainland United States. Passports would be issued to "laborers who have already been in America and to the parents, wives, and children of laborers already resident there." Much of the misunderstanding about the Gentlemen's Agreement arose from the fact that details of the agreement were not made public until 1939.[58]

Whenever people requested information of the State Department about the agreement, they were referred to the 1908 *Annual Report* of the Commissioner General of Immigration. The report noted that the Japanese government had always maintained a policy of regulating emigration to the United States, but many of its subjects had evaded this policy by migrating to Hawaii and then to the United States. On March 14, 1907, President Roosevelt had issued a proclamation excluding Japanese or Korean laborers who had received passports directly to Mexico, Canada, or Hawaii and then tried to enter the United States. The Commissioner General then presented the understanding reached between Japan and the United States:

In order that the best results might follow from an enforcement of the regulations, an understanding was reached with Japan that the existing policy of discouraging emigration of its subjects of the laboring classes to continental United States should be continued, and should, by co-operation with the governments, be made as effective as possible. This understanding contemplates that the Japanese government shall issue passports to continental United States only to such of its subjects as are non-laborers or are laborers who, in coming to the continent, seek to resume a formerly acquired domicile, to join a parent, wife, or children residing there, or to assume active control of an already possessed interest in a farming enterprise in this country, so that the three classes of laborers entitled to receive passports have come to be designated "former residents," "parents, wives, or children of residents," and "settled agriculturists."

With respect to Hawaii, the Japanese government of its own volition stated that, experimentally at least, the issuance of passports to members of the laboring classes proceeding thence would be limited to "former residents" and "parents, wives or children of residents." The said government has also been exercising a careful supervision over the subject of emigration of its laboring class to foreign contiguous territory.[59]

The 1908 report expressed the official views of the United States government that the agreement was a monument to the cooperation and good faith of two governments who sought long-reaching and desirable results. The Commissioner General held that immigration figures showed the agreement was working.[60]

CHAPTER IX

"The Japs Must Go!"
Discrimination and Hostility, 1907-1952

MOST WESTERNERS BELIEVED THAT THE GENTLEMEN'S AGREE-ment would exclude all Japanese. United States Senator George C. Perkins, interviewed in his California home at the close of the 1906-1907 Congressional session, announced that the Japanese coolie influx had been stopped.[1] Without precise information, the susceptible minds of fearful Westerners became prey to the inflammatory propaganda of exclusion organizations, and agitation continued.

The Gentlemen's Agreement did work, as annual immigration figures show. In 1907, 30,226 immigrants arrived. During the first year of the agreement, 15,803 arrivals were registered. Many of these had valid passports issued in advance of the agreement which were honored. A sharp decline was registered in 1909 when only 3,111 were admitted. In 1909, 66 percent of those entering were classified as non-laborers; by 1918 this percentage increased to 77 percent.

San Franciscans, unaware of the terms of the agreement, continued to discriminate. On May 20, 1907, a mob broke into a Japanese restaurant and a bathhouse. Demonstrations against other restaurants continued for four evenings. The Japanese envoy in Washington lodged a protest. A Justice Department investigation coupled these uprisings with the general street railway strike then in progress and felt the attacks were not aimed specifically at the Japanese.[2] Yet no white establishment was invaded. The laborers' pent-up hatred of the Japanese led to violence. The *San Francisco Chronicle* bore out this animosity when it wrote the Japanese had the right to sue for damages but:

> If we are correctly informed, they have next to no chance of proving it in this case, unless upon the theory that the Japanese who insist upon coming here, where they are not wanted, are entitled to some special ... protection. . . . The ordinary citizen is not supposed to be entitled to such extraordinary care, but only to such responsible police service as will suffice, where there is no reason to expect mob violence directed to him.
>
> The Japanese are not liked, nor desired here. We do not see why they do not all clear out and go to Los Angeles or Boston, Mass.[3]

While this latest protest was being investigated, the Tokyo government learned that San Francisco authorities had refused to license Japanese employment agencies or any other Japanese businesses. In 1906 the San Francisco Board of Supervisors had enacted an ordinance granting liquor licenses only to United States citizens. On June 27, 1907, the City Board of Police Commissioners refused to license six Japanese to operate employment agencies. The commission, indicating that it was just following the lead of the Board of Supervisors, claimed no intended injustice to the Japanese but "we want to favor citizens in preference to people who are not citizens."[4]

The State Department still believed that the Gentlemen's Agreement would solve California's problems and end discrimination. Federal pressure was again applied within California to stop San Francisco from its discriminatory activities and to force the board to grant licenses. Roosevelt told Root in July, 1907, that troops massed near San Francisco were to be used if state or local authorities were either unable or unwilling to protect the Japanese.[5]

California racists during 1908 refrained from overt action but the state's Democratic Party, out of power, sought to gain labor's support. It produced a pamphlet showing that the Republicans remained mute on the immigration issue while the Democrats had adopted a plank opposing Asian immigration. William Jennings Bryan said in part when he accepted his party's third call:

> The Chinese Exclusion Act has proven an advantage to this country, and its continuance and strict enforcement, as well as its extension to other similar races, are imperatively necessary. The Asiatic is so essentially different from the American that he can not be assimilated with our population, and is, therefore, not desirable as a permanent citizen.[6]

Following the 1908 elections, the legislative hoppers of California, Nevada, and Oregon received many anti-Japanese bills and resolutions. The opposition in 1909 as in 1907 remained bipartisan. Republican Grove Johnson of Sacramento introduced three such bills—to exclude Japanese from schools attended by white children, to prevent aliens from becoming members of boards of directors of California corporations, and to permit municipalities to segregate into specified areas those "aliens whose presence may be inimical to health and public morals."[7]

Other measures proposed to restrict land ownership by aliens.[8] What had been first an urban problem—white labor's fear—became also a rural one when Japanese agricultural workers became farmers and landowners, threatening white farmers. A rural northwestern California newspaper summarized Californians' feelings in 1909:

> It is a strange condition of affairs if this State has not backbone enough to enact legislation regulating its police affairs. The segregation of Mongolians in our public schools is a police regulation, a regulation governing public morals. Japanese, in fact aliens generally, should not be permitted to monopolize our land. Even the Japanese government realizes the gravity of the situation in the Pacific and has promised to stop coolie immigration. That is good as far as it goes, but the people will not be satisfied if things are left in that condition.[9]

Roosevelt, in his last months as President, worked to restrain the California legislature. He relied upon Governor

James Gillett to point out that the immigration agreement seemed to be working and that:

There is, therefore, no shadow of excuse for action which will simply produce great irritation and may result in upsetting the present agreement and throwing open the whole situation again. These agitators have themselves to thank if trouble comes from what they do, ... Is it not possible to get the legislature to realize the great unwisdom from the standpoint of the country at large, and above all from the standpoint of California, of what is being done?[10]

There was much sound and fury during the 1909 legislative session. Grove Johnson's school bill almost passed; only hard work by party regulars saved the President from embarrassment. Two measures which did pass called for enumeration of Japanese in the state and for extension to the Japanese of the Chinese Exclusion Act.[11]

The 1910 California Democratic State Platform advocated the exclusion of all Asiatic labor and the adoption of State Senator John B. Sanford's measure "preventing Asiatics, who are not eligible to citizenship in America, from owning or leasing land in California."[12]

The United States and Japan in 1911 negotiated a new commercial treaty and Grove Johnson's son, Hiram, who bitterly opposed his father's political views, became Governor of California. As the 1911 California legislative session opened, Governor Johnson sent advance sheets of proposed anti-Japanese bills to Secretary of State Philander Knox. Johnson reported: "I think I can assure you that the committees of both houses that will have in charge measures of this character are wholly sane and trustworthy and that doubtless they will be guided by the wishes of the federal administration."[13] Because of the treaty negotiations, Washington watched Sacramento with an uneasy eye and kept telegraph wires humming between the two capitals. Knox informed San Francisco Mayor Patrick H. McCarthy, head of the Building Trades Council and a leading supporter of the Asiatic Exclusion League, that it would be helpful if

he could assist in heading off the proposed restrictive legislation.[14] On January 31, President William Howard Taft
handed Knox a note which showed that McCarthy had
wired Olaf A. Tveitmoe, exclusion league president, that
"nothing has been proposed which will in any way expose
to danger the American wage earner."[15]

A telegram from Portland, Oregon, reflects well Pacific
Coast fears about the treaty consultations. Portland's Spanish War Veterans telegraphed Taft:

That we hereby protest the dastardly action of the Congress of the
United States in entering into a treaty with Japan by the terms of
which the Pacific Coast will eventually be populated by persons of
an alien race which is unassimilable and are a menace to moral
religious industrial and social traditions of our land and we hereby
denounce the said treaty as being of the interest to the capitalist and
not the common classes of people of our beloved country.[16]

During the Roosevelt years, conservative Republicans
dominated California politics but in 1910 Hiram Johnson
led the Progressive wing to victory. Domestically, the California Progressives were reformers but their program did
not include social equality for the Japanese. They maintained
that they did not wish to create another South in California
and thus to thrust upon the nation another problem of color.
Consequently, the golden rule of reform for middle-class
society did not, or could not, extend to the Japanese.[17]

For a time, the President had held the Californians in
check with the possibility of awarding the Panama-Pacific
Exposition to New Orleans. On February 15, 1911, however, Taft signed the bill awarding the exposition to San
Francisco and thereby lost his advantage. Many in Sacramento felt that California had exchanged a pledge of no
anti-Japanese legislation for the exposition. Tveitmoe immediately repudiated all charges that the Asian Exclusion
League had acquiesced. He informed that California legislature and Secretary of State Knox that the league still de-

sired Sanford's anti-alien land bill and school segregation. He concluded:

We have spent the best years of our lives in an effort to help solve the main problems in cleaning the immigration question which is pressing heavily upon the shoulders of the workers who with their brain and brawn and sinew have wrought the greatness of this state and nation and we shall continue in the same even tenure of our way regardless of whatever noise the little distant drums may make while passing in temporary review. Notwithstanding our consideration we will persevere in our labor the removing of the barricades and obstacles of ignorance and prejudice and clear the way for more toleration and a better understanding of those essential things which help make lives of the masses more replete with happiness.[18]

For Tveitmoe and his small exclusion group, happiness meant elimination of the Japanese.

The climax to California's legal discrimination came in 1913 with passage of the anti-alien land law. Since 1908 California Democrats had favored exclusion but Republican governors, allied with Republican Presidents, had held the exclusionists at bay. The 1913 controversy saw President Woodrow Wilson, a subscriber to the states' rights view, forced to battle California in behalf of Japan, while Hiram Johnson, a disciple of New Nationalism, became in the national eye, the champion of states' rights.

When the California legislature met in January, 1913, it introduced about forty discriminatory measures. Besides the usual school segregation bill, there were bills forbidding Japanese to use power engines in any occupation, subjecting them to poll taxes, prohibiting them from obtaining liquor licenses and employing white women, and increasing their commercial fishing fees.[19]

Several proposed land bills aimed at restricting ownership to "aliens eligible to citizenship" or prohibiting ownership by "those aliens ineligible to citizenship" were introduced. Most legislators were confident that some land law would pass. Governor Johnson at first worked closely with the San

Francisco Exposition leaders to prevent any hostile legislation.

An indication of the temper of Californians is well shown in a letter from A. P. Bettersworth, publisher of the *Elk Grove Citizen,* to Republican Assemblyman Hugh Bradford. Elk Grove was a small farm community near Sacramento in the midst of expanding Japanese farming operations.

Friend Bradford—
Everybody in Elk Grove is complimenting you today on your stand on the Jap question. Stay with it, old boy. There will never be a time when Big Business won't find an excuse to postpone legislation against these Asiatics. Californians should not sell their birthright for a mess of pottage. . . . Were I a Jap I'd welcome to a hospitable grave the American who sought to use me and then stab me in the back after it was over. That is what the exposition crowd are trying to do. I congratulate you on having chosen the nobler and the manlier way.[20]

On April 8, 1913, a *Tokyo Nichi Nichi Shimbun* editorial protested bitterly against the measures pending in the California legislature:

Although the anti-Japanese members of the Legislature plead that the land ownership bill is a general one directed against all aliens not entitled to the right of naturalization, it is well known that the only aliens who do not possess this right are the Japanese and Chinese, and that those who will be most seriously affected by the enactment of the bill are the Japanese, whom it is obviously the real intention of the introducers to expel from the United States in the same manner as they have the Chinese. What a base motive and high-handed lawlessness! Moreover, Mr. Johnson, Governor of California, although occupying a position of responsibility, presumes to declare that, if the bill causes any injury to the Japanese, it will not be the fault of the California Legislature, but that of the Federal Government, which refuses to grant them the right of naturalization. He thus tries to shift the responsibility to the central government and curry the favor of the people of California. . . .[21]

Governor Johnson arranged for an April 2 public hearing in Sacramento on the Japanese issue which gave the Panama-Pacific International Exposition directors an opportunity to argue against anti-Asian legislation. Johnson described the hearing to Theodore Roosevelt:

the farmers appeared, and the debate between the very plain rugged, untutored and uncluttered men from the fields and our astute and educated, plug-hatted brigade who represented the Exposition was most interesting and memorable. When it had ceased the Exposition people retired crestfallen; the audience roared its approval of the farmers and the Committee in charge of the bill immediately and unanimously reported that it "do pass."[22]

One of these farmers, Ralph Newman, was a former Congregational minister.[23] His remarks were circulated widely through the West:

Near my home is an eighty-acre tract of as fine land as there is in California. On that tract lives a Japanese. With that Japanese lives a white woman. In that woman's arms is a baby.

What is that baby? It isn't a Japanese. It isn't white. It is a germ of the mightiest problem that ever faced this state; a problem that will make the black problem of the South look white.[24]

On April 21, the Progressive leadership decided to support an anti-Asian land bill which was much harsher than substitute measures already passed in each house. President Wilson then telegraphed Johnson on April 23 asking if Secretary of State William Jennings Bryan could visit Sacramento. Governor Johnson extended an official welcome. He made it clear that authority was divided between the federal and state governments. California knew its responsibilities, but the state's legal and moral rights would be upheld. Johnson added that much had been said about Japan's dignity, but Californians were concerned over the proposition that "a great State, itself an empire, shall be halted from mere consideration of a legislative act admittedly within its jurisdiction, by the protest of a foreign power which itself has enacted even more stringent regulations on the same subject."[25]

Bryan conferred with the Governor and key Democrats and then addressed the legislators. He brought no new proposals from Washington and Californians knew from the first day that the trip had been in vain. During an executive session of both houses, Governor Johnson closed the debate when he said the issue was not "Is Japan offended today? But is Japan justly offended today?" Johnson contended that California intended no offense against the Japanese people. The U. S. Government had already declared them ineligible to citizenship and Johnson said: "I insist that we are within our rights in enacting a statute of the character that is contemplated; that it is not discriminatory against Japan and that, in enacting that statute, there can be no just cause for offense on the part of Japan, or any other nation that is excluded from citizenship by the laws of the United States."[26]

To avoid possible legal entanglements, California's Attorney General Ulysses S. Webb and Francis Heney, Progressive associates of the governor, prepared a bill substituting the phrase—"aliens eligible to citizenship" for "aliens ineligible for citizenship."[27] On May 3, the Senate passed by a vote of 35 to 2 the Webb bill with an amendment allowing all aliens to lease land for three years.[28] As Bryan was leaving town, the Assembly passed the same bill by a vote of 72 to 3.[29]

In assessing the problem from a distance, the *Independent* noted that the land law applied equally to the Chinese, but no one was concerned about their rights since China did not have a strong navy or a good war record. It suggested that Bryan had "the better side of the poorer case. As a matter of international courtesy or morals, he is all right, but the laws and the precedents are against him." Johnson had demonstrated that the Federal Government made the Japanese and Chinese ineligible for citizenship and this limitation was a greater offense than restriction of land ownership. Bryan was unable to answer why Washington and Arizona alien land laws were acceptable and California's was not.[30]

Californians closed ranks when the Wilson administration suggested dire consequences if Johnson signed the measure. Chester Rowell, a foe of the 1913 measure but Johnson's close political advisor, wrote:

on the larger aspects of the case I think we should agree. This state, on the border between the white man's world and the brown man's world, must be kept absolutely and at any cost a white man's state. If we do not keep it a white man's state it will soon become either a brown man's state or a feudal plutocracy in which there are white and brown aristocrats and brown, yellow and black common people. Neither of these alternatives is too startling to be contemplated.[31]

Hiram Johnson signed the measure on May 19, closing the federal-state issue. Wilson's administration had to deal alone with Japan.

To Governor Johnson were directed expressions of racial hatred against the Japanese from people in all walks of life. He received a copy of a telegram sent by the Pacific Protectorate Society in Los Angeles to President Wilson on May 10:

Japan knew previous to last treaty that our naturalization laws prevented all Orientals from importation, invasion and citizenship. It is not within the jurisdiction of an Alien barred by our laws and our representatives to place fetters on our liberties or subject us to a court of arbitration. This state has been invaded by an army of aliens under generals. . . . Our government for seven years has coerced the State of California and protected its enemies. A solution of the matter reaches you Thursday. Action is demanded or this State will seize the Custom Houses, build forts, and raise an army for protection.[32]

In a similar vein, Fred L. Chase, First Regiment, Moose Patrol, San Bernardino, California, wrote that he had organized a full regiment of well drilled men within the Loyal Order of Moose. He had twelve companies, some fully uniformed but equipped with sword only. He closed saying: "The First Moose Patrol is ready for the command of the Governor."[33] Novelist Kathleen Norris wrote the Governor from Long Island: "Will you permit us to extend to you our heartiest congratulations upon your decision to sign the disputed bill, and our thanks for your courage in making the safety of your own people your first consideration?"[34]

World War I brought a hiatus to California's open hostility. California farmers were not overly concerned about Japanese competition since there were ready buyers for all products. The 1913 alien land law placated many Californians for a time. However, the leasing clause and the growing ownership of land by American-born children of "aliens ineligible for citizenship" negated the effectiveness of the law.

The 1919 California legislature's call for an investigation of land leasing led to a study by the Board of Control, *California and the Oriental*.[35] As fears of the Japanese "peaceful penetration" mounted, the Japanese Exclusion League of California, also known as the California Exclusion League, was organized in September, 1919, in Sacramento.[36] Unlike the earlier anti-establishment labor leaders who had led the anti-Chinese drives of the 1870's and who had launched the anti-Japanese movement, those who directed the 1919 drive came from California's power structure. Racial fear was undisguised. These men did not cloak their arguments with economic or political concerns. They openly advocated a White America. State Senator J. M. Inman of Sacramento was president of the league. John S. Chambers, California State Controller, was chairman of the Executive Committee. United States Senator James D. Phelan and Buron Fitts, a Republican seeking his party's nomination for Governor, were on the committee. Matt I. Sullivan, former chairman of the State Commission for the Panama-Pacific Exposition, and Clarence M. Hunt, editor of the Native Sons of the Golden West's magazine, the *Grizzly Bear*, were on the Finance Committee.[37] The league represented the California State Federation of Labor, the California State Grange, the California Department of the American Legion, and the Native Sons of the Golden West.

The *Grizzly Bear*, in its October, 1919, issue, introduced

Valentine S. McClatchy who became the publicist for the league and in time shared the leadership with Phelan. Mc-Clatchy, who retired as publisher of the *Sacramento Bee* in 1920, was an influential person with a substantial private income who gave full time to the cause. His friendship with United States Senator Hiram Johnson helped prepare the all-out drive for Federal exclusion legislation.[38]

McClatchy set forth in the *Grizzly Bear* the platform of the exclusion league from which it never deviated:

1. Cancellation of the "Gentlemen's Agreement."
2. Exclusion of "Picture Brides."
3. Rigorous exclusion of Japanese as immigrants.
4. Confirmation of the policy that Asiatics shall be forever barred from American citizenship.
5. Amendment of the Federal Constitution providing that no child born in the United States shall be given the rights of an American citizen unless both parents are of a race eligible to citizenship.[39]

Senator James Phelan quickly introduced the league's fifth point in the United States Senate.[40]

Governor William Stephens sent the findings of the California Board of Control on the Oriental in California to Secretary of State Bainbridge Colby:

Again, I deplore the necessity of stating that the spirit of the Anti-Asian Land Legislation passed in 1913 has been evaded and broken through the resort to certain legal subterfuges which have almost frustrated the very purpose of the enactment. These evasions have been accomplished through the medium of corporations, trustee stock ownership, and the device of having native infant children of Japanese parentage made grantees of agricultural lands controlled and operated exclusively by their non-eligible parents.[41]

California was again confronted with the fact that while it could pass discriminatory legislation, it could not prevent the immigration of Asians and their right to work in the state. That power resided in Congress. Stephens reported to Colby that California voters would pass the 1920 initiative measure which would prohibit further transfer of land to Japanese nationals as well as the leasing of land to them and to land corporations in which Japanese were majority stockholders. Most importantly, the measure prevented non-citizen parents of Japanese Americans from serving as guardians for their minor children.[42]

Westerners became highly emotional about Japanese female immigration. Valentine S. McClatchy presented a standard and repetitive argument in a 1921 article in the *Sacramento Bee* entitled: "Picture Brides and their Successors: Japanese Ingenuity in Forcing Peaceful Penetration under the Gentlemen's Agreement":

The intent on the part of the Japanese, it is quite evident, now is to secure upon this continent a foothold for their race, not as individual units to be absorbed and assimilated in the great American melting pot, but as a compact body of loyal subjects of the Mikado, to serve his interests in every way possible. For years the Japanese in California have been appealed to by their leaders and their vernacular newspapers "to beget many children and to secure much land" as the surest means for "permanently establishing the Yamoto race in this country."[43]

On the eve of exclusion in 1924, the *San Francisco Chronicle* editorialized that the Japanese bride was the real menace, for there would be "several Japanese citizens per bride who can become landowners, leading the dual life of American citizens and Japanese subjects."[44]

The issue of picture brides came early to the attention of the United States officials. Robert Devlin, United States Attorney, Northern District, California, reported in 1908 that the Japanese Consul-General wished information about California law regarding marriages contracted between Japanese living in California and Japanese women residing in Japan by exchanging photographs. The Consul-General described the practice as valid under Japanese law. A man mailed a photograph of himself to the woman he intended to marry. She in return sent a photograph back and if both parties agreed, the marriage was registered in an office in Japan. Devlin's preliminary investigation led him to inform the Japanese official that if one of the two parties to the marriage were residing in California prior to the marriage, there was some doubt as to its legality.

The Federal Government concluded that an exchange of photographs could constitute a marriage. The decision was to recommend to Japan that women applying for admission to the United States should "claim to be destined to men in this country to whom they have been married by the photograph method and, shall before being permitted to land, evidence their good faith by being married to the alleged husband under a ceremony whose legality is recognized in the state in which the port of entry is located."[45]

The picture bride controversy came to a head in 1919 when United States Senator James Phelan of California, formerly Mayor of San Francisco and a dedicated Japanese exclusionist, introduced an amendment to the immigration laws to exclude completely Japanese laborers and to end the Gentlemen's Agreement. Phelan informed the State Department that his principal target was the picture bride.[46] Secretary of State Robert Lansing informed the Japanese ambassador that something ought to be done about the picture brides. When the ambassador inquired if a good effect would result if Japan prohibited their entrance, Lansing stated it would.[47] Shortly after this, the Japanese government announced that February 29, 1920, was the last day that passports would be issued to picture brides, and all such passports expired on September 1, 1920.[48]

Roger Daniels aptly summarizes the long-continuing hatred for California's Japanese. They were color visible and physically did not disappear into the myth of the melting pot. The Japanese became too American in competing with whites in many businesses and professions.[49] The Yellow Peril theory which held that Japan was the Germany of Asia convinced many Americans that she was indeed starting her long-range plan of infiltrating California and the Pacific Coast to prepare for the landing of Japanese troops. Richmond Pearson Hobson, the Spanish-American War naval hero, writing for the *San Francisco Examiner,* declared that the Japanese were in 1907 "rushing forward with feverish haste stupendous preparations for war." He declared that that war would be with the United States.[50] Japan's actions in East Asia after World War I did not ease the concern of Americans. Thus her emigrants reaped the harvest of American ill will.

The report by Roland S. Morris, United States Ambassador to Japan, *Japanese Immigration and Alleged Discrimination Against Japanese Resident in the United States,* published in 1921, became the cornerstone of the federal executive's position on the internal Japanese question during the 1920's and 1930's. In a March, 1921, memorandum, John V. A. MacMurray, Chief of the Division of Far Eastern Affairs, wrote that the:

so-called California-Japanese question has two phases, immigration and residence. They are frequently confused, and this confusion is the cause of a good deal of the present misapprehension. The Japanese contention is that under the law of California they are not given the same rights as other aliens in that state. . . .

The Japanese maintained that they had rights under the existing treaty. MacMurray noted that Morris and Japanese Ambassador Shidehara had urged a revision of the Gentlemen's Agreement which should be made public and enforceable by the United States. They suggested that the United States prohibit Japanese immigration and that Japanese residents in the United States receive the same rights and privileges granted by state or federal legislation to other aliens.[51]

MacMurray quoted Morris's conclusion that the solution to the vexing problem internally was one of assimilation:

. . . the next generation of citizens and the present generation of aliens are given without discrimination all the civil rights attached to their status, that we will then lay the groundwork for an earnest effort to Americanize the Japanese and break up the vicious system which now exists among them. Of one thing I feel reasonably sure. Unless we abolish discriminatory treatment, we can never successfully assimilate into our institutions the body of Japanese already here. I think from the national viewpoint any discriminatory legislation against Japanese aliens now will tend only to strengthen the Japanese organization at present existing in California and will draw the Japanese people further apart from American life.[52]

A month later, MacMurray learned that Charles Evans Hughes, the new Secretary of State, felt that the state governments were on "pretty sound ground."[53] For the next two decades, the Federal Government neatly separated the immigration question from the states' rights issue. The executive branch upheld the rights of the states while continuing to talk about the national issue of citizenship and immigration.

In 1921, 7,878 Japanese were admitted; women outnumbered the men. By 1923 the total number declined to 5,809 and Japanese immigration appeared to be leveling off. As noted earlier, the Japanese never constituted a sizeable part of the total annual immigration. But many Americans had long been concerned about the changing characteristics of immigration. In 1924, the United States Congress rewrote the general immigration law because of increasing numbers of non-Nordic immigrants. In the House of Representatives, the fate of the Japanese was decided long before the final vote of 326-71 opposing their further immigration.[54]

The exclusionists were not on such firm ground in the Senate. The West was represented by Senator Hiram Johnson of California, absent much of the time while campaigning for the presidential nomination. There were also only two Southerners in favor of exclusion.[55] When the Senate Committee on Immigration reported out the measure, the Gentlemen's Agreement was left untouched. The debate on the Japanese immigration issue centered about the agreement's secrecy. Secretary of State Charles E. Hughes asked Japanese Ambassador Masano Hanihara to write a letter to him summarizing the agreement.[56] On April 11, 1924,

Hughes sent the letter to the Senate. Henry Cabot Lodge, an advocate of Anglo-Saxonism, seized the letter and turned the tide for exclusionism. The Hanihara letter, after outlining clearly the existing agreement, concluded:

> Relying on the confidence you have been good enough to show me at all times I have stated or rather repeated all this to you very candidly and in a most friendly spirit, for I realize, as I believe you do, the grave consequences which the enactment of the measure retaining that particular provision would inevitably bring upon the otherwise happy and mutually advantageous relations between our two countries.[57]

Lodge picked out the two words "grave consequences" and argued that this was a threat against the United States. The upshot was that the Gentlemen's Agreement was struck from the bill by a vote of 76 to 2. On April 16, 1924, the Senate voted 71 to 4 for exclusion.[58] The Immigration Bill was signed by President Coolidge on May 26, 1924, and the Japanese joined other Asians in being excluded from the United States as aliens ineligible for citizenship.[59] The number of Japanese classified as immigrants dropped from 8,801 in 1924 to 867 in 1925. The Immigration Service recorded small number of entries for the next two decades.[60]

After World War II and the removal of West Coast Japanese, both alien and citizen alike, to interior relocation centers, Congress reconsidered the entire matter of Asian immigration. In 1949, Representative George P. Miller of California, Francis E. Walter of Pennsylvania, Sidney R. Yates of Illinois, and Delegate Joseph Farrington of Hawaii each introduced bills to provide naturalization for those aliens legally in the United States and to extend quotas to Asian and Pacific peoples.[61] In 1950, the House passed a resolution calling for an end to racial restrictions of 90,000 resident Japanese and Korean aliens but the senate refused to adopt the resolution.[62]

In 1952 the McCarran-Walter Immigration Act granted an annual quota to Japan as well as to other Asian countries.

Under the law, Japan had an annual quota of 185. The more important aspect of this legislation was that race was no longer a bar to citizenship.

Suziburo Kujiraoka on February 14, 1953, sent from Tokyo to Senator Pat McCarran his warm appreciation for he had just been chosen as the first Japanese to receive a visa to the United States under the McCarran-Walter Act. Representative Samuel W. Yorty of California reported the same year that hundreds of Issei (first-generation immigrants) had signed up for citizenship classes as a result of the new law. He reported a slight problem since the law provided that persons over fifty who had lived here fifty years did not need to know English. The demand was greater than the availability of interpreters in the Immigration Service.[63]

In 1950, 100 Japanese arrived in the United States; in 1952, the number increased to 3,814. From 1957 through 1959, more than 6,000 a year migrated. In 1960, 5,699 left Japan for the United States.[64]

The Japanese came then in increasing numbers after 1952 as had their predecessors to start a new life in the United States. While this new group encountered some economic discrimination, they were spared much of the bitter persecution levied against the earlier immigrants.

CHAPTER X

Helping America Prosper

BOTH IN HAWAII AND THE WESTERN STATES, THE JAPANESE
first came as agricultural workers. Their attainments in
various economic endeavors earned them both envy and
hatred.

The Hawaiian sugar plantations, from 1890 to the end
of World War II, owed their success to the hands and backs
of Japanese unskilled laborers. In 1902, 31,029 Japanese,
73.5 percent of the total, labored on plantations. This number gradually declined to about 30 percent in 1942.[1] The
Japanese followed the Chinese from the fields into other
activities. In 1910, 33,871 Japanese (76.8 percent) were
classified as laborers. There were 5,183 (9.9 percent) in
1960.[2] The Hawaiian Japanese moved from agriculture and
unskilled work to diversified economic employment ranging from independent farming and horticulture to small
business, civil service, and professions in law, medicine,
and at the University of Hawaii.

As already noted, the Japanese replaced the Chinese
in California as those seasonal field hands who moved from
crop to cop in the Great Central Valley and other fertile
regions. The United States Immigration Commission reported that 40 percent of the mainland Japanese, some
10,000 to 11,000, worked on western farms in sugar beets,
grapes, fruits, berries, vegetables, and hops which required
considerable hand labor at peak periods. The Japanese
formed the backbone of the beet sugar industry in Idaho,

Montana, Colorado, and Utah. In Oregon, Japanese laborers worked on white-owned farms near Portland and the Hood River. Some Japanese farmers raised berries and vegetables and soon most other Japanese laborers began working for them. The same was true in the Washington areas around Tacoma and Seattle.[3]

The United States Immigration Commission found that during the nineteenth century the Chinese had first done the more disagreeable work. By 1910, the Chinese were regular farm employees doing hand work and teaming the horses. Few Chinese became independent farmers, but the Japanese moved quickly to a status of independence.[4]

California sugar beet farmers remembered fondly the Chinese as thoroughly honest, faithful, conscientious, and efficient, if slow, workers who required no watching, kept their contracts, and had their employer's interest at heart. The Japanese, for their part, were praised widely for their industry, eagerness, sobriety, cleanliness, and adaptability to American customs. But they were condemned for a lack of commercial honesty and for the pursuit of their own interests without concern for their employers.[5]

Four Japanese immigrants moved onto Vaca Valley farms during the winter of 1887-88. In 1890 a few worked in the Fresno vineyards while other appeared in the Newcastle fruit areas. In 1892 still others were in the Watsonville area as hop pickers. Wherever farmers needed help the Japanese appeared. By 1900, they were utilized in the Southern California citrus crops.

Thus the Japanese quickly filled the void left by the Chinese. Like the Chinese, they used labor gangs. The Chinese gangs were organizational instruments but the Japanese used theirs for economic betterment moving from laborer to share cropper, manager, and finally independent farmer. Japanese labor agents provided workers to harvest crops. As the real employers, the agents secured the number of men needed and assumed the responsibility of fulfilling the contract. The farm owner had no direct contact with the workers, but paid the agents who in turn paid their men.

Japanese gangs soon dominated seasonal agricultural work as they consistently underbid Chinese and white workers. On one ranch, the lowest harvest bid by an American was $18 an acre while a Japanese agent bid $14.[6] In another locality where Chinese field hands had received $5 a week, the Japanese bid $2.40.[7]

California agriculture simply needed transient labor and turned to Japanese which was more reliable and less expensive than white labor. Even with the rapid increase of Japanese immigrants to meet the West's agricultural needs, labor prices rose.[8]

The Japanese contractors used tactics, familiar to American labor, to increase demands once their competition had been eliminated by low bids. One technique delayed harvesting under the claim of not having enough laborers and then demanding increased wages because the beets had grown in size after the contract was signed. The owner, faced with total crop loss, was forced to accede.[9] Other devices were strikes, threats of strikes, and boycotts of hostile farmers.[10]

The California sugar beet industry, for one, found that once the Japanese monopolized the market, labor costs rose. In 1889, the Japanese worked an 11-hour day for $1.00. By using their tactics, they gained an additional 10¢ a day. By 1908 wages were $1.65 a day.[11]

The profits made from the labor contract system helped transform Japanese seasonal workers into tenant farmers. Some white farmers willingly leased their holdings to secure an adequate labor supply and allowed the tenant farmer to grapple with labor agents.[12] The Japanese, for their part, were eager to lease land for they were ambitious to become independent farmers. Many consequently paid higher shares or cash rents at first. Numbers of white owners were happy to negotiate leases with the Japanese because they made improvements which brought both higher crop yields and cash returns.

The Japanese move to become independent farmers had both economic and social impact. Those white farmers who suffered financially in the face of more efficient farming methods allied with exclusionists because the Japanese quest for farm land caused prices to rise, forcing out marginal farmers. Extensive leasing by the Japanese caused a shift in farming communities as white families moved out or became fearful about buying in the midst of Japanese holdings.[13]

The Japanese specialized in crops which proved to have high profits. The success of these Japanese is one of their major contributions to the United States—and this success came in spite of hostile white farmers. There were thirty-nine Issei farmers in the United States in 1900; thirty-seven were in California. By 1910 there were 1,816 Issei farmers. In 1904 they owned 2,442 acres, leased 35,258 for cash, and farmed 19,572 on crop shares. Five years later, ownership increased to 16,449 acres; 80,232 acres were leased and 59,001 acres were held on shares.[14]

While acreage is indicative of the Japanese move onto the land, the value received for their crops was even more important, for it made possible the acreage expansion. In 1909, their crops had a market value of $16,200,000. In 1920 this had increased to $67,100,000. In spite of anti-Japanese propaganda, this increase did not come completely at the expense of the white farmer. In fact, at this time all of California agriculture was expanding. The Japanese reclaimed swamp and arid lands which California farmers had earlier declared unprofitable. Further, the Japanese did not compete in those commodities in which white farmers were successful—wheat, citrus, walnuts, cattle, and sheep. Their success was in berries and truck crops, 80 to 90 percent of the state's annual total.[15] Whereas much of white agriculture was classified as "resource intensive," Japanese farmers relied upon labor as the basis of operation, or classified as "labor intensive."

Many white Californians watched in horror the growth of Japanese farming in the Florin area outside of Sacramento where only one out of eight farmers was white and generalized that this was the future of California agriculture if left unchecked. Florin's prior extensive cultivation of wheat and hay had exhausted the soil at about the time the Japanese started growing strawberries and grapes. A basket factory, which made containers for the produce, first used white women but the white owners replaced them with Japanese women who proved more reliable.

The Japanese arrived in Florin about 1893. By 1898 they were growing strawberries for crop shares. Their success encouraged others to come while the high price return encouraged white farmers growing marginal crops to lease land to the Japanese. Before long, they controlled strawberry production. Prices fluctuated so that while profits were not constant, the occasional large profits appealed to the immigrants as a way to advance quickly. Starting as tenant farmers with easy credit extended them, the Japanese became landowners by 1901 without much personal capital. Visitors to Florin acknowledged that these farms showed knowledge of agriculture and much industry.[16]

The alien land laws and the exclusion act of 1924 had the desired impact upon Japanese farming during the 1920's. The number of their farms dropped in that decade from 5,152 to 3,956. This proved to be but a temporary setback; by 1940 there were 5,135 with a total acreage of 220,094 as the Nisei came of age and operated their own farms.[17] The Japanese remained largely tenant farmers until World War II, in part because of the uncertainty of the land laws. Money went into equipment and production techniques, not into fixed capital.

In 1940, Japanese farmers on the average cultivated a little over forty acres while the national average was 200.

They continued to make a major contribution as growers of specialty crops. In 1941 their crops returned between thirty and thirty-five million dollars. They produced 90 percent of California's snap beans, celery, peppers, and strawberries; 50-90 percent of the artichokes, cauliflower, cucumbers, spinach, and tomatoes; and 25-50 percent of the asparagus, cabbage, cantaloupes, carrots, lettuce, onions, and watermelons. The Japanese also led in poultry production and nursery crops. Japanese horticulture in the San Francisco and Los Angeles areas expanded until by 1941 they controlled about 65 percent of the flower industry in the latter county.[18]

Following their return to the West Coast after relocation, the Japanese resumed agricultural work. In 1950, the percentage of Japanese employed as farm laborers or foremen was 19.4; this fell to 9.2 percent by 1960. On the other hand, the percentage of farmers and farm managers increased from 17.1 to 21.4 percent during the same decade. In 1960 agriculture was still the largest occupation for California Japanese.[19]

❀   ❀   ❀   ❀

In 1901 Masuo Yasui joined his father, a railroad worker, in Oregon. After a brief reunion, he decided to tour the United States. Fascinated with the Hood River area, he decided to settle there. He joined Japanese crews clearing hillsides for orchards. Later he opened a store and urged other Japanese to buy land and settle. He pioneered the successful Japanese apple and pear industry of that area.[20]

In 1898 George Ushijima appeared among white potato pickers in the San Joaquin Valley. He proved a faster worker and a consistent winner during picking contests. Hoarding his funds, he next became a labor boss and was a successful supplier of Japanese, recognized as prime pickers. Known as George Shima, he purchased cheap and fertile land in the San Joaquin Delta, leasing what he could not buy. The rich and virgin soil required diking and draining. He utilized his countrymen to transform the land into potato farms. Over the years, he continually introduced new techniques to improve production.

By 1912 he controlled 10,000 acres of potatoes worth an estimated $500,000. The *San Francisco Chronicle* reported Shima had for several years made profits of several thousand dollars for a few months work. Characterized as a producer with a good business sense who sold when the market was high and stored crops when prices were low, his success, said the newspaper, "points to the opportunities here to anybody with pluck and intelligence."[21] He added to his holdings yearly until in 1920 he owned 6,000 acres and held an additional 7,000 on long-term lease. In 1920, already known as the Potato King, he cornered the California potato market for a handsome profit. He died in 1926—a typical Horatio Alger hero with an estate of 15 million dollars.[22]

Shima's success in potatoes was equaled by K. Ikuta's pioneering in rice production. At the time of the Gentlemen's Agreement, American farmers, experimenting with rice, utilized some of the Sacramento Valley's best bottom land for paddies. The fertile land produced luxuriant plants but no rice heads. The United States Department of Agriculture installed an experimental station at Biggs, California. Ikuta followed carefully the experiments which proved that hard pan alkali ground was the best for rice. Ikuta led the Japanese in buying up much of this waste land at $2.00 an acre. He associated with the Maxwell and the California Rice Companies. The latter, in 1915, had flourishing rice plantations.

By 1919 rice had become one of the state's most important crops. Japanese, coming from the Island Kingdom's rice culture, saw opportunity and overextended themselves to purchase land. They honored Ikuta with the title of Rice

Wizard.[23] The Japanese Association of America expressed pride in this major agricultural success:

> The Japanese were not the first to try rice in California, but they were the first to make it a commercial proposition. They were the first to apply a practical success to the experimental results of the government rice station at Biggs. And they were the ones to stick to rice through all the years before the industry emerged from its uncertainties and became firmly established. The Japanese demonstrated success and the American farmers, who have since been getting rich out of the industry, and who now greatly outnumber the Japanese rice planters, must admit their prosperity is founded on a structure thrown up by the daring and persistence of the Japanese. This pioneering developed a huge food production on land that in most cases will not grow anything else. It is admitted that the rice industry has been created out of nothing.[24]

The end came suddenly in the fall of 1920 when heavy rains fell for several weeks just as the crops were maturing. Valley fog, low to the ground, closed in after the storms, making harvesting impossible. California banks called in their loans and the Japanese were forced out. Their efforts had laid the foundation for a major California crop. At the time of their departure, what had been worthless land had a valuation of about $200 an acre. By the 1960's, the land was selling at $500 an acre.[25]

Tribute is due the Japanese for their high achievement in California agriculture. Their very success only angered the racists who strove mightily to drive them from the land. As Carey McWilliams says: "For the Japanese to succeed to any degree was an affront; but for them to demonstrate a marked superiority as farmers to their lords and masters was insulting, insubordinate, and essentially subversive."[26]

Other Japanese worked in American industry or entered the business world with varying degrees of success. The *San Francisco Call* in 1896 reported: "Not only are the little brown men from the land of the Mikado making inroads in various lines of trade ... but they are moving into business here." According to the newspaper, there had been the previous year eighteen street peddlers, thirty-two merchants, two restaurants, one hotel, one bank, one billiard parlor, and two employment offices.[27]

In 1908, Japanese in San Francisco worked for sixty-two different white employers. The largest number worked in canneries. Ten hours constituted the work day for both Japanese and Chinese, whether they worked for white or Asian employers. Wages received from white employers ranged from $4 to $16 a week while Japanese working for other Japanese earned wages ranging from $3 to more than $18 a week.[28] A survey, following the San Francisco fire and earthquake, found that the largest number worked as house cleaners. Laundries, oriental shops, and newspapers were the next largest employers of Japanese labor.[29]

This same investigation reported 140 Chinese establishments employing 286 adult males. Cigar making, laundries, meat and fish markets, restaurants, and general merchandising were the major enterprises. The Chinese did not employ minors or females. While the Japanese did not use minors, some females were employed in their oriental shops.[30]

During the first decade of the twentieth century, the Japanese were hired in construction, lumbering, and fishing. The railroads gave employment to more Japanese than any other Western enterprise but could not keep them due to poor living conditions and low wages. In 1909, about 10,000 worked on the railroads.[31]

James J. Hill expressed his complete satisfaction with his Japanese railroad workers in a 1906 letter to Kogoro Takahira, Japanese Ambassador to the United States. Hill requested the Ambassador to find a way to get more workers:

For some years we have had a number of Japanese workmen on our railway. Many of them started as track laborers and are now working in the roundhouses and machine shops, doing their work well and receiving good rates of pay. We have at present 1,200 to 1,400 Japanese workmen employed on the road and would be glad to make it 3,000. We have several Japanese track foremen where those under them are Japanese whose services are very satisfactory. For all of our track gangs we have built special houses where the men can make themselves comfortable. Many of these men come to the United States via Honolulu. The enclosed memorandum from the *Spokesman Review* of Spokane, Washington, would indicate the Japanese Consul in Hawaii is actively working to prevent his countrymen from coming to the United States. . . . It appears to me that if the matter were properly understood at least from 3,000 to 5,000 men could find permanent employment on The Northern Pacific and The Great Northern Railroads. If there is no desire on the part of the Imperial government of Japan to prevent its people from coming to the United States I think it would be worthwhile to let it be known in Japan there is an opportunity on these two railways for permanent employment for a number of men I have suggested.[32]

Hill received his answer from the chargé-d'affaires since the Ambassador had returned to Japan. It is significant to note this reply to Hill preceded the negotiation of the Gentlemen's Agreement by one year:

The Japanese government is putting a restriction upon the immigration of their subjects to this country because they fear, in view of the present attitude of labor organizations in the United States, increased influx of Japanese laborers may not be advantageous for the maintenance and improvement of the existing good relations between the two countries. As to the bringing over of Japanese laborers from Hawaii, I must say that it is not in line with the policy of the Japanese government and therefore the action of the Japanese consul-general in preventing transportation from the islands is proper.[33]

Washington and Oregon lumber mills employed more than 2,200 Japanese in 1909. They had first appeared in the mills around 1890. Widespread entry into this industry was restricted by severe prejudice so that they were hired only at the largest mills where they were used as common laborers, oilers, and teamsters. They were completely excluded if apprentice training were required, such as in the shingle weavers trade.[34]

About 2,000 Japanese were employed in Rocky Mountain coal mines; some 200 worked in Utah and Nevada smelters. Another 200 worked at the Pueblo, Colorado, smelter. In 1907, the United Mine Workers of America extended its organizational activities to the Rocky Mountain region, but the large number of Chinese and Japanese posed a problem to the all-white union. A delegation of Japanese appeared at the Denver mine workers convention to indicate their interest in membership; they stated they would not be used by the owners to cut wages. The union accepted the Asians as equal members—one of the first examples of union integration. The Japanese, proud of their membership, proved loyal union men.[35]

Other Japanese started in 1901 to work in the Columbia River salmon canneries; they later moved to Puget Sound and Alaska. By 1909 some 2,100 worked in Alaska canneries; another 1,468 worked in Washington and Oregon. The Chinese did the skilled jobs. The Japanese did the unpleasant, unskilled work. They cleaned and cut fish, soldered cans, shut and piled cans, and maintained the bathrooms. As in agriculture, the boss and gang system was used.[36] With the Chinese Exclusion Act cutting off replacements, the Japanese moved into skilled positions, much to the concern of white politicians.[37]

Japanese in Western cities were forced into noncompetitive occupations. Time after time, Japanese youth have testified that the white economic world was closed to them. When labor unions refused membership, mainland Japanese formed their own unions. A differential wage scale also existed.[38] A college educated Japanese retail clerk, interviewed in 1942, stated that he was a Hawaiian-born high school graduate. He attended night school at the University of Southern California for three years, studying bookkeeping. The only jobs he could find were in Japanese-owned establishments. He took one of the two or three jobs open to him—a clerk in a vegetable store. The other available jobs were waiters, bell hops, or farm laborers. The firm for which he worked had conducted a survey which found 120 college-trained Japanese men working as vegetable clerks and at wages considerably lower than white clerks. In 1937 the Los Angeles Retail Food Clerks, Local 770, undertook to organize the food industry, both white and Japanese. Results did not reach expectations and in March, 1941, Robert K. Sato was given a charter to organize the "Fruit & Vegetable Store Employees' (Japanese) Union, Local 1510." Unionized Japanese American retail produce workers remained in this local until World War II.[39]

Another Japanese, born in Japan, attended Los Angeles High School where he was well received, but he went to Dixon College in Galesburg, Illinois, because he felt ill at ease in California schools. He graduated in electrical engineering from Harvard in 1924. When he sought a job, firms such as General Electric and Westinghouse said they could not hire him for they had long training programs and he might return to Japan before they received any benefits. He returned from the East to Los Angeles to become an elevator boy in a large apartment house.[40]

Urban Japanese businessmen catered primarily to other Japanese. They operated stores, banks, barber shops, restaurants, newspapers, and pool rooms.[41] These "Little Tokyos" were held together by the interrelationships with residents depending on each other to provide key services.

One highly successful urban business, intertwined with truck gardening, was the marketing of fruits and vegetables. As early as 1901, one Issei had a stall at the Los Angeles City plaza farmers market. In 1909 when the Los Angeles City Market was created, ninety-four Japanese controlled 18 percent of the stock. In 1941, the city had three wholesale markets. Of the 167 commission merchants, twenty-nine were Japanese. There were 232 stall operators; 134 were Japanese. They controlled 37 percent of the distribution business at two terminals and 75 percent of the city's total green vegetable distribution. Following World War II, the Japanese dominated once more the distribution of carrots, beets, celery, and berries. They were also predominant in the retail distribution of fruits and vegetables in California. In 1941 over 1,000 retail outlets or "fruit stands" did a twenty-five million dollar business and employed 5,600 Japanese.[42]

In 1940, agriculture remained the largest single user of Japanese skills, employing 22,027. This was 45 percent of the Pacific Coast total agricultural labor force. The second largest, wholesale and retail stores and restaurants, engaged 11,472 Japanese. Personal service, the third largest category, employed 8,336. Most of these were domestic help.[43]

With the passage of the McCarran-Walter Immigration Act in 1952, overt discrimination largely ended for the Japanese. Nevertheless, they experienced difficulty in reaching high positions in the business world. Small businesses reclaimed most urban Japanese after 1945. They operated apartment houses, grocery stores, laundries, and service stations. Other important services were insurance and real estate, florist shops, travel agencies, and restaurants. The professions saw Nisei increasing in numbers—lawyers, physicians, accountants, engineers, and bankers.[44]

Californians, before and after World War II, relied upon others to help with yard work. The Japanese gardener, an independent small businessman, thrived in this economic area. In Los Angeles in 1958 there were about 5,000 Japanese contract gardeners.[45]

The need for teachers in the expanding West Coast communities opened other doors. Teaching has long been an avenue for emerging social groups. The Nisei found new opportunities in a field closed to them in the 1940's.[46] The willingness to use Japanese teachers in the very same schools which were earlier closed to them as students is indeed a significant measure of assimiliation or acceptance.

Perhaps the best example of Japanese assimilation into the American economic stream is in Hawaii. In 1910, about half of the 79,675 Hawaiian Japanese constituted 77 percent of the territory's gainfully employed males classified as laborers. In 1960, Japanese were .2 percent of the total laborer group with 5,183 of them thus classified. In 1910, there were only 221 Japanese professionals, while in 1960 there were 5,286, or 10 percent of the state's total.[47] Thirty percent of employed male Japanese in 1960 were engaged as craftsmen or foremen; 13 percent were classified as operatives. With the abolition of race as a bar to membership, union employment was possible for all. Another 30 percent were about evenly divided between clerical and sales, management, and equipment operators.[48] The Hawaiian Japanese have had better opportunities for economic success than those living elsewhere in the United States.

CHAPTER XI

The Search for Citizenship

THE FIRST JAPANESE IMMIGRANTS, LIKE THE CHINESE AND some European immigrants, were mostly single males. When the picture brides arrived, the Japanese did what most Chinese never could—they began to lead normal family lives. Issei families settled in "Japtowns" or "Little Tokyos" where traditional cultural life was maintained and, like Chinese communities, became even more conservative than similar communities in Japan.

A young Japanese has left the following description of a 1920 Japanese family:

In California, about half of the adult Japanese are married, and the rest of the people have no way to get wives. . . .

The Japanese family life in America is almost the same as that in Japan, except that the new environment has caused changes in some respects. . . .The wives are treated more fairly and are happier in their homes here than in their own country. The women are most self-sacrificing of their own time for the welfare of the families; they cook, clean house, wash, take care of the children, and sometimes help their husbands on the farms or in business.

The children are very highly prized in the Japanese home. . . . and the natural responsibility of the parents is the main reason why there are very few cases of juvenile delinquency among the Japanese. This problem of parental control in the Japanese home, however, is becoming very complex, because of the lack of English knowledge on the part of the parents, and the lack of Japanese on the part of the children. There is no way for them to communicate to their parents the ideas and ideals which they get at the public schools. This creates an alarming gulf between the second generation and their parents. . . .[1]

Kitano notes that in spite of arranged marriages, separation or divorce was uncommon and there were few broken homes. One major reason was that there were few other choices. Although life was hard for the picture bride, family obligation overrode the disillusionment.[2]

In Japan, the larger community was more important than family or individual. The Issei had long understood the proper relationships between family, prefecture, nation, and emperor. In the United States, discrimination led the Japanese to rely upon familiar communal organizational patterns. Consequently, the Japanese Association of America was created in 1900 in San Francisco. There were at first a few local branches elsewhere, but by 1905, following the anti-Japanese agitation, it was recognized as the central organization to which others affiliated. By 1921 there were four major Japanese associations:

1. United Northwestern Japanese Association in Seattle comprised of fifteen local associations in Washington and Montana with a membership of 8,860;
2. Japanese Association of Oregon in Portland with three or four locals in Oregon and Idaho;
3. Japanese Association of America, San Francisco, which had forty locals with some 16,000 members in Northern California, Nevada, Utah, and Colorado;
4. Central Japanese Association of Southern California with nineteen locals and 8,000 members in eight counties.[3]

The purposes of the Japanese Association of America were to educate newcomers about their new home and provide information on birth and baby care. An Americanization project encouraged learning about the United States and using English as a second language. Legal aid was available to fight the numerous anti-Japanese laws. The association also provided political information about the alien land laws. Agricultural experts advised about crops and soils. All associations established graveyards, arranged for translation services, and in general took care of local community needs.[4]

Anti-Japanese agitators continually claimed that the associations were secret arms of the Japanese government. These associations did have ties with the home government and in particular kept track of the Issei. They provided statistical material and also channeled reports of discrimination and indignities to local consulates. Depending on this information, the Japanese government lodged protests with the State Department. Since the Japanese could not become citizens of the United States, they remained Japanese citizens and were truly the responsibility of the government of Japan.[5]

In 1918 a group of San Francisco Nisei, discussing their future as American citizens, formed the American Loyalty League. The league gradually extended into the San Joaquin Valley. The Seattle Progressive Citizens League, formed in 1921, combatted anti-Japanese movements in that area. As the decade closed, Dr. Thomas A. Yatabe of Fresno, Saburo Kido of San Francisco, and Clarence Arai of Seattle arranged for a national Nisei organization, the Japanese American Citizens League. The founding convention was held in Seattle in 1930.[6]

During the 1930's the league held biennial conventions in major western cities. The leaders were frustrated by the larger community and by the fact that most young Nisei looked upon JACL local chapters as social organizations. The league leadership in the summer of 1941 appointed its first full-time executive secretary, Mike Masaoka of Salt Lake City, a graduate of the University of Utah.[7] At the age of twenty-six, Masaoka was ready to guide the Nisei organization during the trying days of relocation and postwar readjustment. Through the pioneering efforts of the JACL leaders in the late 1930's, the Nisei were able to assume a significant place in their communities in the 1950's and thereafter.

An important aspect of all American immigrant groups has been their religion. Most Issei were largely Buddhists who brought concepts featuring the ceremonial and emphasizing an ethical code. These first immigrants were susceptible to conversion to Christianity as one step perhaps to adapting to living in America. The Methodist Church established missions throughout the West, from California north to Seattle and east to Denver. A 1936 survey made in Seattle showed that 1,200 Japanese attended Christian churches while 800 belonged to two Buddhist sects with fewer than 200 in other Japanese religious groups. The efforts of the American Christian ministers in befriending the Japanese and helping them find entry level jobs brought the Japanese to the churches. The educational function of the churches aimed at the Americanization of the Asians cannot be overemphasized.[8]

Buddhism did not make an organized effort in the mainland United States until the late 1890's. Two Buddhist missionaries, Shuyei Sonoda and Kukuyro Nishijima, arrived in San Francisco on September 2, 1899, to offer spiritual guidance. The Buddhist Churches of America date their beginning from this day. Buddhist churches sprang up throughout the San Joaquin Valley and in Seattle—wherever there was a sizeable Japanese community. There are presently four sects in the United States—Zen, Nichiren, Shingon, and Jodo Shinshu. In 1968, the Jodo Shinshu Buddhists chose an American Nisei as bishop for the first time. This particular sect, under the title Buddhist Churches of America, has fifty-seven churches.[9]

Recent studies point out how whites have stereotyped the Japanese into certain categories. To some extent the Japanese have striven to fulfill those positive stereotypes believed in by the whites. Success and frustration of the Japanese in America have stemmed from what on the surface appears to be a similar value structure. The Japanese have moved to acculturation not because their culture is identical to white middle-class America but because traditional Japanese culture closely parallels rural nineteenth-century American culture.[10]

The Issei naturally wanted equality of treatment and they wanted the possibility of American citizenship which had constantly been denied. The Issei first relied upon the government of Japan to demand equality of treatment; later they utilized the courts. In 1916, Takao Ozawa sought to determine whether he was eligible for citizenship. He had lived for about twenty years in the United States. He had graduated from Berkeley High School and attended the University of California. Ozawa held before the United States District Court, Territory of Hawaii, that only those persons whose quality of goodness and worthiness were doubtful might be denied citizenship. He noted that the Japanese were not specifically excluded. The court conceded that Ozawa was "well qualified by character and education for citizenship," but concluded that the immigration laws pertained only to "free white persons and aliens of African nativity." Since the Japanese were not mentioned, it could be assumed they were to be excluded. Ozawa appealed the case to the United States Supreme Court which upheld the decision of the lower court.[11]

On the same day, the Supreme Court denied the right of citizenship to two Washington residents, Kono and Yamashita. Their application for articles of incorporation had been refused because, as Japanese, they were not entitled to become citizens. The two men had countered that a Washington State Superior Court had admitted them to citizenship. The case wended its way to the Supreme Court. Justice Sutherland read the court opinion which held that the Japanese were not eligible for naturalization or citizenship and that the Superior Court's granting of citizenship was void.[12]

The U. S. Supreme Court in 1925 repudiated a 1919 Congressional law which read in part: "Any person of foreign birth who served in the military or naval forces of the

United States during the present war who was honorably discharged shall have the benefits" of citizenship. On May 16, 1921, H. Toyota was granted a certificate of naturalization. Shortly after, the United States asked a Massachusetts court to cancel the certificate. The court, basing its decision upon the recent 1922 cases, agreed in May, 1923, that the law covered Toyota only if the law applied to the Japanese. But the court fell back on the established precedent that only whites or persons of African descent were entitled to citizenship. Toyota consequently was denied his citizenship.[13]

The first JACL convention in 1930 passed a resolution calling for citizenship for those Asians who served in World War I. Tokutaro Slocum, a sergeant-major in the war, led the lobbying for the Issei veterans. His effective efforts led to a Congressional act in 1935 which granted to aliens ineligible for citizenship the right to apply for naturalization if they had served in the armed forces between April 6, 1917, and November 11, 1918, had received an honorable discharge, and had been permanent residents of the United States. Before the January 1, 1937, expiration date, some 700 Issei became citizens.[14]

Of equal concern to the Issei was the jeopardy faced by their children as a consequence of the alien land laws. A series of important cases seeking to guarantee the future for their children were fought through the courts. A landmark case which tested the validity of the California alien land laws was Porterfield and Mizuno v. U. S. Webb, California Attorney General, and Thomas Woolwine, Los Angeles County District Attorney. Porterfield and Mizuno applied for a preliminary injunction against the 1921 alien land law which restricted leasing rights. Porterfield claimed that he was deprived the right to lease eighty acres to Mizuno. The lower court upheld the denial of leasing. Porterfield and Mizuno's appeal to the U. S. Supreme Court was in vain. The high court held that alien land laws did not deprive aliens of the right to engage in agricultural pursuits and were therefore not unconstitutional.[15]

A second agricultural case was heard at the same 1922 Supreme Court session. The State of California appealed a federal district court decision which found for I. J. O'Brien and J. Inouye of Santa Clara County. O'Brien owned property used for raising berries and truck crops. O'Brien and Inouye, a qualified farmer, wanted to enter into a crop contract, but were restrained from doing so in fear of legal action by the Santa Clara County District Attorney and U. S. Webb. The district court agreed that they could enter into a crop contract, but could not negotiate a lease, and that aliens lawfully in the United States could pursue such activities unless specifically prohibited from doing so. Attorney General Webb argued before the high court that the entire purpose of the alien land laws was to reserve California agricultural lands for United States citizens and that crop contracts were an evasion of state law. Justice Butler, delivering the opinion overturning the district court's decision, held that "Aliens ineligible to citizenship may own or lease houses, manufactories, warehouses, and shops for residential or commercial purposes. These things, but no possession or enjoyment of land otherwise are permitted."[16]

Another landmark case protected the property rights of minor American citizens—the Nisei. In December, 1919, owners of Butte County property sold by deed fifteen acres of land to H. Yano, the guardian of his four-year-old daughter, Tetsudumi Yano. The State of California held that Yano, an alien ineligible for citizenship, had paid for the property with his own funds in an attempt to evade the alien land law. The Superior Court heard arguments from U. S. Webb and ruled that Yano sought to control the land that the young girl in effect was holding for her father. Yano's appeal to the State Supreme Court in 1922 was successful. This court held that under the Fourteenth Amendment Japanese American minors were entitled to have their alien parents as guardians.[17]

Following the 1924 Immigration Act, which incorporated Japanese exclusion, most white Americans along the Pacific Coast accommodated well to the few Japanese they saw. When whites talked about a Japanese problem, it was largely a California problem for 95 percent of the total mainland population was in that state in 1930 and in 1940. In 1930, 42 percent of California's Japanese lived in Los Angeles County; this increased to 45 percent in 1940.[18] Even in California in 1940, most whites had less contact with the Japanese than did their ancestors with the Chinese during the Gold Rush Years of the 1850's.

CHAPTER XII

World War II and Its Aftermath

A SIGNIFICANT ASPECT OF THE JAPANESE STEREOTYPE PRE-sented by white exclusionists was the "Yellow Peril." While some early concern had been expressed about the Chinese threat of overrunning California, the Japanese military threat seemed real, reinforced by Japan's victories over China and Russia. The belief that all Japanese immigration was part of the Japanese government's secret plan was fre-quently emphasized. Alabama Democratic Congressman Richmond Pearson Hobson, a Spanish-American War hero, launched an attack in 1907 against the Japanese "Yellow Peril" in the Hearst newspapers and detailed in lurid fashion the coming attack upon the Pacific Coast. In 1909, Homer Lea gained considerable attention with his book, *The Valor of Ignorance,* which outlined how the Japanese would first seize the Philippine Islands and then overrun the Pacific Coast.[1] The "Yellow Peril" continued as a major weapon in the exclusionists's arsenal to 1941.

As Japanese imperial forces moved through China in the 1930's, Americans became apprehensive about the possibil-ity of war. Anti-Japanese groups in California used the occa-sion to create trouble for the American Japanese. At the same time, Japan's imperialism caused deep splits within the Issei-Nisei communities as pro and con views about the Island Empire surfaced.

In Southern California, a Committee of One Thousand was formed for the purpose of boycotting Japanese goods. Its publication, the *American Defender,* dredged up old charges that Japanese truck gardeners used human excrement as fertilizer to spread dysentery epidemics throughout the white society. A variant of this was the story that they used lead arsenic spray on their vegetables to poison their customers. The Japanese were also accused of selling opium to subvert white America.

↵ ⟶ In 1935, a widespread story claimed there was an enormous Japanese fishing fleet operating out of California harbors using ships constructed in Japan which could be transformed immediately into minelayers and torpedo boats. The myth held that the fleet was manned by Japanese naval officers disguised as fishermen. Carey McWilliams investigated these charges and found that of all fishing boats over 115 feet in length only two were Japanese owned. The rest belonged to Italians, Finns, and Portuguese. Only ten Japanese boats were in the 85-110 foot range. At the same time, some Americans charged that there were 500,000 armed Japanese in the United States and 2,000 trained naval officers operating fishing boats. In 1935, actually there were only 158,834 Japanese in the United States, and only 680 of them were licensed fishermen out of California's total of 5,399.[2]

The significance of the "Yellow Peril" became monumental on December 7, 1941, when the Japanese Navy attacked Pearl Harbor and the Philippines. The resulting internment of all West Coast Japanese carried exclusionists' goals to the ultimate—the forcible removal of the Japanese from the coast. In the weeks and months following the attack, the national leadership succumbed to the arguments of the exclusionists. The Federal Government failed to protect property rights during the war and was reluctant to assume much responsibility after the war. The most serious act of ⟵ the government was the repudiation of Japanese American citizenship rights. The 1942 claim of military necessity and the subsequent apology of war hysteria do not mitigate the injustices meted out against the American Japanese.

In 1941 there were about 40,000 Issei on the Pacific Coast of an average age of 52. The War Relocation Authority found in 1942 that they "were a tired, hopeless, and bewildered group of people who retained a sentimental attachment for the Japan they had known as children or adolescents in the earlier years of the century, but who wanted nothing more acutely than to live the rest of their lives in comfort and peace."[3] The fact that they suddenly became enemy aliens was not of their own choosing, for it was the United States who had declared them ineligible for citizenship. In the days that followed Pearl Harbor, federal and state officials reported time after time that it was impossible to tell a loyal Japanese from a disloyal one. Yet identifying disloyal Germans and Italians never seemed a problem. In May, 1942, the assistant chief of the Army's Western Defense Command's Civil Affairs Division wrote:

In the case of the Japanese, their oriental habits of life, their and our inability to assimilate biologically, and what is more important, our inability to distinguish the subverts and saboteurs from the rest of the mass made necessary their class evacuation on a horizontal basis. In the case of the Germans and the Italians, such mass evacuation is neither necessary nor desirable.[4]

There was never any question about the wisdom or legality of interning dangerous enemy aliens. Japanese, German, and Italian aliens had already been identified by the FBI and Naval Intelligence before December 7. But the major issue and the sharp break with what had been recognized as constitutional guarantees was the treatment of Japanese American citizens. Our law courts still tell prospective jurors that the defendant is innocent until proven guilty. But early in 1942 all Japanese, aliens and citizens alike, were judged by the executive and legislative branches of the Federal Government to be potentially guilty and their rights were violated.

The West Coast Nisei numbered about 70,000 and were predominately between fifteen to twenty-five years of age.

Leadership of Japanese communities still resided with the Issei. Cultural strife between first and second generations, common to immigrant groups, had already begun. For example, in 1930 the Nisei had barred the Issei from membership in the Japanese American Citizens League. Postwar resettlement hastened the end of the tight Issei family structure; evacuation destroyed Issei control and brought the Nisei to the fore.

In 1940, the total Japanese population in the continental United States was 126,947.[5] Of these, about 15,000 residing in other than Pacific Coast states, did not lose their constitutional rights. In light of the treatment of Pacific Coast Japanese, it is important to see what happened to the Hawaiian Japanese. In 1941, 157,000 Japanese comprised 37 percent of the Islands' total population. Of these, 37,000 were Issei. Martial law was immediately declared on December 7. Suspected individuals were picked up; Nisei in the National Guard were soon deactivated. Of the total population, 1,118 were eventually evacuated to mainland relocation centers.[6]

On December 21, 1941, General Delos C. Emmons indicated that loyal Hawaiian Japanese would be treated fairly.[7] But in Washington, D. C., Secretary of Navy Frank Knox advocated their removal from Oahu to Molokai. President Franklin D. Roosevelt, in a February 26, 1942 memo, eight days after signing the executive order relocating Pacific Coast Japanese, agreed with Knox:

> Like you, I have long felt that most of the Japanese should be removed from Oahu to one of the other islands. . . .
> I do not worry about the constitutional question—first, because of my recent order and second, because Hawaii is under martial law. The whole matter is one of immediate and present war emergency.
> I think you and Stimson can agree and then go ahead and do it as a military project.[8]

General Emmons received several direct orders to develop an evacuation plan about which he was unenthusiastic, for there were counter pressures in Hawaii. The Japanese, a vital segment of the labor force, could not be easily replaced. There was no strong race prejudice against them. Finally, it appears that Emmons and his staff were not convinced that the Japanese posed any military or subversive threat.[9]

On December 19, 1941, General John L. De Witt recommended that *all* enemy aliens be removed from the Pacific Coast military zone.[10] However, on December 26, the general indicated that he was opposed to evacuating citizens: — "An American citizen, after all, is an American citizen. And while they may not be loyal, I think we can weed the disloyal out of the loyal and lock them up if necessary."[11] Yet on April 13, 1943, he testified before the House Naval Affairs Subcommittee that "A Jap's a Jap. They are a dangerous element, whether loyal or not. There is no way to determine their loyalty.... It makes no difference whether he is an American; theoretically, he is still a Japanese and you can't change him...."[12] Clearly, the general vacillated as he tried to trim to the winds of change.

By 1943, De Witt was still responding to political considerations. The pressures for change upon him and the Army came from California state and Congressional officials and exclusion advocates as well as from Washington. It is true that the Army because of a sense of fear and uncertainty about the Japanese had earlier grasped at straws.

World War II gave West Coast exclusionists the chance to achieve their goal—exclusion of the Japanese to which the "establishment" gave support. De Witt reported on January 27, 1942, that pressure to remove the Japanese is "not being instigated or developed by the people who are not thinking but by the best people of California."[13] Late in January and early February, 1942, the Bureau of Intelligence, U. S. Office of Facts and Figures, conducted interviews in the three Western states which supported later findings that exclusionists capitalized on the war.[14] Those Caucasians who met the Japanese as economic competitors held the greatest hostility and insisted upon removal. The Los Angeles area, for example, was a leading center of agitation; however, the feeling was manifested statewide. Years of race hatred led to perennial slogans, "Once a Jap, always a Jap," and "It's in their blood." Yet the survey's sample gave no indication of an overwhelming demand for removal. A memorandum sent by this agency to the War Department summarized the situation as "loaded with potential dynamite; but it is not as desperate as some people believe."[15]

Official attitudes reacted to increasingly hostile public opinion by moving from a program of control of aliens to complete removal of the Japanese. Lieutenant Colonel Karl R. Bendetsen of the Provost Marshal General's office was active both in Washington and San Francisco. At an early January meeting, he informed De Witt that the Army must have stricter control measures for enemy aliens than those proposed by the Justice Department.[16]

De Witt met with Governor Culbert Olson and Attorney General Earl Warren. He reported on January 29, 1942, that he concurred with the view of both men that all Japanese should be removed from the state. On February 4, De Witt reported that Olson and other state officials then thought that voluntary relocation within the state was both desired and possible. In March, Olson testified before the Tolan Committee that the Japanese were loyal.[17] He agreed with the current view that it could not be determined which Japanese were loyal or disloyal. He agreed with the solution of internment. After meeting with DeWitt, Warren, on February 2, revealed his fear of the Japanese. He found it sinister that they were located near strategic areas and that no acts of sabotage had been committed. His curious logic led him to predict that the Japanese were awaiting the proper moment.[18] There is reason to suspect that Warren, an astute student of California politics, chose to use this means to advance his gubernatorial candidacy. Strikingly, the U. S. Army's *Final Report* on evacuation expressed identical ideas to Warren's.[19] In fact, the statements verge on plagiarism.

On January 30, 1942, when West Coast Congressmen met informally with representatives of the Justice and War Departments, Bendetsen was a key figure. He presented De Witt's position about removal and added that while not authorized to speak for the War Department, he thought the Army would be willing to handle the evacuation program. The Congressmen approved of evacuation of enemy aliens and "dual" citizens without mentioning the Japanese. Bendetsen then reported to his superior that the Congressmen were "calling for the immediate evacuation of all Japanese from the Pacific coastal strip including Japanese citizens of the age of twenty-one and under, and calling for an Executive order of the President imposing full responsibility and authority (with the power to requisition the services of other Federal agencies) upon the War Department."[20]

Recommendations, adopted on February 13 by a subcommittee in behalf of West Coast Congressmen, were sent to the President. In part the subcommittee said:

> We recommend the immediate evacuation of all persons of Japanese lineage and all others, aliens and citizens alike, whose presence shall be deemed dangerous or inimical to the defense of the United States from all strategic areas.[21]

Warren in California and these Congressmen had adopted the position of the agitators and had made their stance known to the War Department.

Events now happened quickly. Bendetsen had been to California to confer with De Witt and to indicate the War Department's position. On February 11, Secretary of War Henry M. Stimson conferred with Roosevelt by telephone on the responsibilities of the Justice and War Departments. Roosevelt agreed that the War Department should undertake evacuation of aliens and citizens on the basis of military necessity. The one qualification was, "Be as reasonable as you can." John McCloy, Assistant Secretary of War, informed Bendetsen immediately that the President would sign the order.[22] On February 19, the President signed Executive Order No. 9066 authorizing evacuation.

In the light of the treatment of the Hawaiian Japanese, it seemed that the Army was on uncertain ground in demanding evacuation and that political overtones were more important. The position of the FBI and Naval Intelligence seems to indicate the situation was under control. During the summer of 1941, the Army searched for trained Japanese linguists. The hope was that these would be found among the Nisei. After a survey of 3,700 Nisei, only 470 were of any use and most of these had to be schooled intensively in the language. This Army project proved that Americanization of the Nisei had advanced more rapidly than was realized. The Army established its school at the Presidio of San Francisco, November 1, 1941. Classes were held there until May, 1942. Because the students were Japanese Americans and had been excluded from the West Coast, the school had to be moved to Camp Savage, Minnesota.[23]

By late March, 1942, the first large movement of Japanese commenced with little advance notice to the Manzanar Reception Center in Owens Valley, California. By the end of May, 1942, all but a few thousand were confined in sixteen Assembly Centers—fair grounds, race tracks, and stadiums. Thirteen of these were in California. They were next moved from Assembly Centers to the Relocation Centers.

The table on page 162 lists the Relocation Centers and their approximate population.

There have been many excellent studies of the treatment of the Japanese in the centers and their efforts to adapt to this dislocation. Most Japanese Americans strove to demonstrate their support of the United States. The most notable

TABLE III

RELOCATION CENTERS[24]

LOCATION	POPULATION
CALIFORNIA	
Manzanar	10,046
Tule Lake	18,789
ARIZONA	
Poston	17,814
Gila River	13,348
UTAH	
Topaz	8,130
IDAHO	
Minidoka	9,397
COLORADO	
Granada	7,318
WYOMING	
Heart Mountain	10,767
ARKANSAS	
Rohwer	8,475
Jerome	8,497

---

contribution was the outstanding military service first provided by Hawaii's 100th Battalion. Later, the 442nd Regimental Combat Team was formed of Nisei volunteers from Hawaii and Relocation Centers. When the 442nd arrived in Italy, it absorbed the 100th Battalion and the reorganized unit continued to demonstrate bravery and heroism.[25]

Some Issei and Nisei were discouraged and disillusioned by relocation orders. Some understandably became surly and unruly; these and others refused to sign loyalty pledges. These persons were concentrated at Tule Lake.[26] On December 17, 1944, the War Department announced that on January 2, 1945, the mass exclusion orders would end and that the Japanese could return to the West Coast. This decision preceded by one day the United States Supreme Court ruling in *Endo v. United States.* The court found that the indefinite retention of citizens of Japanese ancestry who were of proven loyalty was not authorized by law.[27] This was not what the exclusionists wanted and a round of minor terrorism started. On January 8, 1945, an attempt was made to burn and dynamite the packing shed of a returned Japanese in Placer County, California.[28] There were many other hostile incidents.

During the war, the Japanese had few friends in the United States. Both conservatives and liberals seemed in agreement with the explanation of military necessity. The Native Sons of the Golden West and the California Joint Immigration Committee led the opposition while the legislature enacted key measures. In May, 1942, Clarence Hunt, editor of the *Grizzly Bear,* proposed in his usual anti-Japanese editorial that the Japanese be dispossessed of every foot of land, urban and rural; challenged the citizenship of every Japanese; and urged the closing of every Japanese language school. In 1943 and 1945, the legislature tightened the alien land law and denied alien Japanese the right to fishing licenses.[29]

Senator Hugh Burns of Fresno in 1945 introduced a bill placing the burden of proof upon an individual that he did not possess dual citizenship. This bill would divest Japanese Americans of the right to own land until proof was furnished. Burns said his measure was the result of a two-year study by the legislature of un-American activities.[30] The bill did not pass.

In 1946, California voters renounced a Senate constitutional amendment which would have ratified the 1943 and 1945 alien land statutes. As the Japanese returned to the coast in 1945, the land laws were enforced.[31] On July 6, 1945, the San Joaquin County Superior Court ruled that the war had invalidated the 1911 commercial treaty and that alien Japanese could not enter into commercial property leases. Two years later, this decision was reversed in the Court of Appeals.[32]

During 1946 California Attorney General Robert Kenny and county district attorneys using the 1943 law, started fifty cases to confiscate the property of Japanese Americans for alleged violations.[33] From 1913 to 1948 there were seventy-nine escheat cases; four were against Hindus; two against Chinese and seventy-three against Japanese—fifty-nine after 1942.

Having been impounded during the war, the Nisei in the last half of the 1940's fought to regain their rights. An early aspect of relocation was the confiscation of Japanese property which had been stored or sold. In 1948 President Harry S Truman signed the Japanese American Evacuation Claims Act allowing reimbursement. Some 23,689 claims were filed asking for $131,949,176. Of these, about 2,400 claims were for less than $500. There were about 11,700 claims for amounts between $501 and $2,500. Another 4,500 ranged between $5,001 and $100,000 while only seventy-seven exceeded the larger amount.[34]

By the time this sad affair wound through federal procedures of providing itemized claims and receipts, the Federal Government, based upon 1942 prices, recompensed the Japanese Americans $38,000,000—about 15¢ for every dollar. Bill Hosokawa states that in actuality the evacuees received only a nickel for every dollar.[35]

The most spectacular example was the payment made to the estate of Keisabura Koda. Koda had purchased worthless alkali hardpan land near Dos Palos, California, in 1927 and turned it into valuable rice fields. He developed the largest rice growing, milling, and packaging operation in California which he was forced to abandon during the war. When he returned, it was discovered that the white managers, given the power of attorney, had divested all but 987 acres for profit. Koda's share of the profit would have been $100,000 but state law forbade the payment of proceeds to any alien stockholder and the money went to the state. This was returned to Koda after the war. He filed a federal claim of $2,400,000. In 1965 the Federal Government paid $362,-500 which went mostly to pay court fees.[36]

The Japanese American Citizens League legal defense committee, meeting in Stockton in December, 1945, launched a program to "defend their property rights in current land seizure proceedings by the State of California."[37] The first case to test the long-standing alien land laws was the case of *The People v. Oyama*. In 1934, Kajiro Oyama, an Issei, had purchased six acres of land in the name of his six-year-old boy, Fred Oyama. Kajiro Oyama petitioned the county superior court to be named guardian and was so appointed. In 1942, the family was evacuated and in 1944, when Fred was sixteen years of age, Attorney General Robert Kenny filed escheat proceedings to revoke the original deed on the grounds that the land had been purchased "with intent to violate and evade the alien land law." The San Diego County court ruled for the state and when Oyama appealed, the State Supreme Court held that the state could exclude ineligible aliens from any interest in agricultural land. The case was appealed to the United States Supreme Court which found for Oyama's claim that he was deprived equal protection but the decision turned on the point that aliens could make gifts of real estate if they were for the benefit of their children.[38]

Two other cases cleared up the long-standing issue of constitutionality of the alien land laws. Sei Fujii, an important figure in the Issei Los Angeles community, purchased an unimproved city lot and sought title to it. The State of California undertook escheat proceedings. In the case *Sei Fujii v. State of California* a state district court of appeals found that the alien land law was unenforceable under the United Nations Charter.[39] The Fujii case tested the land law as it applied to the Issei and won. In the case *Masaoka v. California*, a test case created by the Masaoka

family, one of Mrs. Haruye Masaoka's sons and his wife
transferred title to a Pasadena unimproved city lot to her.
This case determined that it was not possible for the State
of California to relegate some citizens to a secondary position because of racial origin. With this case, a court finally
declared the land law unconstitutional.[40]

One last example of harassment was the action of the
California legislature during 1943 and 1945 which restricted
the right of aliens ineligible to citizenship from securing
commercial fishing licenses. In a major decision for the
Japanese, *Takahashi v. Fish and Game Commission,* the
United States Supreme Court in 1948 held that denying
an alien the right to earn a living was unconstitutional.[41]

With the passage of the McCarran-Walter Immigration
Act, the matter of aliens ineligible for citizenship ended.
More importantly, the attitudes of white California had
changed. The watchdog work of the JACL paid off. Faced
with a lifelong struggle, the Issei and Nisei have held fast
and have provided opportunities, denied them, to the Sansei,
the third generation Japanese. Interestingly, as with other
immigrant groups, the younger generation has begun to
challenge the values of the Issei and Nisei. Both in California and Hawaii, Third World Movements and ethnic studies
are attracting more Sansei and the Yonsei, the fourth generation.

Part III

Joining the Pluralistic Society

CHAPTER XIII

Contributions to American Society

CHINESE AND JAPANESE IMMIGRANTS AND THEIR CHILDREN have added significantly to the pluralistic dimensions of American society. In view of their original desire to return home and the hatred and hostility of whites aimed at driving them out, the accomplishments of these Asian immigrants are truly outstanding.

When immigration studies note contributions of immigrants and measure them against standards of the majority society, they are apt to point to those few members of an ethnic group who have achieved unusual success. Defenders of the uniqueness of minority groups maintain that the use of this yardstick subverts the value structure of such groups. But one characteristic of American pluralistic society is that the various groups' economic, social, and political values have tended to coalesce. In Hawaii, an emerging college-educated Chinese group disdains the pretensions and strivings of the new rich. "These young people," claims a local newspaper, "shun the rigidity of their heritage, but they embrace and perpetuate the strengths, combining them with their Western learning."[1] There may well be developing a true amalgam balancing the cultural characteristics of East and West.

In the case of those Chinese and Japanese who can be singled out because of noteworthy contributions to American society, it is equally important to remember the fathers, mothers, brothers, and sisters of these outstanding individuals. The results of the back-breaking labor of the Chinese, still visible throughout the West, were achieved by nameless thousands of men hacking away at the face of the land. Unnamed Japanese equally transformed Western unproductive lands into national garden baskets. The first newcomers among both groups provided hand and back muscle for the nation's development.

As the need for hand labor decreased and as white labor led in discriminatory legislation, both Asian groups moved to noncompetitive economic areas. The 1930 and 1940 censuses indicated that large numbers of Chinese were associated with laundries, restaurants, or domestic service.[2] In 1940 and 1950 most Japanese were still employed in agriculture as laborers or as clerical personnel.[3]

These Chinese and Japanese who received a college education and then sought professional careers found the doors closed for many years. The vast industrial expansion during World War II and increasing national needs for skilled and professional people changed this for the Chinese. They found more and more opportunities throughout the business and professional world. The Japanese did not reap the same benefits until after 1950. But by the 1960's it was still rare to find top management personnel in white business and industry being selected from the ranks of Asians. Elsewhere in our society, most Chinese and Japanese, like other Americans, have pursued occupations ranging from the professions to unskilled labor, living their own lives with family and friends in anonymity.

The one exception to restrictive career opportunities is the state of Hawaii. This has occurred in part because Asians constitute a majority of the population. Caucasians are a large minority about equal to the number of Japanese in the state. Both Chinese and Japanese immigrants arrived to become plantation workers. In a little more than fifty years, their descendants have moved to the world of business and the professions. An interesting and important indicator of their economic success in Hawaii can be seen in a study of male income in 1949 and 1959. The median income for all ethnic groups in 1949 was $2,340 and $3,717 in 1959. Caucasian medians were $2,856 and $3,649. The Chinese medians were $2,964 and $5,096 while Japanese medians were $2,427 and $4,302.[4]

The list of Chinese who have contributed to the fabric of our multi-hued society in some noteworthy manner is long. It is possible to provide only a representative sampling.

In Hawaii, the name of Chin Ho comes readily to mind in the world of business and finance. Born in Waikiki, he translated traditional Chinese love and concern for land into a financial empire on the island of Oahu. In 1944, he formed the Capital Investment Company which has built major real estate developments in Honolulu and on Oahu. Two outstanding projects, typical of Hawaii's 1960 resort development were Ilikai Hotel and the Makaha Valley Resort. Ho is also chairman of the board of directors of Honolulu's evening daily newspaper and director of a variety of trusts and corporations. In a state where land is a premium investment, Chin Ho symbolizes the escape of a people from a plantation economy to positions of major economic importance.[5]

In 1907, Joe Shoong started a merchandise business in San Francisco following the fire and earthquake. Through the years, the Shoong family expanded its operations to the larger cities of the West creating the National Dollar Stores, Ltd. The capital stock was owned by the family and all principal officers remained Chinese.[6] Shoong became one of the wealthiest Chinese in the United States and an outstanding philanthropist. The Chinese hospital in San Francisco and the Oakland Chinese Community Center have been recipients of his gifts. The Chung Hwa School in San Francisco and the Joe Shoong School in Lodi, California, have also benefitted. The University of California has a $1,400 scholarship for American Chinese students and there is a Joe Shoong Foundation to help finance other deserving American Chinese students.[7]

Another success in America's business world has been K. C. Li who created an important tungsten operation in the United States. In 1916, his Wah Chang Company of New York traded in and processed tungsten. After World War II, the firm expanded its operations until in 1953 it built the world's largest tungsten refinery. It moved into allied operations in tin and zirconium. K. C. Li, educated in the Royal School of Mines in London came to the United States in 1916 to form his company. He helped develop the Li process for tungsten carbide.[8]

One of the more significant results of the 1943 repeal of the Chinese Exclusion Act was the migration of intellectuals to the United States. Science, medicine, engineering, and other academic areas owe much to these recent immigrants.[9]

Tsung Dao Lee and Chen-Ning Yang, graduates of the Southwest Associated University, Kummin, China, earned doctorates at the University of Chicago. Dr. Lee was born in Shanghai, China, in 1926, the son of a successful businessman. Dr. Yang was born in Peking in 1922. His father was a Professor of Mathematics at Tsing Hua University at Peking.[10] Lee joined the Physics Department at Columbia University in 1953, while Yang had become a member of the Institute for Advanced Study at Princeton in 1948. In 1957 the two men were recipients of the Nobel Prize for their new studies of the principle of the conservation of parity, a long accepted physics principle.[11] The experiments to prove their theories were performed by Dr. Chien-Shiung Wu, one of the world's leading experimental physicists. In 1958, she was the first woman to receive an honorary Doctor of Science Degree from Princeton University. Dr. Wu received her B.S. degree from the National Central University in Nanking, China, and did graduate work at the University of California in 1936. There she met and married

Chia-lui Yuan.[12] Dr. Yuan, a senior physicist at Brookhaven, was one of those responsible for the cosmotron, an accelerator.[13]

Chinese Americans also point with pride to Dr. Choh Hao Li, a biochemist who in 1962 won the Albert Lasker Medical Research Award as the world's leading authority on the pituitary gland. A professor of biochemistry and experimental endocrinology at the University of California, he has done outstanding research on the composition of ACTH molecules. Li, born in Canton in 1913, arrived at the University of California in 1935. His family's affluence made it possible for him to study at the University and achieve professional success.[14]

In 1964, the Republican National Convention, meeting in San Francisco, arrived at the precise moment when the roll of the states was called for nominations for the office of President of the United States. When Hawaii's name was called, the spokesman for that new state placed into nomination Hiram L. Fong, the first American of Asian ancestry to be elected to the United States Senate.

Senator Fong was born in the Kalihi slums of Honolulu in 1907 of immigrant parents who had come to Hawaii to work on the sugar plantations. As a young boy he worked at odd jobs such as shining shoes and selling fish, newspapers, and poi. After graduation from high school, he worked three years to finance his education at the University of Hawaii. He graduated from the university, earning a Phi Beta Kappa key. He worked at other odd jobs for two more years in order to attend Harvard Law School. He graduated in 1935 and returned to Honolulu to found the law firm of Fong, Miho, Choy and Robinson. Over the years Fong became wealthy through investments in real estate, shopping centers, and in a banana plantation. He also organized finance and insurance companies.

Fong entered public service as a deputy attorney for the City and County of Honolulu. In 1938 he was elected

to the Territorial Legislature where he served continuously
for fourteen years. In 1942 he was Vice Speaker of the
House of Representatives and became Speaker in 1948.
Over the years, Senator Fong has maintained an interesting political alliance with the International Longshoremen's
and Warehousemen's Union. Many of Fong's early constituents from the slums of Kalihi worked on the docks. The
union supported Fong for the speakership and in 1964 en-
dorsed him for reelection against Democrat Tom Gill. Fong
was a key figure in the first Hawaii State Constitutional
Convention. In 1959, he became one of the state's first
United States Senators and has been successful in his two
reelection bids.[15]

Many times in the nineteenth and twentieth centuries,
white exclusionists predicted that unrestricted Asian immigration would bring the downfall of American institutions
and that Asians would steal the Anglo-Saxon birthright by
being elected to public office. In California, Chinese Americans have been successful in winning office through the elective process. Alfred H. Song from Monterey Park was reelected in 1970 to a second term as state senator. Born in
Hawaii, he received his law degree from the University of
Southern California. Before serving his state in the Senate,
he was a city councilman and when elected to the Assembly
in 1962, he served two terms. Song was joined in the Assembly in 1966 by Mrs. March K. Fong of Alameda County.
She was elected to a third term in 1970. She holds degrees
from the University of California, Berkeley, and Mills College, and has a doctorate in education from Stanford University. For ten years she was a member of the Alameda
County Board of Education.

In 1966, Governor Edmund Brown appointed Harry W.
Low to the San Francisco Municipal Court. Low became
the first Chinese American to hold such a position. He had
earlier served as member of the State Workman's Compen-
sation Appeals Board and for ten years was in the Califor-

nia Attorney General's Office. In 1971, Herbert Y. C. Choy of Honolulu became a member of the Federal Ninth Circuit Court of Appeals. Choy was a law partner of Senator Hiram Fong for several years and was the first person from Hawaii to be appointed to this level of federal judgeships.[16]

Arizona elected Wing F. Ong as a state legislator in 1946. When he first arrived in San Francisco, he worked in a laundry and studied at a mission school. He later moved to Phoenix, Arizona, where he worked his way through high school and junior college. He entered the grocery business in the 1930's. In 1940, in his first race for the Arizona State Legislature, he lost by only seventeen votes. He then enrolled in the University of Arizona law school, graduating in 1943. He was successful in his second attempt for elective office in 1946.[17]

The cultural contributions of the Chinese to American life have been numerous. Chinese food is commonplace throughout the nation, even though many Americans have limited their epicurean experience to chop suey and chow mein. But today, Chinese frozen food is available at the supermarkets and the nation's newspapers from time to time feature Chinese recipes. In recent years, the number of Chinese restaurants, serving dishes of China's three major regions, has increased. Restaurants specializing in Cantonese, Northern, and Szechwan dishes are available in those cities with large numbers of Chinese.

The Chinese Americans have sustained American interest in Chinese art by providing stores featuring Oriental art. The very name chinaware is indicative of our debt to the Chinese for their craft of creating and glazing dishes. Most Americans know Blue Willowware which has become mass produced. Beautiful Chinese porcelains, such as figurines, vases, and bowls, have long remained popular. Temple bells and statues of Chinese gods have found their way into many American homes.[18]

An important artist who migrated to the United States

in 1947 was Chen-Chi, born in Wusih, China, in 1902. Outstanding as a watercolor artist, he has won numerous awards in this country. His work has attracted national attention including a grand award and gold medal from the American Watercolor Society. His work may best be seen in a 1965 published collection of *Chen-Chi—Paintings*.[19]

An American-born artist of national repute is Dong Kingman, born in Oakland, California, in 1911. Well known for his watercolors of San Francisco and as a story illustrator, he has exhibited in the Whitney Museum, the Metropolitan Museum, the Museum of Modern Art, and the De Young Museum in San Francisco.[20]

Two leading American Chinese architects are Ieoh Ming Pei and Worley K. Wong. Pei was born in Canton in 1917. After attending private school in China, he enrolled at the Massachusetts Institute of Technology for a Bachelor's degree in Architecture. In 1946 he received the degree of Master of Architecture from Harvard. He has practiced in Boston, Los Angeles, and New York and is well known for his outstanding designs—Mile High Center, Denver, Colorado; John Fitzgerald Kennedy Library, Cambridge, Massachusetts; East-West Center, University of Hawaii, Honolulu, Hawaii; Dallas City Hall; National Airlines Terminal at John F. Kennedy International Airport; and the total campus design for the State University of New York at Fredonia.[21]

Worley K. Wong, born in Oakland in 1912, has become a successful California architect. He graduated from the University of California with honors in 1936. His firm of Campbell, Wong & Associates has won important assignments from the University of California campuses, Stanford University, and the California State Colleges. It might be considered a symbolic defeat for exclusionist politicians that Wong won the California Governor's Mansion competition to design a new home for the state's governors, whose predecessors had worked so hard against Wong's ancestors.[22]

The careers of the Japanese in the United States parallel those of the Chinese. Once more, it must be pointed out that for each individual selected for mention here, there are many more persons who have become successful in their own ways. Culturally, the Japanese contribution to the American scene has been manifested by an artistic cuisine, noted for its epicurean delights and colorful simplicity. Japanese flower arranging, gardens, housing, and art have become integral parts of American life.

In May, 1971, Tetsuo Toyama, long proclaimed in Hawaii as a publisher-patriot, died at the age of eighty-eight. Like many other Hawaiian Japanese, Toyama was from Okinawa where he attended high and normal schools. He arrived on the island of Kauai in 1906 to work in the canefields. After several other jobs, he started publishing *Jitsugyono Hawaii Journal,* a magazine. With the bombing of Pearl Harbor, Toyama was one of those Hawaiians interned on the mainland. He was released in April, 1944. On February 26, 1953, he was with the first group of Japanese aliens to be naturalized under the McCarran-Walter Act. In 1954, he founded *The Citizen,* a bilingual newspaper which encouraged the elderly Japanese to seek citizenship. For many years he offered free citizenship classes in his office. He was well respected in Honolulu for his love of his adopted country.[23]

Following World War II, returning veterans of the 442nd Regimental Combat Team prepared to enter civilian life. One of these was Daniel K. Inouye. Born in Honolulu, he graduated from McKinley High School and was a premedical student at the University of Hawaii. In early 1943 at the age of eighteen, he volunteered for military service and was sent with other Nisei to Italy. Just before the end of the war in Italy, Inouye, wounded in the stomach, led a charge up a ridge. During the fight, his right arm was shattered and he was wounded in the leg. Much decorated, he returned home a captain. While recuperating in a military hospital, he talked at length with his friend, Sakae Takahasi, who later became a Hawaii State Senator representing West Honolulu. These two men, along with other Nisei, determined to make a place for themselves in Hawaii through political action. Working hard during the 1950's, they helped make the Democratic Party the dominant party in the territory. When statehood was granted in 1959, Inouye was elected as the state's first Member of the House of Representatives. He was reelected in 1960. Two years later he was elected to the United States Senate and was reelected in 1968. During that latter year, he gained additional national attention when he delivered the Democratic National Convention's keynote address in Chicago.[24]

When Inouye moved to the Senate, he was succeeded in the House of Representatives by a fellow veteran of the 442nd, Spark M. Matsunaga. Matsunaga, educated in Hawaii's schools, graduated from the University of Hawaii in June, 1941. Volunteering for duty after graduation, he served in both the 100th Battalion and the 442nd Combat Team. After the war, he received his law degree from Harvard Law School. He sat in the Hawaii Territorial Legislature from 1954 to 1959. He has been reelected four times to the House of Representatives and has advanced to the powerful House Rules Committee and has been a key figure on the Agriculture Committee.[25]

Following the 1960 census, Hawaii became eligible for a second representative and in 1964 Patsy Takemoto Mink, Hawaii's first Nisei woman lawyer, won that seat and has been reelected three times. She attended Wilson College, University of Nebraska, and the University of Hawaii, and received her law degree from the University of Chicago in 1951. Mrs. Mink served one term in the territorial House and two split terms in the Senate, once during the last territorial session and once during statehood. Mrs. Mink has become an important Congresswoman, serving on the Education and Labor Committee as well as the Interior and Insular Affairs Committee.[26]

These three have gained national attention by virtue of their Congressional service. In Hawaii, in 1970, George Ariyoshi became the first Nisei to be elected lieutenant governor. The 1971 state legislature had thirteen Japanese and four Chinese in the Senate; the House, led by Speaker Taddu Beppu, had thirty-three Japanese and five Chinese.

A brief study of the family of Senator Robert Taira, representing West Honolulu, is perhaps a typical example of the state's political leaders. Taira's father came from Okinawa in 1908 to work as a cane cutter on Kauai for 69¢ a day, ten hours a day. His wife, a picture bride, came from the same Okinawa community. They worked together, she running a community kitchen and doing laundry for her boarders at $1.25 a month plus $6.00 for groceries. An attempt at independence as a butcher failed and the senior Taira became a contract labor broker for Filipino labor. The family moved in 1928 to Honolulu to engage in various jobs. The father worked with a fertilizer company for a time and for the Hawaiian Meat Company while the mother worked at the Hawaiian Pineapple Cannery. In 1957 he leased some Kalihi Valley land to operate a hog farm. Much earlier, in 1935, Taira had purchased an agricultural plot in Kalihi Valley at 8¢ a square foot. In 1957, he and his neighbors formed Kalihi Valley Enterprises, Limited, which quickly reached a worth of $250,000.

The Tairas had six children; Robert was the eldest. At the age of twelve he worked in the pineapple cannery at 8¢ an hour during the summer. At the age of fifteen, he sold newspapers in downtown Honolulu, netting 50¢ a day, and worked with his father in the fertilizer plant. Later he attended Mid-Pacific Institute in Honolulu on a work scholarship. At the University of Hawaii he excelled on the debate and forensics team and upon graduation became a teacher. During World War II he volunteered with the first group of Nisei and went with other Hawaiians to Italy. After the war, he taught at Farrington High School but left to work for the Veterans Administration. Much later he joined his father to form Taira and Associates.

In 1962, he ran successfully for the State House of Representatives and was reelected three times. In 1970 he gained a seat in the State Senate.[27] The Taira family story, with minor variations, could be repeated several times.

In the field of fine arts, the name of Sessue Hayakawa is renowned in the motion picture industry. Arriving in the United States before World War I, he became a star instantly with a salary ranging between $3,500 and $5,000 a week. He had an up-and-down career during the 1920's but went into eclipse during the 1930's. Rediscovered in the 1940's he capped his career with the picture *Bridge over the River Kwai*.[28]

In 1968, Dr. Samuel I. Hayakawa was appointed President of San Francisco State College, the first such administrative appointment for a Japanese American. Hayakawa, born in Vancouver, British Columbia, received his early education in Canada as well as his Bachelor of Arts and Master of Arts degrees. He earned his Ph.D. at the University of Wisconsin in English. He was associated with the University of Wisconsin, the Armour Institute, and the University of Chicago. In 1955, he joined the faculty of San Francisco State College. He had a world reputation as a semanticist and had written some highly regarded works on the subject. In 1968, the state college was torn asunder by faculty discontent and the demands of blacks, Chicanos, Chinese, and Japanese. In the midst of this turmoil, S. I. Hayakawa was appointed President. Although at first a controversial figure, he has restored the reputation of the college as one of the major assets of the California State College System.[29]

Of more recent vintage is Pat Suzuki, singing stage star of *Flower Drum Song* and recording star. Tomi Kanazawa, a Californian, became the first Nisei to appear in a leading role with the Metropolitan Opera Company and was widely known as a concert performer.

Other people of outstanding creative power have come from the Nisei ranks. Harry A. Osaki of Pasadena, California, is a silversmith whose work is widely displayed and who has traveled in U. S. State Department shows in Europe. Isamu Noguchi has gained a world reputation as a sculptor. Born in Los Angeles, he attended Columbia University and has studied in Paris, China, and elsewhere. His works have been displayed from New York to Hawaii. In 1963, he received a Fine Arts Medal from the American Institute of Architects and the following year was consulted about the Arlington Cemetery tomb for John F. Kennedy. Two other important artists are sculptor George Tsutakawa and Paul Horiuchi, a painter. Both live in Seattle. Tsutakawa is best known for fountains in numerous parks and buildings.[30]

In 1962, the Japanese American Citizens League named Minoru Yamasaki as the Nisei of that biennium. His citation read:

by artfully blending his understanding of Japanese art and culture with that of Western architecture, he has attained in his profession a philosophy of humanism which seeks to elevate the dignity of man in his environment, a philosophy dedicated to and consistent with the highest ideals of democracy.[31]

Yamasaki was born in Seattle in 1912. He graduated from the University of Washington in 1934 and then studied in New York. He has designed outstanding buildings throughout the United States such as the Federal Science Pavilion at Seattle's Century 21 Exposition and the World Trade Center for the Port Authority of New York. At Princeton University he planned the Woodrow Wilson School of Public and International Affairs.[32]

Nisei in the mainland political arena have also made outstanding contributions. Unlike the Hawaiian Japanese and Chinese, they have had to overcome their minority status and the prejudiced opinions of the majority whites. Any such listings must include at the top the name of Mike

Masaoka. In 1950 when the JACL convention honored him for his leadership, his citation read:

> Rarely can a history of one decade of people be identified with a single individual. But uniquely and unmistakenly the history of American citizens of Japanese ancestry during the ten most crucial and tumultuous years of their existence is the story of Mike M. Masaoka. Appointed national secretary of the Japanese American Citizens League in 1941, his statesmanship, courage and vision during the evacuation, relocation and resettlement not only helped guide the organizations and persons of Japanese ancestry through their most difficult years, but also brought him recognition as their outstanding spokesman. Following his discharge from the Army, in which he served with the famed 442nd Regimental Combat Team, he became the national legislative director of the JACL Anti-Discrimination Committee in Washington, D. C. Largely through his vigorous efforts the vast reservoir of goodwill which the *Nisei* veterans won for persons of Japanese ancestry was translated into positive legislation for their common good. . . .[33]

The only Nisei to be elected to a mainland legislature has been Seiji Horiuchi of Brighton, Colorado. After serving one term in the Colorado legislature he retired to return to his private business. In California, Ken Nakaoka was elected Mayor of Gardena and Frank Ogawa has served on Oakland's City Council. In San Jose, Norman Mineta became the first non-Caucasian to serve on that nearly 100-year-old city council.[34] In 1971, Mineta won election as mayor. His victory showed, he claimed, "that political success is not just a possibility for Japanese Americans in Hawaii but on the mainland as well."[35]

The United States of America is a nation of immigrants. All groups have left their mark upon the country's fabric. As the Chinese and Japanese like other immigrant groups sought success, they were confronted both by opportunity and by serious obstacles. Their physical stamina and intellectual abilities have enabled them to make their mark and to add measurably to the American heritage.

Appendix

TABLE I

CHINESE IMMIGRANTS AND RESIDENTS

YEAR	ARRIVALS[1]	U.S. CENSUS REPORTS[2]	CALIF.[3]	HAWAII[4]	NEW YORK[5]
1820	1	——	——	——	——
1850	3	758	——	——	——
1860	5,467	34,933	34,933	816	——
1870	15,740	63,199	49,277	——	——
1880	5,802	105,465	75,132	——	909
1890	1,716	107,488	72,472	16,752	2,935
1900	1,247	89,863	45,753	25,767	7,170
1910	1,968	71,531	36,248	21,674	5,266
1920	2,330	61,639	28,812	23,507	5,793
1930	1,589	74,954	37,361	27,179	9,665
1940	643	77,504	39,556	28,774	13,731
1950	1,289	117,140	58,324	32,376	20,171
1960	3,672	237,292 (199,095)*	95,600	38,119	37,573
1970	14,093[6]				

[1]*Statistical History of the United States,* pp. 58-59, 66D; Kung, *Chinese in America,* Table VI, p. 270.

[2]U.S. Bureau of the Census, *Reports,* 1850-1960.

[3]Kung, Table XI, p. 275.

[4]Lind, Table 2, p. 28.

[5]Kung, Table XI, p. 275.

[6]U.S. Commissioner of Immigration and Naturalization, *Annual Report,* 1970, p. 64.

*This is the 1960 total, excluding Hawaii. Hawaiian Chinese are not included in any other decade.

TABLE II

CHINESE AND JAPANESE IMMIGRANTS
ARRIVAL BY DECADES[1]

YEAR	TOTAL ADMITTED CHINESE	TOTAL ADMITTED JAPANESE
1851-60	61,397	—
1861-70	64,301	186
1871-80	123,201	149
1881-90	61,711	2,270
1891-1900	14,799	25,942
1901-10	21,605	129,797
1911-20	21,907	83,837
1921-30	29,907	33,462
1931-40	4,928	1,948
1941-50	16,709	1,555
1951-60	24,226	46,550
1961-70[2]	96,702	38,521

[1]*Statistical History of the United States,* pp. 58-59, 66D; Kung, *Chinese in America,* Table VI, p. 270.

[2]U.S. Commissioner of Immigration and Naturalization, *Annual Report,* 1970, p. 64.

TABLE III

CHINESE POPULATION IN U. S. BY GEOGRAPHICAL REGION

GEOGRAPHICAL AREA	1870	1880	1890	1900	1910	1920	1930	1940	1950	1960[1]
North Atlantic	137	1,628	61,707	14,693	11,688	12,414	17,799	19,646	28,931	53,654
South Atlantic	11	74	669	1,791	1,582	1,824	1,869	2,047	4,755	8,555
North Central	9	813	2,357	3,668	4,610	6,721	8,078	6,092	10,646	18,413
South Central	211	848	1,447	1,982	1,717	2,076	2,325	2,879	5,713	8,284
West	62,831	102,102	96,844	67,729	51,934	38,604	44,883	46,840	67,584	148,386
	(99%)*	(99%)	(90%)	(75%)	(72%)	(63%)	(60%)	(60%)	(58%)	(63%)
California	49,277	75,132	72,472	45,753	36,248	28,812	37,361	39,556	58,324	95,600
	(77%)	(71%)	(67%)	(51%)	(51%)	(47%)	(50%)	(51%)	(50%)	(40%)
Hawaii	2,038	18,254	16,752	25,767	21,674	23,507	27,179	28,774	32,376	38,119[2]
	(1872)	(1884)								

[1]U. S. Bureau of the Census, *Reports*, 1870-1960.

[2]Lind, p. 28.

*The West's and California's share of the total mainland Chinese population is indicated by percentages for the years 1880-1950. The 1960 percentages include Hawaiian Chinese.

TABLE IV

CHINESE POPULATION IN U. S. BY CITIES

CITIES	1870	1880	1890	1900	1910	1920	1930	1940	1950	1960
San Francisco	12,022	21,745	25,833	13,954	10,582	7,744	16,303	17,782	24,813	36,445[1]
New York				6,321	4,614	5,042	8,414	12,753	18,327	32,831
Los Angeles				2,111	1,954	2,062	3,009	4,736	8,067	15,443
Oakland				950	3,609	3,821	3,048	3,201	5,531	5,264
Chicago				1,209	1,778	2,353	2,757	2,013	3,334	5,082
Sacramento				1,065	1,054	831	1,366	1,508	2,885	5,551
Boston				1,186	1,192	1,075	1,595	1,383	2,101	3,592
Washington, D. C.				455	369	461	398	656	1,825	2,632
Stockton				593	359	341	991	1,052	1,825	2,291
Portland				7,841	5,699	1,846	1,416	1,569	1,467	1,869
Philadelphia				1,165	997	869	1,672	922	1,242	1,810
Honolulu			7,693 (1896)	9,061	13,724	13,383	12,334	22,445	26,724	30,078[2]

[1]Kung, p. 43; Tow, pp. 42-43.
[2]Lind, p. 50; U. S. Bureau of the Census, *Reports*, 1900-1940.

TABLE V

JAPANESE IMMIGRANTS AND RESIDENTS

YEAR	ARRIVALS[1]	U.S. CENSUS REPORTS[2]	CALIF.[3]	HAWAII[4]	WASHINGTON[5]
1870	48	55	––	––	––
1880	4	148	86	116 (1884)	1
1890	691	2,039	1,147	12,610	360
1900	12,635	24,326	10,151	61,111	5,617
1910	2,720	72,157	41,356	79,675	12,929
1920	9,432	111,010	71,952	109,274	17,387
1930	837	138,834	97,456	139,631	17,838
1940	102	126,947	93,717	157,905	14,565
1950	100	141,758	84,956	184,598	9,694
1960	5,699	464,468 (260,195)*	157,317	203,876	16,652
1970[6]	4,485				

[1]*Statistical History of the United States*, pp. 58-59, 66D.

[2]U.S. Bureau of the Census, *Reports*, 1870-1960.

[3]Kitano, Table 13, p. 162.

[4]Lind, Table 2, p. 28.

[5]Kitano, Table 13, p. 163.

[6]U.S. Commissioner of Immigration and Naturalization, *Annual Report*, 1970, p. 64.

*This is the 1960 total, excluding Hawaii. Hawaiian Japanese are not included in any other decade.

TABLE VI

JAPANESE POPULATION IN U.S. BY GEOGRAPHICAL REGION

Geographical Area	1880	1890	1900	1910	1920	1930	1940	1950	1960[1]
North Atlantic	41	247	535	1,885	3,613	4,014	3,400	7,443	18,098
South Atlantic	5	55	29	156	360	393	442	1,393	5,730
North Central	8	117	349	1,482	2,007	1,931	1,571	18,207	27,845
South Central	—	61	37	454	748	827	607	2,189	10,255
West	94 (64%)*	1,559 (77%)	23,376 (96%)	68,150 (94%)	104,282 (93%)	131,310 (95%)	120,927 (95%)	112,541 (80%)	198,267 (77%)
California	86 (58%)	1,147 (57%)	10,151 (41%)	41,356 (57%)	71,952 (65%)	97,456 (70%)	93,717 (73%)	84,956 (59%)	157,317 (60%)
Hawaii	——	12,610	61,111	79,675	109,274	139,631	157,905	184,598	203,876[2]

[1]U.S. Bureau of the Census, *Reports*, 1880-1960.

[2]Lind, Table 2, p. 28.

*The West's and California's share of the total mainland Japanese population is indicated by percentages for the years 1880-1950. The 1960 percentages include Hawaiian Japanese in the total.

Notes and References

INTRODUCTION

1. *Statistical History of the United States from Colonial Times to the Present* (Stamford, Conn.: Fairfield Publishers, Inc., 1965), "Series C 103 Immigrants, by Country: 1820-1957," pp. 56-59.
2. *Ibid.*

CHAPTER I

1. George M. Beckmann, *The Modernization of China and Japan* (New York: Harper & Row, 1962), pp. 2-18; L. Carrington Goodrich, *A Short History of the Chinese People*, 3rd ed. (New York: Harper Torchbook, 1963), pp. 1-142.
2. Goodrich, pp. 171-88.
3. *Ibid.*, pp. 189-213.
4. *Ibid.*, pp. 214-31; Beckmann, pp. 51-63.
5. Beckmann, pp. 26-28; John King Fairbank, *The United States and China* (New York: Viking Press, 1958), pp. 82-86.
6. George B. Cressey, *China's Geographic Foundations*, 1st ed. (New York: McGraw-Hill, 1934), p. 15; Fairbank, pp. 15-17.
7. Fairbank, pp. 19-20.
8. Cressey, p. 349.
9. *Ibid.*, p. 351.
10. *Ibid.*, pp. 348, 361-63.
11. *Ibid.*, pp. 352-53.
12. *Ibid.*, pp. 353-58; Gunther Barth, *Bitter Strength* (Cambridge: Harvard Univ. Press, 1964), pp. 13-15.
13. Cressey, p. 356.
14. Barth, pp. 13, 19-21; Fairbank, pp. 15-17.
15. Barth, pp. 16-19.
16. Thos. W. Chinn, ed., *A History of the Chinese in California* (San Francisco: Chinese Historical Society of America, 1969), p. 4.
17. *Ibid.*, pp. 102-5.
18. *Ibid.*, p. 30.
19. *Ibid.*, p. 31.
20. Herrlee G. Creel, *Confucius, the Man and the Myth* (New York: John Day Co., 1949); Arthur Wright, *Confucianism and Chinese Civilization* (New York: Atheneum, 1964).

21. Fairbank, pp. 97-99; Holmes Welch, *The Parting of the Way: Lao Tzu and the Taoist Movement* (Boston: Beacon Press, 1957).

22. Fairbank, pp. 99-102; Arthur F. Wright, *Buddhism in Chinese History* (Stanford Univ. Press, 1959).

23. Fairbank, pp. 146-47.

24. Chinn, p. 31.

25. Fairbank, pp. 54-64.

26. *Ibid.*, pp. 94-97.

27. *Ibid.*, p. 71.

28. Goodrich, p. 32.

29. *Ibid.*, p. 218.

30. Barth, pp. 21-22.

31. Chinn, p. 2.

32. *Ibid.*, p. 4; Betty Lee Sung, *Mountain of Gold* (New York: Macmillan Co., 1967), pp. 11-16.

33. Sung, p. 19; Barth, p. 22.

34. Barth, pp. 24-25.

35. *Ibid.*, pp. 25-26.

36. Samuel Eliot Morison, *The Maritime History of Massachusetts, 1783-1860* (Boston: Houghton Mifflin Co., 1921), p. 45.

37. *Ibid.*, p. 64; Fairbank, pp. 115-20.

38. Morison, p. 71; Edward T. Williams, *China Yesterday and To-Day* (New York: Thos. Y. Crowell, 1932), pp. 432-34.

39. Morison, p. 66; Williams, p. 433.

40. Alexander DeConde, *A History of American Foreign Policy* (New York: Charles Scribner's Sons, 1963), pp. 225-27.

41. *Ibid.*, pp. 227-31.

42. *Ibid.*, pp. 232-33.

43. Mary R. Coolidge, *Chinese Immigration* (New York: Holt & Co., 1909), pp. 15-17.

44. Chinn, p. 11.

45. *Ibid.*, pp. 10-11.

46. *Ibid.*, pp. 12-13.

CHAPTER II

1. Barth, pp. 50-55.

2. Persia C. Campbell, *Chinese Coolie Emigration to Countries Within the British Empire* (London: P. S. King & Son, Ltd., 1933), pp. 86-97.

3. *Ibid.*, pp. 144-59; 12 *U. S. Statutes* (1862), pp. 340-41.

4. U. S. *Congressional Record*, 47th Cong., 1st Sess., March 20, 1882, p. 2030. Representative Flower, a Democrat, was elected to replace Levi P. Morton for the 1881-83 term. He was reelected to Congress in 1889. In 1891 he became Governor of New York.

5. *Sacramento Union*, February 5, 1859, p. 2.

6. Yung Wing returned to China in 1855 but was unable to find a suitable position. In 1872 he returned to the United States as co-commissioner of the Chinese Education Commission. Appointed associate minister from China to the United States, Spain, and Peru, he helped open the legation in 1878 and was present in Washington, D. C., during the critical years leading to Chinese exclusion. See Edmund H. Worthy, Jr., "Yung Wing in America," *Pacific Historical Review*, XXXIV (1965), 265-87; Thomas E. La-Fargue, *China's First Hundred* (Pullman, Wash.: Washington State College, 1942), pp. 17-24; Rose Hum Lee, *The Chinese in the United States of America* (Hong Kong: Hong Kong Univ. Press, 1960), p. 86.

7. See Appendix A, Tables I, II, and III; *Statistical History of the United States*, pp. 58-59.

8. Hubert Howe Bancroft, *History of California* (San Francisco: 1890), VII, 336; Barth, pp. 55-59; Chinese Historical Society of America, *Bulletin* V. (March, 1970), p. 1.

9. *San Francisco Star*, April 1, 1848, p. 2.

10. Walton Bean, *California, An Interpretive History* (New York: McGraw-Hill Book Co., 1968), pp. 108-23.

11. James O'Meara, "The Chinese in Early Days," *Overland Monthly*, n.s., III (1884), 477-81.

12. C. V. Gillespie wrote to Thomas Larkin on March 6, 1848, on the subject of contract labor. He said in part that "any number of mechanics agriculturists and servants can be obtained. They would be willing to sell their services for a certain period to pay their passage across the Pacific. . . ." See Thos. O. Larkin, *The Larkin Papers*, Geo. P. Hammond, ed. (Berkeley: Univ. of Calif. Press, 1964), p. 167. Once the Chinese came under contract, it was difficult to keep them. Edward Lucatt has written that "the fifteen coolies I brought from China, and who were under a bond for two years . . . were no sooner ashore than they resisted their contract, and each turned his separate way." See Edward Lucatt, *Rovings in the Pacific from 1837 to 1849* (London: Longman, Brown, Green and Long-mans, 1851), II, 263.

13. H. Brett Melendy and Benjamin F. Gilbert, *The Governors of California: Peter H. Burnett to Edmund G. Brown* (Georgetown, Calif.: Talisman Press, 1965), p. 40.

14. *Daily Alta California* (San Francisco), March 8, 1852, p. 2.

15. See note 12 above.

16. California, *Senate Journal*, 3rd Sess., 1852, pp. 373-78.

17. *Ibid.*, p. 731.

18. Winfield J. Davis, *History of Political Conventions in California, 1849-1892* (Sacramento: State Library, 1892), p. 23.

19. Elmer C. Sandmeyer, *The Anti-Chinese Movement in California* (Urbana, Ill.: Univ. of Illinois Press, 1939), p. 26.

20. *Congressional Record,* 47th Cong., 1st Sess., March 8, 1882, p. 1717.

21. Thomas C. Cochran and William Miller, *The Age of Enterprise, a Social History of Industrial America* (New York: Macmillan Co., 1942); Edward C. Kirkland, *Industry Comes of Age: Business, Labor, and Public Policy 1860-1897* (New York: Holt, Rinehart and Winston, 1961), pp. 342-98.

22. Henry Pelling, *American Labor* (Chicago: University of Chicago Press, 1960), pp. 48-102; Alexander Saxton, *The Indispensable Enemy Labor and the Anti-Chinese Movement in California* (Berkeley: Univ. of Calif. Press, 1971), pp. 293 ff.; Robert F. Heizer and Alan J. Almquist, *The Other Californians* (Berkeley: Univ. of Calif. Press, 1971), pp. 154-77.

23. U. S. Senate, *Report of the Joint Special Committee to Investigate Chinese Immigration,* 44th Cong., 2nd Sess., Report No. 689, 1877, pp. 1-1253. Hereafter cited as Joint Committee, *Report.*

24. *Ibid.,* p. 15.

25. *Ibid.,* pp. 175-76.

26. Campbell, pp. 28-29; Joint Committee, *Report,* p. 44.

27. Joint Committee, *Report,* pp. 111, 827.

28. Campbell, p. 29.

29. *Ibid.,* p. 31.

30. *Ibid.,* p. 32.

31. *Ibid.,* p. 33.

32. Joint Committee, *Report,* pp. 38-39.

33. Barth, pp. 57-61; Chinn, p. 16.

34. John H. Kemble, transcriber, "Andrew Wilson's 'Jottings' on Civil War California," *California Historical Society Quarterly,* XXXII (1953), 209, 212-14.

35. Albert S. Evans, "From the Orient Direct," *Atlantic Monthly,* XXIV (1869), 543-47.

36. See Appendix A, Table II.

37. Ralph S. Kuykendall, *The Hawaiian Kingdom* (Honolulu: Univ. of Hawaii Press, 1968 reprint), I, 27.

38. *Ibid.,* pp. 328-29.

39. *Ibid.,* pp. 76-77.

40. *Ibid.,* pp. 177-84.

41. *Ibid.,* pp. 190-91.

42. *Ibid.,* III, pp. 117-22.

43. *Ibid.,* pp. 142-53.

CHAPTER III

1. Francis J. Brown and Joseph S. Roucek, ed., *One America— The History, Contributions, and Present Problems of Our Racial and National Minorities,* 3rd ed. (New York: Prentice-Hall, 1952), p. 471.

2. Fred W. Riggs, *Pressures on Congress A Study of the Repeal*

of Chinese Exclusion (New York: King's Crown Press, 1950), pp. 90-91.

3. Joint Committee, *Report*, p. 31.

4. Melendy and Gilbert, p. 45.

5. Rodman Paul, "The Origins of the Chinese Issue in California," *Mississippi Valley Historical Review*, XXV (1938), 181-96.

6. *Daily Alta California*, May 12, 1852, p. 2.

7. Charles W. Brooks, "The Chinese Labor Problem," *Overland Monthly*, o.s., III (1869), 407-19; Sandmeyer, p. 42.

8. 1 *U. S. Statutes* (1790), p. 103.

9. California, *Senate Journal*, 7th Sess., 1856, p. 401; *The Oriental* (San Francisco), January 4, 1855, p. 2.

10. *Sacramento Union*, January 23, 1855, p. 2.

11. *Ibid.*, April 25, 1855, p. 2; January 5, 1858, p. 4; March 5, 1858, p. 2; February 2, 1859, p. 2; February 26, 1859, p. 2; *Oriental*, April 14, 1855, p. 2; *San Francisco Evening Bulletin*, April 3, 1858, p. 1.

12. *Daily Alta*, May 21, 1853, p. 2.

13. *Ibid.*, August 19, 1854, p. 2.

14. *Ibid.*, September 4, 1854, p. 2.

15. *Ibid.*, October 19, 1859, p. 4.

16. California, *Assembly Journal*, 6th Sess., 1855, pp. 463-65; *Oriental*, March 29, 1855, p. 2.

17. California, *Statutes*, 6th Sess., 1855, pp. 194-95.

18. *Ibid.*, 1st Sess., 1850, p. 455.

19. California, *The People* v. *Hall*, 4:399.

20. *Oriental*, January 18, 1855, p. 2; February 22, 1855, p. 2.

21. Sandmeyer, pp. 46-47.

22. Melendy and Gilbert, p. 149.

23. *Sacramento Union*, May 30, 1872, p. 2.

24. William N. Slocum, "Revolution The Reorganization of Our Social System Inevitable, An Address before the Anti-Monopoly Association, San Francisco, February 24, 1878," Appendix, "The Chinese Question," pp. 25-26.

25. California, Superintendent of Public Instruction, *Ninth Annual Report*, 1859, p. 14.

26. *Ibid.*, *Thirteenth Annual Report*, 1863, p. 67; *Ibid.*, *First Biennial Report*, 1864-65, p. 57; California, *Statutes*, 16th Sess., 1865-66, p. 398.

27. California, *Senate Journal*, 19th Sess., 1872, pp. 113-14; *Sacramento Union*, August 22, 1877, p. 3.

28. *Sacramento Union*, January 10, 1885, p. 8.

29. California, *Statutes*, 26th Sess., 1885, p. 100.

30. See Appendix A, Table III.

31. *San Francisco Chronicle*, May 17, 1873, p. 2; The Friends of International Right and Justice, "How the U. S. Treaty with China

is Observed in California," 2nd ed., San Francisco, September 13, 1877.

32. *Daily Alta,* February 5, 1871, p. 1.

33. *Ibid.,* June 10, 1873, p. 1; June 24, 1873, p. 1; *San Francisco Bulletin,* May 27, 1873, p. 3.

34. *Sacramento Union,* May 28, 1873, p. 1.

35. *Ibid.,* July 1, 1873, p. 3; *San Francisco Bulletin,* May 27, 1873, p. 3; Sandmeyer, p. 52.

36. U. S. Circuit Court for California, "Opinion in Ho Ah Kow vs. Matthew Nunan Delivered July 7, 1879" in "The Invalidity of the 'Queue Ordinance' of the City and County of San Francisco" (San Francisco, J. L. Rice & Co., 1879).

37. Paul Mason, compiler, *Constitution of the State of California Annotated, 1946* (Sacramento: Calif. State Printing Office, 1946), pp. 1299-301.

38. Bean, pp. 136-48, 236-37.

39. *Daily Alta,* February 13, 1867, p. 1; February 2, 1867, p. 1; March 5, 1867, p. 1.

40. Paul M. De Falla, "Lantern in the Western Sky," *Historical Society of Southern California Quarterly,* XLII (1960), 57-88, 161-85.

41. *Sacramento Union,* May 2, 1876, p. 3.

42. *Ibid.,* June 20, 1876, p. 1; October 6, 1876, p. 2.

43. *Ibid.,* December 29, 1875, p. 1.

44. "How the Treaty is Observed," Appendix, ii; *Daily Alta,* March 16, 1877, p. 1; *Sacramento Union,* March 19, 1877, p. 1.

45. "How the Treaty is Observed"; Bean, pp. 236-37; William Tell Coleman, "Statements and Other Materials Assembled in Preparing his Biography for Chronicles of Builders," University of California Bancroft Library Manuscript Collection.

46. Bean, pp. 237-38.

47. *Daily Alta,* December 17, 1877, p. 1.

48. California, *Appendix to Journals, Senate and Assembly,* 23rd Sess., 1880, p. 36.

49. Coolidge, p. 123.

50. U. S., *Papers Relating to Foreign Relations of U. S., 1881,* pp. 318, 323-25.

51. U. S., *Papers Relating to Foreign Relations, 1885,* pp. 110-15; Wen Hwan Ma, *American Policy Toward China* (Shanghai, China, 1934), pp. 177-82.

52. "Anti-Chinese Riots of 1885," *Papers Relating to the History of State of Washington,* Part V, *Washington State Historical Society Publications* (Olympia: State Historical Society, 1915), II, 388-97; *Sacramento Union,* November 9, 1855, p. 1; Mrs. S. L. Baldwin, "Must the Chinese Go? An Examination of the Chinese Question" (Boston: Rand, Avery and Co., 1886).

53. U. S., *Papers Relating to Foreign Relations of U. S., 1888,* pp. 363-64.

54. *Ibid.,* pp. 391-92.

55. James D. Richardson, compiler, *A Compilation of the Messages and Papers of the Presidents, 1789-1905* (Bureau of National Literature and Art, 1908), IX, 5083.

56. U. S., *Papers Relating to Foreign Relations of U. S., 1886,* p. 158.

57. Samuel Gompers and Herman Gutstadt, *Meat vs. Rice, American Manhood Against Asiatic Coolieism* (San Francisco: Asiatic Exclusion League, 1908).

58. Arthur Mann, "Gompers and the Irony of Racism," *Antioch Review,* XIII (June, 1953), 203-14.

CHAPTER IV

1. J. Douglas Borthwick, *Three Years in California* (Edinburgh: W. Blackwood and Sons, 1857), pp. 117-18.

2. *Ibid.,* pp. 215-18.

3. *Ibid.,* p. 118.

4. Ping Chui, *Chinese Labor in California, 1850-1880* (Madison, Wis.: State Historical Society of Wisconsin, 1963), pp. 24-25.

5. *Ibid.,* p. 12.

6. *Ibid.,* p. 27; U. S., 8th Census, I, 611-15; 9th Census, I, 722.

7. Chinn, pp. 33-34.

8. *Ibid.,* pp. 35-36.

9. *Sacramento Union,* June 15, 1858, p. 2.

10. Chui, pp. 41-42; Ira B. Cross, *A History of the Labor Movement in California* (Berkeley: Univ. of Calif. Press, 1910), p. 74.

11. Joint Committee, *Report,* p. 667.

12. *Ibid.,* p. 78.

13. Chui, p. 45.

14. *Ibid.,* pp. 45-46.

15. Barth, pp. 191-96. Barth details the career of Cornelius Koopmanschap as a contractor of Chinese labor.

16. Joint Committee, *Report,* p. 674.

17. *Ibid.,* p. 675.

18. Chui, p. 46.

19. Joint Committee, *Report,* p. 669.

20. Chinn, p. 44.

21. *Ibid.,* p. 45.

22. Wesley S. Griswold, *A Work of Giants* (London: Muller, 1963), p. 123.

23. *Ibid.,* pp. 160-61.

24. Joint Committee, *Report,* p. 667.

25. Bean, pp. 217-18.

26. Chui, p. 26.

27. Vincent Carosso, *The California Wine Industry 1830-1895* (Berkeley: Univ. of Calif. Press, 1951), p. 71; California State Agriculture Society, *Transactions*, 1866-67 (Sacramento, 1867), p. 447.

28. Claude B. Hutchinson, *California Agriculture* (Berkeley: Univ. of Calif. Press, 1946), p. 445; Victor N. Cone, *Irrigation in the San Joaquin Valley, California* (United States Department of Agriculture, Office of Experimental Stations, Bulletin 239, 1911), pp. 22-26.

29. Joint Committee, *Report*, p. 439.

30. Augustus W. Loomis, "How Our Chinamen are Employed," *Overland Monthly*, o.s., II (March 1869), pp. 231-40.

31. *Pacific Rural Press*, June 10, 1893, p. 3; September 16, 1893, p. 3.

32. Chui, p. 72; Joint Committee, *Report*, pp. 54, 441.

33. Henryk Sienkiewicz, "The Chinese in California," *California Historical Society Quarterly*, XXXIV (1955), 301-16.

34. Chinn, pp. 60-61.

35. *San Francisco Chronicle*, January 5, 1902, p. 12.

36. "Chinese Fisheries in California," *Chamber's Journal*, I (1854), 48.

37. Robert F. G. Spier, "Food Habits of the Nineteenth Century California Chinese," *California Historical Society Quarterly*, XXXVII (1958), 79-81, 128-36; George B. Goode, *The Fisheries and Fishing Industries of the U. S.* (Washington: U. S. Printing Office, 1887), I, 735-39; California, *Report of the State Board of Fish Commissioners, 1891-1892* (Sacramento, 1892), pp. 20-24.

38. John S. Hittell, *The Commerce and Industries of the Pacific Coast of North America* (San Francisco: A. L. Bancroft and Co., 1882), p. 366; Goode, II, 809; Chinn, pp. 38-40.

39. Goode, II, 623-25.

40. Chui, pp. 119-28; Chinn, pp. 49-50.

41. Chui, pp. 89-102; Chinn, pp. 50-51, 53-55.

42. Chui, pp. 103-8; Chinn, pp. 51-53.

43. George F. Seward, *Chinese Immigration in its Social and Economic Aspects* (New York: Chas. Scribner's Sons, 1881), p. 134.

44. *Ibid.*, p. 135.

45. Alexander McLeod, *Pigtails & Golddust* (Caldwell, Ida: Caxton Printers, 1947), p. 111.

46. Hubert H. Bancroft, *Essays and Miscellany* (San Francisco: A. L. Bancroft Co., 1890), p. 348.

47. *New York Illustrated News*, June 4, 1853, p. 359.

48. Chinn, p. 63.

49. Sung, p. 191.

50. Lee, p. 226.

51. Noah Brooks, "Restaurant Life in San Francisco," *Overland Monthly*, o.s., I (1868), 472-73; Samuel Bowles, *Our New West* (Hartford, Conn.: Hartford Pub. Co., 1869), pp. 407-13.

52. Chinn, p. 62.

53. Chinn, p. 62; Sung, p. 202-3. Another description of chop suey is that the dish is food familiar to a common laborer—a liquid stew poured over rice. See Emily Hahn, *The Cooking of China* (New York: Time-Life, 1968), p. 178.

54. Sung, p. 203.

55. Pardee Lowe, *Father and Glorious Descendant* (Boston: Little Brown and Co., 1943), pp. 146-47.

56. Kung, pp. 179-96.

CHAPTER V

1. 22 *U. S. Statutes* (1882), pp. 58-61.

2. Sandmeyer, p. 95; Stuart C. Miller, *The Unwelcome Immigrant* (Berkeley: Univ. of Calif. Press, 1969), p. 3. Miller's monograph properly questions assumptions made by earlier historians of the Chinese in California that the Eastern establishment was won over by the West. Miller holds that the East had as a consequence of the China Trade developed its own stereotype of the Chinese and needed no help from Californians.

3. 23 *U. S. Statutes* (1884), p. 115.

4. 25 *U. S. Statutes* (1888), p. 476.

5. See Appendix A, Tables I and II.

6. *Ibid.*

7. 27 *U. S. Statutes* (1892), p. 25.

8. 149 U. S., 698-763.

9. 30 *U. S. Statutes* (1898), p. 751; 31 *U. S. Statutes* (1900), p. 161.

10. Richardson, *Messages and Papers of the Presidents*, X, 425-26.

11. 32 *U. S. Statutes* (1902), pp. 176-77.

12. 33 *U. S. Statutes* (1904), p. 428.

13. Sung, pp. 73-75, 100-3.

14. Fu Chi Hao, "My Reception in America," *The Outlook*, LXXXVI (August 10, 1907), 770-73.

15. 39 *U. S. Statutes* (1917), p. 874.

16. 43 *U. S. Statutes* (1924), p. 153-69.

17. Lee, p. 14.

18. 43 *U. S. Statutes* (1924), pp. 153-69.

19. S. W. Kung, *Chinese in American Life* (Seattle: Univ. of Washington Press, 1962), p. 98.

20. Sung, pp. 98-100; Lee, pp. 300-7.

21. *Time,* January 20, 1958, p. 17; *New York Times,* January 15, 1957, p. 18; February 20, 1957, p. 13; May 6, 1957, p. 23.

22. 71 *U. S. Statutes* (1957), pp. 639-44.

23. Robert A. Divine, *American Immigration Policy, 1924-1952* (New Haven: Yale Univ. Press, 1957), pp. 147-48; Riggs, pp. 47-64.

24. Riggs, pp. 65-84.

25. U. S. Cong. 78th, 1st Sess., Comm. on Immigration and Naturalization, Hearings, "Repeal of The Chinese Exclusion Acts," pp. 31, 37, 56, 68-70, 78-80, 92-93, 119-23, 133-34, 145, 153, 197.

26. *Grizzly Bear* (Los Angeles), LXXIII (May, 1943), Supplement, p. 6.

27. U. S. Cong. 78th, 1st Sess., Hearings, pp. 217-19.

28. *Ibid.*, p. 206.

29. *Congressional Record*, 78th Cong., 1st Sess., 1943, pp. 8199-200.

30. 57 *U. S. Statutes* (1943), pp. 600-1.

31. Sung, pp. 81-82.

32. 66 *U. S. Statutes* (1952), p. 277.

33. Sung, p. 112.

34. Chinn, p. 29; Kung, pp. 118-26.

35. Chinn, p. 29.

36. *New York Times*, October 6, 1965, p. 1; 79 *U. S. Statutes* (1965), pp. 911-22.

37. *San Francisco Chronicle*, October 21, 1966, pp. 1, 6.

38. U. S. Commissioner of Immigration and Naturalization, *Annual Report*, 1970, p. 64.

39. *Ibid.*, pp. 59-60.

CHAPTER VI

1. Sung, p. 134.

2. Borthwick, p. 61.

3. Augustus Loomis, "Chinese in California, Their Sign-board Literature," *Overland Monthly*, o.s., I (1868), 152-55.

4. Lee, pp. 61-63; Charles C. Dobie, *San Francisco's Chinatowns* (New York: D. Appleton-Century Co., 1936), pp. 225-32.

5. See Appendix A, Table III.

6. Kung, pp. 198, 319.

7. Augustus Loomis, "The Six Chinese Companies," *Overland Monthly*, o.s., I (1868), 222.

8. Barth, pp. 88-90; Dobie, pp. 119-37; Kung, pp. 76-77.

9. *Daily Alta California*, April 5, 1856, p. 3.

10. Loomis, "The Six Chinese Companies," pp. 222-27.

11. *Ibid.*, p. 223.

12. Barth, p. 97.

13. Chinn, p. 65.

14. *Ibid.*

15. Sung, p. 12.

16. *Ibid.*, p. 135.

17. Kung, p. 222.

18. Dobie, p. 136.

19. *Honolulu Star-Bulletin*, November 26, 1970, p. E12.

20. Lowe, pp. 298-99.

21. Lee, pp. 359-60. Her chapter on "Imagery by Eras" reviews ably the stereotyping of Chinese by white America.

22. Dobie, pp. 144-45; Augustus Loomis, "Chinese Women in California," *Overland Monthly*, o.s., II (1869), 344-51; Richard Dillon, *The Hatchetmen* (New York: Coward-McCann, Inc., 1962), pp. 223-39; M. G. C. Edholm, "A Stain on the Flag," *California Illustrated Magazine*, I (1891-92), 159-70; Frederick J. Masters, "Opium and its Votaries," *California Illustrated Magazine*, I (1891-92), 631-45.

23. Dobie, p. 145.

24. Barth, pp. 100-8; Dobie, pp. 138-76; Frederick J. Masters, "Among the Highbinders," *California Illustrated Magazine*, I (1891-92), 62-74; Lee, 161-73.

25. Lee, p. 282.

26. Chinn, pp. 73-74.

27. *Ibid.*, pp. 74-75.

28. Augustus Loomis, "Holiday in California Quarter," *Overland Monthly*, o.s., II (1869), 148-49.

29. Chinn, p. 76.

30. *Ibid.*, pp. 76-77.

31. F. R. Dresslar, "Chinese Pedagogies in Practice," *Education*, XX (1899), 136-42.

32. Chinn, p. 69.

33. Lowe, pp. 107-8.

34. *Honolulu Star-Bulletin*, November 26, 1970, p. E12.

35. Lee, pp. 64-68.

36. *Ibid.*, pp. 247-51.

37. Kung, p. 217; Sung, pp. 139-40.

38. *Time*, September 8, 1967, p. 18; *Newsweek*, February 23, 1970, pp. 57-58; *San Francisco Chronicle*, August 5, 1971, pp. 1, 22; August 6, 1971, pp. 1, 22.

39. Tom Wolfe, "The New Yellow Peril," *Esquire*, LXXII (1969), 190-99, 322.

CHAPTER VII

1. Edwin O. Reischauer, *The United States and Japan*, 3rd ed. (Cambridge: Harvard Univ. Press, 1965), pp. 5-9.

2. Glen T. Trewartha, *A Reconnaissance Geography of Japan* (Madison, Wis.: Univ. of Wisconsin, 1934), pp. 9-11; *The Japan Times Year Book, 1933*, 2nd ed. (Tokyo: Japan Times, 1933), p. 1.

3. Reischauer, p. 102.

4. *The Japan Times Year Book, 1933*, p. 1.

5. *Ibid.*, pp. 3-4.

6. Trewartha, pp. 155-202.

7. Beckmann, pp. 72-80.

8. *Ibid.*

9. *Ibid.*, pp. 81-85.

10. *Ibid.*, pp. 85-86.

11. Milton W. Meyers, *Japan, A Concise History* (Boston: Allyn and Bacon, 1966), p. 49.

12. Beckmann, pp. 93-97.

13. *Ibid.*, pp. 100-1.

14. W. G. Beasley, *The Modern History of Japan* (Frederick A. Praeger, 1963), pp. 76-97.

15. *Ibid.*, p. 99.

16. *Ibid.*, p. 97.

17. *Ibid.*, pp. 141-51; Reischauer, pp. 87-97.

18. *Ibid.*, pp. 134-95; Reischauer, pp. 53-68.

19. Reischauer, pp. 62-66.

20. Ralph S. Kuykendall, *The Hawaiian Kingdom, 1874-1893* (Honolulu, Hawaii: Univ. of Hawaii Press, 1967), III, 153-72.

21. U. S. Immigration Commission, *Reports of the Immigration Commission* (Washington, 1911), XXIII, 62-68.

22. Reischauer, pp. 116-19, 134.

23. Beasley, pp. 125-27; Yosaburo Yoshida, "Sources and Causes of Japanese Immigration," *Annals of the American Academy of Political and Social Science*, XXXIV (September, 1909), 157-67.

24. Beasley, pp. 141-43; Reischauer, pp. 60-65.

25. Beasley, pp. 109-12.

26. Reischauer, pp. 91-97.

27. *Ibid.*, pp. 133-41, 159-63.

28. *Ibid.*, p. 144.

29. *Ibid.*, pp. 144-50.

30. *Ibid.*, pp. 172-77.

31. *Ibid.*, pp. 119-25.

32. *Ibid.*, pp. 125-26.

33. *Ibid.*, pp. 126-27.

34. *Ibid.*, pp. 127-29.

35. See Daniel Holton, *Modern Japan and Shinto Nationalism; a Study of Present-Day Trends in Japanese Religions*, rev. ed. (Chicago: University of Chicago Press, 1967).

36. Ernest D. Saunders, *Buddhism in Japan, with an Outline of its Origins in India* (Philadelphia: Univ. of Pennsylvania Press, 1964),

37. Chikao Fujisawa, *Zen and Shinto; the Story of Japanese Philosophy* (New York: Philosophical Library, 1959).

38. Reischauer, p. 14.

CHAPTER VIII

1. Minutes of Bureau of Immigration, March 19, 1868, Public Archives of Hawaii, Honolulu, Hawaii.

2. Ralph S. Kuykendall, *The Earliest Japanese Labor Immigration to Hawaii* (Honolulu: University of Hawaii Occasional Papers, No.

25, 1935); F. Hilary Conroy, *The Japanese Frontier in Hawaii, 1868-1898* (Berkeley: Univ. of California Press, 1953).

3. Kuykendall, *The Hawaiian Kingdom,* III, 155-59.

4. *Ibid.,* p. 162.

5. Conroy, pp. 82-83; Yoshida, pp. 159-62.

6. Kuykendall, III, 165-66.

7. *Ibid.,* p. 167.

8. *Ibid.,* p. 170.

9. *Ibid.,* p. 172.

10. *Sacramento Union,* June 18, 1869, p. 2; *San Francisco Chronicle,* June 17, 1869, p. 3.

11. *Sacramento Union,* June 18, 1869, p. 2.

12. *Daily Alta California,* October 23, 1869, p. 2.

13. Bill Hosokawa, *Nisei, The Quiet Americans* (New York: William Morrow and Co., 1969), pp. 31-33.

14. *San Jose News,* June 4, 1969, p. 4.

15. *Sacramento Union,* February 9, 1870, p. 3.

16. Hosokawa p. 38.

17. U. S. Immigration Commission, *Reports of the Immigration Commission,* XXIII (1911), 63.

18. Raymond L. Buell, "The Development of the Anti-Japanese Agitation in the United States," *Political Science Quarterly,* XXXVII (1922), 606-7.

19. Hisaakira Kano, *Tunnels under the Pacific* (New York, 1919), p. 21.

20. Harry H. L. Kitano, *Japanese Americans—The Evolution of a Subculture* (Englewood Cliffs, N. J.: Prentice-Hall, Inc., 1969), p. 23.

21. Hosokawa, pp. 47-50.

22. *Ibid.,* p. 48.

23. U. S. Superintendent of Immigration, *Annual Report, 1892,* p. 13; U. S. Commissioner General of Immigration, *Annual Report, 1897,* p. 6.

24. Hosokawa, p. 51.

25. *San Francisco Call,* May 4, 1892, p. 8.

26. *Ibid.,* May 6, 1892, p. 3.

27. *Ibid.,* May 30, 1892, p. 3.

28. U. S. State Dept., *Foreign Relations of the United States, 1897,* pp. 367-68.

29. U. S. Commissioner General of Immigration, *Annual Report, 1899,* p. 29.

30. *Statistical History of the United States from Colonial Times to the Present,* pp. 56, 58.

31. Buell, "The Redevelopment of the Anti-Japanese Agitation in the United States," pp. 608-9.

32. *San Francisco Chronicle,* May 8, 1900, p. 1.

33. *Ibid.*, p. 3.

34. *Congressional Record,* 57th Cong. 1st Sess., 1901, pp. 135, 308.

35. *San Francisco Chronicle,* February 23-March 6, 1905.

36. California, *Senate Journal,* 1905, pp. 1164-65.

37. Roger Daniels, *The Politics of Prejudice: The Anti-Japanese Movement in California and the Struggle for Japanese Exclusion* (Berkeley: Univ. of Calif. Press, 1962), pp. 27-28. In 1907, the league changed its name to the Asiatic Exclusion League (Daniels, p. 126). See too Walter MacArthur, "Opposition to Oriental Immigration," *Annals of the American Academy of Political and Social Science,* XXXIV (September, 1909), pp. 223-30.

38. Asiatic Exclusion League, *Proceedings* (San Francisco, 1907-12), May, 1910, pp. 13-14.

39. Letter, Roosevelt to George Kennan, May 6, 1905, Theodore Roosevelt MSS, Library of Congress, Manuscript Division. (Hereafter cited as LCMD.)

40. Letter, Roosevelt to Cecil Arthur Spring-Rice, July 24, 1905, Roosevelt MSS., LCMD.

41. Richardson, *Messages and Papers of the Presidents,* XI, 7008.

42. For a full account of the school controversy, see Thomas A. Bailey, *Theodore Roosevelt and the Japanese-American Crises* (Stanford: Stanford University Press, 1934).

43. *San Francisco Call,* December 6, 1902, p. 14. This opinion leaned heavily on *Plessy v. Ferguson* 136 U. S. 537, 16 Sup. Ct., 1138, 412. Ed. 256 (1896) and the cases cited therein.

44. *Pacific Citizen,* February 23, 1946, p. 4.

45. *Ibid.; San Francisco Chronicle,* December 16, 1945, p. 9; *Deering's Annotated* [California] *Education Code,* II, 126.

46. Letter, Roosevelt to Baron Kentaro Kaneko, October 26, 1906, Roosevelt MSS., LCMD.

47. Root to Metcalf, "Confidential Memorandum for Secretary Metcalf regarding exclusion of Japanese children from public schools and boycotting of Japanese restaurants in San Francisco, Oct. 27, 1906," U. S. State Dept., Numerical File 1797/13. (Hereafter cited as Numerical File.)

48. Metcalf to Roosevelt, November 2, 1906, Numerical File 1797/37.

49. Victor H. Metcalf, Scrapbooks on Dept. of Labor and Commerce, Univ. of California Bancroft Library, IV, 101.

50. U. S. Cong., Senate, *Japanese in the City of San Francisco,* 59th Cong., 2nd Sess., Doc. 147, p. 15.

51. George Kennan, "The Japanese in the San Francisco Public Schools," *Outlook,* June 1, 1907.

52. U. S. Cong., Senate, *Japanese in the City of San Francisco,* pp. 3-7.

53. Richardson, *Messages and Papers of the Presidents,* XI, 7054.

54. *Ibid.,* pp. 7055-76.

55. *San Jose Mercury,* February 9, 1907, p. 1.

56. Telegrams, Root to Wright, February 1, 1907, and February 5, 1907, in Roland S. Morris, *Report of the Honorable Roland S. Morris on Japanese Immigration and Alleged Discriminatory Legislation Against Japanese Residents in the United States* (Washington, 1921), pp. 96-97, U. S. State Dept. Decimal File 711.945/1249. (Hereafter cited as Decimal File.)

57. "San Francisco School Board Resolution Adopted March 13, 1907," Numerical File 2542/48.

58. Letter, Japanese Foreign Office to American Embassy, February 18, 1908, U. S. State Dept., *Foreign Relations of the United States, 1924* (Washington, 1939), p. 365.

59. U. S. Commissioner General of Immigration, *Annual Report, 1908,* p. 125.

60. *Ibid.,* pp. 125-28.

CHAPTER IX

1. *Humboldt Standard,* March 16, 1907, p. 4.

2. Telegram, Root to Gillett, May 25, 1907, Numerical File 1797/206-7; telegram, Gillett to Root, May 25, 1907, 1797/308; telegram, Devlin to Attorney General, May 27, 1907, 1797/309.

3. *San Francisco Chronicle,* June 7, 1907, p. 6.

4. Report of Robert Devlin, U. S. Attorney at San Francisco relative to the refusal of the Board of Police Commissioners to issue licenses to Japanese employment agencies—received in State Department, July 16, 1907, Numerical File 1797/256-59.

5. Letter, Roosevelt to Herman Speck Von Sternberg, July 13, 1907; Letter, Roosevelt to Root, July 26, 1907, Roosevelt MSS., LCMD.

6. Charles Gildea, "Asiatic Immigration and the Japanese Question Issued by the Democratic State Central Committee for the 1908 Presidential Election" (San Francisco, 1908).

7. California, *Assembly Journal,* 38th Sess., 1909, pp. 72, 74; *Humboldt Standard,* January 4, 1909, p. 3; January 7, 1909, p. 1.

8. California, *Assembly Journal,* 38th Sess., 1909, pp. 61, 78; *San Francisco Chronicle,* January 9, 1909, p. 3.

9. *Humboldt Standard,* January 9, 1909, p. 2.

10. Letter, Roosevelt to Gillett, January 16, 1909, Roosevelt MSS., LCMD.

11. *California Statutes,* 38th Sess., 1909, pp. 227, 719, 1146.

12. John B. Sanford was the Democratic Senate Minority Leader from Ukiah, Calif. Franklin Hichborn, *The Story of the Session of the California Legislature of 1911* (San Francisco: James H. Barry Co., 1911), pp. 223-24.

13. Hiram Johnson to Knox, January 6, 1911, Decimal File 811.52;

see also Johnson Papers, Univ. of Calif. Bancroft Library, Part II, Box 41.

14. Letter, Knox to Mayor of San Francisco, January 19, 1911, correspondence of Philander Knox, LCMD, XIII, 2096-97.

15. Memorandum, Taft to Knox, January 31, 1911, Papers of William Howard Taft, Presidential Series No. 2, File 749, LCMD.

16. Scout Young Camp #2, United Spanish War Veterans, Portland, Ore., to President, Taft, Decimal File 711.942/81.

17. For the standard work on the California Progressives, see George Mowry, *The California Progressives* (Berkeley: Univ. of Calif. Press, 1951).

18. Hichborn, *1911 Session*, p. 344.

19. The fishing fee bill required Japanese fishermen to pay $100 a year for commercial licenses while other aliens paid $10 and citizens paid $2.50. The Senate Committee on Federal Relations felt correctly that the bill violated the 1911 treaty and thus did not report out the bill. *San Jose Mercury*, May 6, 1913, p. 2; Eleanor Tupper and George E. McReynolds, *Japan in American Public Opinion* (New York: Macmillan Co., 1937), p. 58; Jabez T. Sunderland, *Rising Japan* (New York: G. P. Putnam's Sons, 1918), pp. 160-61.

20. Letters, A. P. Bettersworth to Assemblyman Hugh Bradford, January 8, 1913, Hugh Bradford "Scrapbook of Clippings," California Section, California State Library, Sacramento, Calif.

21. Newspaper Clippings, U. S. Tokyo Legation to Sec. of State, April 11, 1913, Decimal File 811.52/72.

22. Letter, Hiram Johnson to Theo. Roosevelt, June 21, 1913, Johnson Papers, Part II, Bancroft Library.

23. Daniels, p. 59.

24. Hichborn, *Story of the 1913 Legislative Session* (San Francisco: James H. Barry Co., 1913), pp. 230-31.

25. *Humboldt Standard*, April 24, 1913, p. 1.

26. "Transcript of the Executive Session of California Legislature with Bryan, April 28, 1913," Johnson Papers, Part II, Box 41; Hichborn, *1913 Session*, pp. 257-58.

27. Letter, Johnson to Roosevelt, June 21, 1913, Johnson Papers, Box 41; Daniels, p. 61.

28. *San Francisco Chronicle*, May 3, 1913, p. 1.

29. *Humboldt Standard*, May 5, 1913, p. 1; Hichborn, pp. 269-72; Thomas A. Bailey, "California, Japan, and the Alien Land Legislation of 1913," *Pacific Historical Review*, I (1934), 45.

30. *The Independent*, LXXXIV (May 1, 1913), 945.

31. Letter, Chester Rowell to Payson J. Treat, May 3, 1913, Rowell Papers, Carton 1, Outgoing, Univ. of Calif. Bancroft Library.

32. Telegram, N. C. Newerf, President, Pacific Protectorate Society, Los Angeles, to Woodrow Wilson, May 10, 1913, Johnson Papers.

33. Letter, Fred Chase to Hiram Johnson, May 12, 1913, Johnson Papers.

34. Letter, Kathleen Norris to Johnson, May 11, 1913, Johnson Papers.

35. California, Board of Control, *California and the Oriental* (Sacramento, Calif., 1920), p. 19.

36. B. C. Haworth to Director of Naval Intelligence Re: Reply to State Dept. March 24, 1920, on California Japanese Question, Decimal File 811.5594/1.

37. Letter, John S. Chambers to Chester Rowell, September 10, 1919, Rowell Papers; Letterhead of the Japanese Exclusion League of California, Decimal File 811.5294/357.

38. Daniels, p. 91.

39. *Ibid.*, p. 85.

40. *San Francisco Chronicle,* January 23, 1920, p. 1.

41. Board of Control, *California and the Oriental,* p. 21.

42. Daniels, p. 88.

43. *Sacramento Bee,* November 28, 1921, pp. 1-2, 4-5, 8.

44. *San Francisco Chronicle,* May 17, 1924, p. 26.

45. Letter, Acting Attorney General to Sec. of State, July 31, 1908; Memo, Division of Far Eastern Affairs, October 7, 1908, Numerical File 14932.

46. Memorandum for Mr. MacMurray, November 20, 1919; "The Picture Bride Question and the Japanese Question," Memo, Division of Far Eastern Affairs, November 19, 1919, Decimal File 711.94/310.

47. Darrell H. Smith and J. Guy Herring, *The Bureau of Immigration* (Baltimore: The Johns Hopkins Press, 1924), p. 27.

48. Memo, Division of Far Eastern Affairs, March 18, 1921, Decimal File 811.5294/352.

49. Daniels, p. 106.

50. *San Francisco Examiner,* November 3 and November 10, 1908.

51. Memorandum by John V. S. MacMurray, March 18, 1921, Decimal File 811.5294/352.

52. *Ibid.*

53. Dearing to MacMurray, April 22, 1921, Decimal File 811.5294/352.

54. Rodman Paul, *The Abrogation of the Gentlemen's Agreement* (Cambridge, Mass.: Harvard Univ. Press, 1936), p. 33.

55. *Ibid.*, p. 34.

56. U. S. Dept. of State, *Foreign Relations of the United States, 1924,* p. 338.

57. *Ibid.*, pp. 372-73.

58. Paul, p. 82.

59. 46 *U. S. Statutes* (1924), pp. 153-69.

60. *Statistical History of the United States,* p. 58.

61. *Congressional Record,* 81st Cong., 1st Sess., 1949, pp. 15, 17, 19, 167, 296.

62. *Ibid.,* 81st Cong., 2nd Sess., 1950, Appendix A, 1334-35.

63. *Ibid.,* 83rd Cong., 1st Sess., 1953, p. 1677; Appendix A, 3101.

64. *Statistical History of the United States,* p. 660.

CHAPTER X

1. Lind, p. 75.

2. *Ibid.,* p. 77.

3. U. S. Immigration Commission, *Reports,* I, 61, 68, 70.

4. *Ibid.,* II, 31.

5. *Ibid.,* II, 108-10.

6. Lloyd H. Fisher, *The Harvest Labor Market in California* (Cambridge, Mass.: Harvard Univ. Press, 1953), pp. 25-26; Masakazu Iwata, "The Japanese Immigrants in California Agriculture," *Agricultural History,* XXXVI (1962), 28.

7. U. S. Immigration Commission, *Reports,* I, 63.

8. *Ibid.,* pp. 68-70.

9. *Ibid.,* II, 109.

10. *Ibid.,* I, 67.

11. *Ibid.,* II, 109.

12. Iwata, p. 28.

13. U. S. Immigration Commission, *Reports,* I, 81-82, 86.

14. Iwata, p. 29.

15. Bruce Bliven, "The Japanese Problem," *The Nation,* CXII (February 2, 1921), 171-72.

16. H. A. Millis, *The Japanese Problem in the United States* (New York: Macmillan Co., 1915), pp. 152-72.

17. U. S. Census Bureau, *Sixteenth Census, 1940, Agriculture,* III, 224; Iwata, p. 50.

18. Iwata, p. 33.

19. California, Division of Labor Statistics and Research, *Californians of Japanese, Chinese and Filipino Ancestry* (San Francisco, June, 1965), p. 13.

20. Hosokawa, p. 137.

21. *San Francisco Chronicle,* June 25, 1912, p. 6.

22. Hosokawa, p. 63.

23. Emil T. H. Bunje, "The Story of Japanese Farming in California," WPA Project, University of California, Berkeley, 1937, pp. 44-52.

24. *Ibid.,* p. 50.

25. Hosokawa, pp. 661-62.

26. Carey McWilliams, *Brothers Under the Skin,* rev. ed. (Boston: Little, Brown and Co., 1964), p. 154.

27. *San Francisco Call,* April 7, 1896, p. 9.

28. California, Bureau of Labor Statistics, *Thirteenth Biennial Report,* 1907-1908, p. 218.

29. *Ibid.*, pp. 208-9.

30. *Ibid.*, pp. 218-19.

31. U. S. Immigration Commission, *Reports*, I, 2, 36-41.

32. Letter, James J. Hill to Honorable Kogoro Takahira, March 26, 1906, St. Paul, Minn., Numerical File 2542/18B.

33. *Ibid.*

34. U. S. Immigration Commission, *Reports*, I, 35, 46-48.

35. *Ibid.*, pp. 52-55.

36. *Ibid.*, pp 48-51.

37. Washington, Bureau of Labor, *Special Report on the Salmon Canning Industry in the State of Washington and the Employment of Oriental Labor* (Olympia, 1915).

38. U. S. Office of Facts and Figures, "Exploratory Study of West Coast Relations to the Japanese" (Washington, 1942), p. 10.

39. *Ibid.*, p. 8; John Modell, "Class or Ethnic Solidarity: The Japanese American Company Union," *Pacific Historical Review,* XXXVIII (1969), 197-206.

40. Social Science Institute, Fisk University, "Orientals and Their Cultural Adjustment," Social Science Source Documents No. 4, 1946.

41. Mears, pp. 284-316.

42. Iwata, p. 34.

43. U. S. Congress, 77th Cong., 2nd Sess., House Select Committee Investigating National Defense Migration, *Findings and Recommendations on Evacuation of Enemy Aliens and Others from Prohibited Military Zones*, 4th Interim Report, 1942, p. 104.

44. Al Erickson, "Los Angeles Nisei Today," *California Sun Magazine* (Summer, 1958), p. 3.

45. *Ibid.*

46. Kitano, pp. 21-22, 53-56.

47. Lind, pp. 77, 80.

48. *Ibid.*, p. 82.

Chapter XI

1. Mears, pp. 342-43.

2. Kitano, pp. 62-65.

3. K. K. Kawakami, *The Real Japanese Question* (New York: Macmillan Co., 1921), pp. 193-94.

4. Michinari Fujita, "Japanese Associations in America," *Sociology and Social Research*, XIII (1929), 211-28; Kitano, p. 81.

5. Daniels, pp. 26-27; Mears, p. 357.

6. Hosokawa, pp. 191-98.

7. *Ibid.*, pp. 203-5.

8. *Ibid.*, pp. 126-29.

9. *Ibid.*, pp. 130-31.

10. Kitano, pp. 99-115; Dennis Ogawa, *From Japs to Japanese* (Berkeley, Calif.: McCutchan Pub. Co., 1971), pp. 47-67.

11. *Ozawa* v. *United States,* 260 U. S. 189

12. Consulate General of Japan, *Documentary History of Law Cases Affecting Japanese in the United States, 1916-1924* (San Francisco, 1925), I, 121-75.

13. *Ibid.,* pp. 211-21; Hosakawa, p. 91.

14. 50 U. S. *Statutes* (1937), pp. 743-44; Hosakawa, pp. 198-99.

15. *Porterfield v. Webb,* 44 Sup. Ct. Rep. 21.

16. *Webb v. O'Brien,* 263 U. S. 313.

17. *Yano Guardianship Case,* 188 Cal. 645.

18. See Appendix A, Table V; Kitano, p. 165.

CHAPTER XII

1. Daniels, pp. 71-73.

2. Carey McWilliams, "Once Again the Yellow Peril," *The Nation,* CX (June 26, 1935), 735-36.

3. U. S. Dept. of Interior, War Relocation Authority, *WRA, A Story of Human Conservation,* 1946, p. 2.

4. Stetson Conn, Rose C. Engelman, Byron Fairchild, *Guarding the United States and Its Outposts* (Washington, D. C.: U. S. Dept. of Army, Office of the Chief of Military History, 1964), p. 144.

5. See Appendix A, Tables IV, V.

6. Allan R. Bosworth, *America's Concentration Camps* (New York: W. W. Norton & Co., 1967), pp. 121-24; WRA, *The Evacuated People a Quantitative Description,* 1946, p. 8.

7. Conn, *Guarding the United States . . . ,* p. 267.

8. *Ibid.,* pp. 207, 209-10.

9. *Ibid.,* p. 207.

10. Stetson Conn, "The Decision to Evacuate the Japanese from the Pacific Coast," *Command Decisions* (Washington, 1960), p. 127. Hereafter cited as *Command Decisions.*

11. *Ibid.,* p. 128.

12. U. S. Department of Interior, War Relocation Authority, "Myths and Facts About the Japanese Americans Answering Common Misconceptions Regarding Americans of Japanese Ancestry," Mimeographed, 1945, p. 21.

13. *Command Decisions,* p. 133.

14. U. S. Office of Facts and Figures, "Exploratory Study of West Coast Reactions to the Japanese," February 4, 1942; ————, "Pacific Coast Attitudes Toward the Japanese," February 28, 1942, "Summary Section," pp. 1-9; Morton Grodzins, *Americans Betrayed* (Chicago: University of Chicago Press, 1949).

15. *Command Decisions,* p. 138.

16. Conn, *Guarding the United States . . . ,* p. 118; Bendetsen, born in Aberdeen, Washington, received his baccalaureate and law degrees from Stanford. He practiced law in the state of Washington from 1932 to 1940 and was prominent in the Taxpayers' Association.

He was a lieutenant in the Reserve Officer Corps 1929-40. In 1940 he was a captain in the Judge Advocate General's Department. The next year he was transferred to the General Staff Corps and helped organize the Provost Marshal General's office. He was placed in charge of the alien custody program. He was now a major. Bendetsen described himself in the 1948-49 *Who's Who in America* as the person who "conceived method, formulated details, and directed evacuation of 120,000 persons of Japanese ancestry." After the war, he became vice president of the Champion Paper and Fibre Company. In 1950-52 he was Assistant Secretary of the Army and Director General, U. S. Railroads. In 1952 he was Under Secretary of the Army. More recently, living in Ohio, he was the director of several banks and corporations—*Who's Who in America*, 1948-49 (Chicago: A. N. Marquis Co., 1948), p. 181. See subsequent editions for other entries regarding Bendetsen.

17. *Command Decisions,* p. 133; Conn, *Guarding the United States . . . ,* p. 125; U. S. Congress, House of Representatives, Select Committee Investigating National Defense Migration, *Fourth Interim Report,* H.R. 2124, 77th Cong., 2nd Sess., 1942, p. 143.

18. War Relocation Authority, "Wartime Exile. The Exclusion of the Japanese Americans from the West Coast," mimeographed, 1946, pp. 52-53.

19. U. S. War Department, *Final Report Japanese Evacuation From the West Coast,* 1942, pp. 9-10.

20. *Command Decisions,* p. 134; Conn, *Guarding the United States . . . ,* pp. 122-23.

21. *Command Decisions,* p. 144.

22. *Ibid.,* p. 143.

23. U. S. Military Intelligence Service Language School, *MISLS Album, 1946* (Fort Snelling, Minn., 1946), pp. 28, 30, 36.

24. Edward H. Spicer *et al., Impounded People* (Tucson, Ariz.: Univ. of Arizona Press, 1969), p. 67.

25. Thomas D. Murphy, *Ambassadors in Arms* (Honolulu, Hawaii: Univ. of Hawaii Press, 1954); Hosokawa, pp. 393-422.

26. Dorothy S. Thomas and Richard Nishimoto, *The Spoilage* (Berkeley, Calif.: Univ. of Calif. Press, 1946).

27. *Ex parte Endo* v. *United States,* 323 U. S. 283. Two other cases, *Hirabayashi* v. *United States* and *Korematsu* v. *United States,* revolved around the questions of detention and attending restrictions. The legal points are well detailed in ten Broek, Barnhart and Matson, *Prejudice, War and the Constitution.* The important fact is that in all three cases, the court sidestepped any constitutional determination regarding the government's harassment of the Nisei. See *Hirabayashi v. United States,* 320 U. S. 81, and *Korematsu v. United States,* 323 U. S. 215.

28. War Relocation Authority, *WRA, A Story of Human Conservation*, pp. viii-xiii.

29. California, *Statutes* (1943), pp. 1059, 1100; *Statutes* (1945), pp. 181, 1129.

30. *San Francisco Chronicle*, May 20, 1945, p. 10; See Edward L. Barret, Jr., *The Tenney Committee* (Ithaca: Cornell Univ. Press, 1951) for background on un-American investigations during and after World War II.

31. *Pacific Citizen*, January 6, 1945, p. 2; February 10, 1945, p. 1.

32. *Ibid.*, July 14, 1945, p. 1; *San Francisco Chronicle*, August 27, 1947, p. 13.

33. *Pacific Citizen*, February 2, 1946, p. 1.

34. Hosokawa, p. 445.

35. *Ibid.*, pp. 447-48.

36. Audrie Girdner and Anne Loftis, *The Great Betrayal* (New York: Collier-Macmillan Co., 1969), p. 430; Hosokawa, p. 446.

37. *Pacific Citizen*, December 1, 1945, p. 1.

38. Girdner and Loftis, p. 431; Hosokawa, p. 448.

39. Girdner and Loftis, p. 431; Hosokawa, p. 449.

40. Hosokawa, pp. 449-50.

41. *Ibid.*; Girdner and Loftis, p. 432.

CHAPTER XIII

1. *Honolulu Star-Bulletin*, July 13, 1970, p. B-6.

2. Kung, p. 181.

3. Kitano, p. 172.

4. Lind, p. 11.

5. *Who's Who in America* (Chicago: A. N. Marquis Co., 1968-69), XXXV, 1033.

6. Kung, pp. 250-51.

7. *Ibid.*, p. 327.

8. *Ibid.*, p. 251.

9. *Ibid.*, pp. 228-52; Sung, pp. 290-98.

10. Sung, pp. 295-96.

11. Kung, pp. 238-39.

12. Sung, p. 297.

13. Kung, pp. 239, 325.

14. *Ibid.*, p. 239.

15. U. S., *Congressional Directory*, 91st Cong., 2nd Sess., 1970, p. 44; *Who's Who in America*, 1968-69, p. 753.

16. *San Francisco Chronicle*, December 30, 1966, p. 1; *Honolulu Advertiser*, June 1, 1971, p. A-9.

17. Sung, pp. 291-92.

18. Lee, pp. 414-15.

19. *Who's Who in America*, 1968-69, p. 415.

20. *Ibid.*, p. 1213.

21. *Ibid.,* p. 2389.

22. *Ibid.*

23. *Honolulu Advertiser,* June 1, 1971, p. B-1; *Honolulu Star-Bulletin,* May 31, 1971, p. A-10.

24. *Who's Who in America,* 1968-69, p. 1104; *Congressional Directory, 1970,* p. 44; Hosokawa, pp. 416-17, 468-69.

25. *Congressional Directory, 1970,* pp. 44-45; Hosokawa, p. 470.

26. *Congressional Directory, 1970,* p. 45; Hosokawa, pp. 470-71.

27. *Honolulu Star-Bulletin,* May 30, 1964, p. B-11.

28. Hosokawa, p. 145-46.

29. *Who's Who in America,* 1968-69, p. 980.

30. Hosokawa, p. 485.

31. *Ibid.,* p. 481.

32. Noel L. Leathers, *The Japanese in America* (Minneapolis, Minn.: Lerner Publications Co., 1967), pp. 23-25.

33. Hosokawa, p. 475.

34. *Ibid.,* pp. 483, 487.

35. *Honolulu Star-Bulletin,* April 14, 1971, p. 2.

Bibliography

A. Manuscripts

Hugh Bradford. Scrapbook pertaining to the Alien Land Law of 1913 and other matters. California State Library, Sacramento, Calif.

Hiram Johnson. MSS. Bancroft Library.

California Joint Immigration Committee. MSS. Documents Division, University of California, Berkeley.

Philander Knox. MSS. Library of Congress Manuscript Division, Washington, D. C.

Victor H. Metcalf. Scrapbooks on Department of Labor and Commerce. Bancroft Library.

Panama-Pacific International Exposition. MSS. Bancroft Library.

Theodore Roosevelt. MSS. Library of Congress Manuscript Division.

Chester H. Rowell. MSS. Bancroft Library.

William Howard Taft. MSS. Presidential Series No. 2. Library of Congress Manuscript Division.

United States Department of State. Decimal File. National Archives, Washington, D. C.

————. Numerical File. National Archives, Washington, D. C.

Bureau of Immigration, Kingdom of Hawaii. Minutes of 1868. Public Archives of Hawaii. Honolulu, Hawaii.

B. Government Documents

1. *Federal*

Congressional Record, 47th-83rd Cong., 1882-1953.

U. S. Statutes at Large, 1790-1965.

a. Congressional Documents

44th Cong., 2nd Sess., 1877, Senate. Report No. 689. *Joint Special Committee on Chinese.*

45th Cong., 2nd Sess., 1878, House. Report No. 62. *Chinese Immigration.*

46th Cong., 2nd Sess., 1879, House. Report No. 572. *Depression in Labor and Business and Chinese Immigration.*

47th Cong., 1st Sess., 1881-1882, House. Report No. 67. *Chinese Immigration.*

————. Report No. 1017. *Chinese Immigration.*

52nd Cong., 1st Sess., 1891-1892, House. Report No. 407. *Exclusion of Chinese.*

57th Cong., 1st Sess., 1902. Senate Document No. 304. *Exclusion of Chinese Laborers.*

59th Cong., 2nd Sess., 1906. Senate Document No. 147. *Japanese in the City of San Francisco, Cal.*

66th Cong., 2nd Sess., 1920, House. Committee on Immigration and Naturalization. *Hearings on Japanese Immigration.*

69th Cong., 1st Sess., 1926, House. Committee on Immigration and Naturalization. *Hearings on Admission of Wives of American Citizens of Oriental Ancestry.*

70th Cong., 1st Sess., 1928, House. Committee on Immigration and Naturalization. *Hearings on Wives of American Citizens of Oriental Race.*

77th Cong., 2nd Sess., 1942, House. Select Committee Investigating National Defense Migration, 4th Interim Report. *Findings and Recommendations on Evacuation of Enemy Aliens and Others from Prohibited Military Zones.*

78th Cong., 1st Sess., 1943, House. Special Committee on Un-American Activities. *Investigation of Un-American Propaganda Activities in the United States.*

————. Committee on Immigration and Naturalization. Report No. 732. *Hearings on Repeal of the Chinese Exclusion Acts.*

82nd Cong., 1st Sess., 1951, Senate. Report No. 601. *Compromise and Settlement of Japanese Evacuation Claims.*

83rd Cong., 2nd Sess., 1954, House. Committee on Judiciary—Subcommittee No. 5. *Hearings on H. R. 7435 to Amend the Japanese-American Evacuation Claims Act of 1948.*

91st Cong., 2nd Sess., 1970. *Congressional Directory.*

b.   Executive Documents

Department of Commerce. Bureau of Census. *Eighth-Eighteenth Census,* 1860-1960.

Department of Interior. War Relocation Authority. "Myths and Facts About the Japanese Americans Answering Common Misconceptions Regarding Americans of Japanese Ancestry." Washington, D. C., Mimeographed, 1945.

————. "Wartime Exile. The Exclusion of the Japanese Americans from the West Coast." Washington, D. C., Mimeographed, 1946.

————. *WRA, A Story of Human Conservation.* Washington, D. C., no date.

————. *The Evacuated People, a Quantitative Description.* Washington, D. C., 1946.

Department of Justice. Superintendent of Immigration. *Annual Report*, 1892.

—————. Commissioner General of Immigration. *Annual Report*, 1895-1908.

—————. Commissioner of Immigration and Naturalization. *Annual Report*, 1964-1970.

Department of State. *Papers Relating to Foreign Relations of the United States, 1881-1924*. Washington, D. C., 1881-1939.

—————. *Report of The Honorable Roland S. Morris on Japanese Immigration and Alleged Discriminatory Legislation Against Japanese Residents in the United States*. Washington, D. C., 1921.

Department of War. *Final Report Japanese Evacuation from the West Coast*. Washington, D. C., 1942.

—————. U. S. Military Intelligence Service Language School. *MISLS Album*, 1946. Fort Snelling, Minn., 1946.

U. S. Immigration Commission. *Reports of the Immigration Commission*, 25 vols. Washington, D. C., 1909-1911.

U. S. Industrial Commission. *Reports of the Industrial Commission*. 15 vols. Washington, D. C., 1901.

U. S. Office of Facts and Figures. *Pacific Coast Attitudes Toward the Japanese Problem*. Denver: National Opinion Research Center, 1942.

—————. Bureau of Intelligence. "Exploratory Study of West Coast Relations to Japanese (Preliminary Results)." Dittoed, 1942.

2. State

California. *Journal of the Assembly of the State of California*. Sacramento, 1851-1953.

—————. *Journal of the Senate of the State of California*. Sacramento, 1851-1953.

—————. *Statutes*, 1855-1943.

—————. Senate. 55th Sess., 1944. "Partial Report of Senate Fact Finding Committee on Japanese Resettlement."

—————. Board of Control. *California and the Oriental: Japanese, Chinese, and Hindus*. Sacramento, 1920.

—————. Board of Fish Commissioners. *Report, 1891-1892*. Sacramento, 1892.

—————. Bureau of Labor Statistics. *Thirteenth Annual Report, 1907-1908*. Sacramento, 1908.

—————. Division of Labor Statistics and Research. *Californians of Japanese, Chinese and Filipino Ancestry*. San Francisco, 1965.

—————. State Agricultural Society. *Transactions*, 1866-67. Sacramento, 1867.

—————. Superintendent of Public Instruction. *Ninth Annual Report*. Sacramento, 1859.

—————. *First Biennial Report, 1864-1865*. Sacramento, 1865.

Paul Mason, compiler. *Constitution of the State of California, Annotated.* Sacramento, 1946.

Oregon. Frank Davey. *Report on the Japanese Situation in Oregon investigated for Governor Ben W. Olcott, August, 1920.* Salem, 1920.

Washington. Bureau of Labor. *Special Report on the Salmon Canning Industry in the State of Washington and the Employment of Oriental Labor.* Olympia, 1915.

c.   Foreign

Consulate General of Japan, San Francisco. *Documentary History of Law Cases Affecting the Japanese in the United States, 1916-1924.* 2 vols. San Francisco, 1925.

C.   NEWSPAPERS

Daily Alta California (San Francisco)
Honolulu Advertiser
Honolulu Star-Bulletin
Humboldt Standard (Eureka, California)
Humboldt Times (Eureka)
Los Angeles Times
Oriental (San Francisco)
New York Illustrated News
New York Times
Pacific Citizen (Salt Lake City)

Pacific Rural Press (San Francisco)
Sacramento Bee
Sacramento Union
San Francisco Call
San Francisco Chronicle
San Francisco Evening Bulletin
San Francisco Examiner
San Francisco Times
San Jose Mercury
San Jose News

D.   PERIODICALS

Chinese Historical Society of America Bulletin (San Francisco).

E.   ALMANACS AND HANDBOOKS

Deering's Annotated [California] *Education Code.* San Francisco. Whitney-Bancroft Publishers, 1946.

Japan Times Year Book, 1933, 2nd ed. Tokyo: Japan Times, 1933.

Statistical History of the United States from Colonial Times to the Present. Stamford, Conn.: Fairfield Publishers, Inc., 1965.

F.   BOOKS

ABBOTT, JAMES FRANCIS. *Japanese Expansion and American Policies.* New York: Macmillan Co., 1916.

BAILEY, THOMAS A. *Theodore Roosevelt and the Japanese-American Crises.* Stanford, Calif.: Stanford University Press, 1934.

BALDWIN, MRS. S. L. *Must the Chinese Go? An Examination of the Chinese Question*. Boston: Rand, Avery and Co., 1886.

BANCROFT, HUBERT HOWE. *Essays and Miscellany*. San Francisco: A. L. Bancroft Co., 1890.

————. *History of California*. 7 vols. San Francisco: A. L. Bancroft Co., 1890.

BARTH, GUNTHER. *Bitter Strength*. Cambridge, Mass.: Harvard University Press, 1964.

BEASLEY, W. G. *The Modern History of Japan*. New York: Frederick A. Praeger, 1963.

BECKMANN, GEORGE M. *The Modernization of China and Japan*. New York: Harper & Row, 1962.

BOSWORTH, J. DOUGLAS. *Three Years in California*. Edinburgh: W. Blackwood and Sons, 1857.

BROOM, LEONARD AND RIEMER, RUTH. *Removal and Return The Socio-Economic Effects of the War on Japanese Americans*. Berkeley: University of California Press, 1949.

BROOM, LEONARD, AND RIEMER, RUTH. *Removal and Return The Japanese American Family in World War II*. Berkeley: University of California Press, 1956.

BROWN, FRANCIS J., AND ROUCEK, JOSEPH S., ED. *One America—The History, Contributions, and Present Problems of Our Racial and National Minorities*, 3rd ed. New York: Prentice-Hall, 1952.

CAMPBELL, PERSIA CRAWFORD. *Chinese Coolie Emigration to Countries Within the British Empire*. London: P. S. King & Sons, Ltd., 1923.

CHINN, THOS. W., ED. *A History of the Chinese in California*. San Francisco: Chinese Historical Society of America, 1969.

CHUI, PING. *Chinese Labor in California, 1850-1880*. Madison, Wisconsin: State Historical Society of Wisconsin, 1963.

COLEMAN, ELIZABETH. *Chinatown U.S.A.* New York: John Day, 1946.

COMAN, KATHERINE. *The History of Contract Labor in the Hawaiian Islands*. New York: Macmillan, 1903.

CONN, STETSON, ET AL. *Guarding the United States and Its Outposts*. ing Office, 1960.

CONN, STETSON ET AL. *Guarding the United States and Its Outposts*. Washington, D. C.: U. S. Printing Office, 1964.

CONROY, F. HILARY. *The Japanese Frontier in Hawaii, 1868-1898*. Berkeley: University of California Press, 1953.

COOLIDGE, MARY R. *Chinese Immigration*. New York: Henry Holt, 1909.

CREEL, HERRLEE G. *Confucius, the Man and the Myth*. New York: John Day, 1949.

CRESSEY, GEORGE B. *China's Geographic Foundations*, 1st ed. New York: McGraw-Hill, 1934.

CROSS, IRA B. *A History of the Labor Movement in California.* Berkeley: University of California Press, 1910.

DANIELS, ROGER. *The Politics of Prejudice: The Anti-Japanese Movement in California and the Struggle for Japanese Exclusion.* Berkeley: University of California Press, 1962.

DAVIS, WINFIELD J. *History of Political Conventions in California, 1849-1892.* Sacramento: California State Library, 1892.

DILLON, RICHARD. *The Hatchetmen.* New York: Coward-McCann, 1962.

DIVINE, RORERT A. *American Immigration Policy, 1924-1952.* New Haven: Yale University Press, 1957.

DOBIE, CHARLES C. *San Francisco's Chinatowns.* New York: Appleton-Century, 1936.

ESBERG, A. I., ED. *Forty-Nine Opinions on Our Japanese Problem.* San Francisco: Grabhorn Press, 1944.

FAIRBANK, JOHN KING. *The United States and China,* rev. ed. New York: Viking Press, 1958.

FLOWERS, MONTAVILLE. *The Japanese Conquest of American Opinion.* New York: George H. Doran, 1917.

FUJISAWA, CHIKAO. *Zen and Shinto; the Story of Japanese Philosophy.* New York: Philosophical Library, 1959.

GIBSON, OTIS. *The Chinese in America.* Cincinnati: Hitchcock and Walden, 1877.

GIRDNER, AUDRIE, AND LOFTIS, ANNE. *The Great Betrayal.* New York: Collier-Macmillan, 1969.

GOODRICH, L. CARRINGTON. *A Short History of the Chinese People,* 3rd ed. New York: Harper Torchbook, 1963.

HICHBORN, FRANKLIN. *The Story of the Session of the California Legislature of 1911.* San Francisco: James H. Barry Co., 1911.

————. ———— *of 1913.* San Francisco: James H. Barry, 1913.

HIGHAM, JOHN. *Strangers in the Land: Patterns of American Nativism, 1860-1925.* New York: Atheneum, 1969.

HINMAN, GEORGE WARREN. *The Oriental in America.* New York: Missionary Education Movement of the United States and Canada, 1913.

HOLTON, DANIEL. *Modern Japan and Shinto Nationalism—A Study of Present Day Trends in Japanese Religions,* rev. ed. Chicago: University of Chicago Press, 1967.

HOSOKAWA, BILL. *Nisei, The Quiet Americans.* New York: William Morrow, 1969.

HOY, WILLIAM. *The Chinese Six Companies.* San Francisco: Chinese Consolidated Benevolent Association, ca. 1942.

ICHIHASI, YAMOTO. *Japanese in the United States—A Critical Study of the Problems of the Japanese Immigrants and their Children.* Stanford, Calif.: Stanford University Press, 1932.

INOUYE, DANIEL. *Journey to Washington.* Englewood Cliffs, N. J.: Prentice-Hall, 1967.

IYENAGA, T., AND SATO, KENOSKE. *Japan and the California Problem,* 2nd ed. New York: Putnam, 1921.

KANO, HISAAKIRA. *Tunnels under the Pacific.* New York: no pub., 1919.

KAWAKAMI, K. K. *The Real Japanese Question.* New York, Macmillan, 1921.

KITANO, HARRY H. L. *Japanese Americans—The Evolution of a Subculture.* Englewood Cliffs, N. J.: Prentice-Hall, 1969.

KONVITZ, MILTON R. *The Alien and the Asiatic in American Law.* Ithaca: Cornell University Press, 1946.

KUNG, S. W. *Chinese in American Life.* Seattle: University of Washington Press, 1962.

KUYKENDALL, RALPH S. *The Earliest Japanese Labor Immigration to Hawaii.* Honolulu: University of Hawaii Occasional Papers, No. 25, 1935.

————. *The Hawaiian Kingdom.* 3 vols. Honolulu: University of Hawaii Press, 1966-67.

LA FARGUE, THOMAS E. *China's First Hundred.* Pullman, Washington: Washington State College Press, 1942.

LEATHERS, NOEL L. *The Japanese in America.* Minneapolis: Lerner Publications, 1967.

LEE, ROSE HUM. *The Chinese in the United States of America.* Hong Kong: University of Hong Kong Press, 1960.

LIND, ANDREW W. *Hawaii's People,* 3rd ed. Honolulu: University of Hawaii Press, 1967.

LUCATT, EDWARD. *Rovings in the Pacific from 1837 to 1849.* 2 vols. London: Longman, Brown, Green and Longmans, 1851.

LOWE, PARDEE. *Father and Glorious Descendant.* Boston: Little, Brown, 1943.

MCLEOD, ALEXANDER. *Pigtails and Golddust.* Caldwell, Idaho: Caxton Printers, 1947.

MCWILLIAMS, CAREY. *Brothers Under the Skin,* rev. ed. Boston: Little, Brown, 1951.

————. *Prejudice Japanese Americans: Symbol of Racial Intolerance.* Boston: Little, Brown, 1944.

MA, WEN HWAN. *American Policy toward China.* Shanghai, China: Kelly and Walsh, Ltd., 1934.

MARTIN, RALPH G. *Boy from Nebraska—The Story of Ben Kuroki.* New York: Harper, 1946.

MEARS, ELIOT G. *Resident Orientals on the American Pacific Coast.* Chicago: University of Chicago Press, 1928.

MELENDY, H. BRETT, AND GILBERT, BENJAMIN F. *The Governors of California: Peter H. Burnett to Edmund G. Brown.* Georgetown, Calif.: Talisman Press, 1965.

MEYERS, MILTON W. *Japan, A Concise History.* Boston: Allyn and Bacon, 1966.

MILLER, STUART C. *The Unwelcome Immigrant.* Berkeley: University of California Press, 1969.

MILLIS, H. A. *The Japanese Problem in the United States.* New York: Macmillan, 1915.

MURPHY, THOMAS D. *Ambassadors in Arms.* Honolulu, Hawaii: University of Hawaii Press, 1954.

OGAWA, DENNIS. *From Japs to Japanese.* Berkeley: McCutchan Publishing Co., 1971.

PAJUS, JEAN. *The Real Japanese California.* Berkeley, Calif.: James J. Gillick, 1937.

PAUL, RODMAN W. *The Abrogation of the Gentlemen's Agreement.* Cambridge, Mass.: Harvard University Press, 1936.

—————. *Mining Frontiers of the Far West, 1848-1880.* New York: Holt, Rinehart and Winston, 1963.

PITKIN, WALTER B. *Must We Fight Japan?* New York: The Century Co., 1921.

PURCELL, VICTOR. *The Chinese in Southeast Asia.* Oxford: Oxford University Press, 1961.

REISCHAUER, EDWIN O. *The United States and Japan,* 3rd ed. Cambridge, Mass.: Harvard University Press, 1965.

RIGGS, FRED W. *Pressures on Congress—A Study of the Repeal of Chinese Exclusion.* New York: King's Crown Press, 1950.

SANDMEYER, ELMER C. *The Anti-Chinese Movement in California.* Urbana, Illinois: University of Illinois Press, 1939.

SAUNDERS, ERNEST D. *Buddhism in Japan, with an Outline of its Origins in India.* Philadelphia: University of Pennsylvania Press, 1964.

SAXTON, ALEXANDER. *The Indispensable Enemy Labor and the Anti-Chinese Movement in California.* Berkeley: University of California Press, 1971.

SCHUYLER, LAMBERT. *The Japs Must Not Come Back!* Winslow, Washington: Herron House, 1944.

SCHWANTES, ROBERT S. *Japanese and Americans—A Century of Cultural Relations.* New York: Harper, 1955.

SEWARD, GEORGE F. *Chinese Immigration in its Social and Economical Aspects.* New York: Charles Scribner's, 1881.

SMITH, BRADFORD. *Americans from Japan.* New York: Lippincott, 1948.

SMITH, DARRELL HEVENOR, AND HERRING, H. GUY. *The Bureau of Immigration—Its History, Activities and Organization.* Baltimore: The Johns Hopkins Press, 1924.

SONE, MONICA. *Nisei Daughter.* Boston: Little, Brown, 1953.

SOYEDA, J., AND KAMIYA, T. *A Survey of the Japanese Question in California.* San Francisco, no pub., 1913.

SPEER, WILLIAM. *China and California: Their Relations, Past and Present.* San Francisco: John O'Meara, 1853.

SPICER, EDWARD H., ET AL. *Impounded People.* Tucson, Ariz.: University of Arizona Press, 1969.

SUNDERLAND, JABEZ T. *Rising Japan.* New York: G. P. Putnam's, 1918.

SUNG, BETTY LEE. *Mountain of Gold.* New York: Macmillan, 1967.

TENBROEK, JACOBUS, ET AL. *Prejudice, War and the Constitution.* Berkeley: University of California, 1954.

THOMAS, DOROTHY S. *The Salvage.* Berkeley: University of California Press, 1952.

————, AND NISHIMOTO, RICHARD. *The Spoilage.* Berkeley: University of California Press, 1946.

TOW, J. S. *The Real Chinese in America.* New York: Academy Press, 1923.

TREAT, PAYSON J. *Japan and the United States 1853-1921.* Stanford, Calif.: Stanford University Press, 1928.

TREWARTHA, GLEN T. *A Reconnaissance Geography of Japan.* Madison, Wis.: University of Wisconsin, 1934.

TUPPER, ELEANOR AND MCREYNOLDS, GEORGE E. *Japan in American Public Opinion.* New York: Macmillan, 1937.

WELCH, HOLMES. *The Parting of the Way: Lao Tzu and the Taoist Movement.* Boston: Beacon Press, 1957.

WILLIAMS, EDWARD T. *China Yesterday and To-day.* New York: Thos. Y. Crowell, 1932.

G.   PAMPHLETS

ADAMS, ROMANZO. *The Japanese in Hawaii.* New York, 1924.

AMERICAN FRIENDS SERVICE COMMITTEE. *Bulletin on Minorities in the United States—Japanese and Japanese-Americans, May 15, 1942.*

ASIATIC EXCLUSION LEAGUE. *Proceedings.* San Francisco, 1907-1912.

BALCH, JOHN ADRIAN. *Shall the Japanese be allowed to dominate Hawaii?* Honolulu, 1943.

BALDWIN, MRS. S. L. *Must the Chinese Go?* Boston: Rand Avery and Co., 1886.

BUNJE, EMIL T. H. "The Story of Japanese Farming in California," Berkeley, 1937.

CONE, VICTOR N. *Irrigation in the San Joaquin Valley, California.* Washington, D. C.: U. S. Dept. of Agriculture, Office of Experimental Stations, Bulletin 239, 1911.

CONMY, PETER T. *The History of California's Japanese Problem and the Part Played by the Native Sons of the Golden West in its Solutions.* 1942.

FRIENDS OF INTERNATIONAL RIGHTS AND JUSTICE. *How the U. S. Treaty with China is Observed in California.* 2nd ed., San Francisco, 1877.

GILDEA, CHARLES. *Asiatic Immigration and the Japanese Question Issued by the Democratic State Central Committee for the 1908 Presidential Election.* San Francisco, 1908.

GOMPERS, SAMUEL, AND GUTSTADT, HERMAN. *Meat vs. Rice—American Manhood Against Asian Coolieism.* San Francisco: Asiatic Exclusion League, 1908.

LECHNER, JOHN. *Playing with Dynamite—Inside Story of Our Domestic Japanese Problem.* No Date. No Pub. A report filed with the Western Defense Command October 30, 1944, at the request of the American Legion, 23rd District.

SLOCUM, WILLIAM N. *Revolution—The Reorganization of Our Social System Inevitable.* Address before the Anti-Monopoly Association, San Francisco, 1878.

SOCIAL SCIENCE INSTITUTE, FISK UNIVERSITY. *Orientals and Their Cultural Adjustments.* Nashville, Tenn. Social Science Source Documents No. 4, 1946.

The Invalidity of the "Queue Ordinance" of the City and County of San Francisco. San Francisco: J. L. Rice & Co., 1879.

H.   ARTICLES

"Anti-Chinese Riots of 1885," *Papers Relating to the History of the State of Washington,* Part V. *Washington State Historical Society Publications.* Olympia, Washington: State Historical Society, 1915.

"Chinese Fisheries in California," *Chamber's Journal,* I (1854), 48.

ADAMS, ROMANZO C. "Japanese Migration Statistics," *Sociology and Social Research,* XIII (May-June, 1929), 436-45.

BAILEY, THOMAS A. "California, Japan and the Alien Land Legislation of 1913," *Pacific Historical Review,* I (1932), 36-59.

BLIVEN, BRUCE. "The Japanese Problem," *Nation,* CXII (February 2, 1921), 171-72.

BOGARDUS, EMORY S. "Japanese and the Quota," *Sociology and Social Research,* XV (May-April, 1931), 472-78.

————. "The Japanese Return to the West Coast," *Sociology and Social Research,* XXXI (January-February, 1947), 226-33.

BROOKS, CHARLES W. "The Chinese Labor Problem," *Overland Monthly,* old series, III (1869), 407-19.

BROOKS, NOAH. "Restaurant Life in San Francisco," *Overland Monthly,* o.s., I (1868), 472-73.

BUELL, RAYMOND L. "Again the Yellow Peril," *Foreign Affairs,* II (1923), 295-309.

————. "The Development of the Anti-Japanese Agitation in the United States," *Political Science Quarterly,* XXXVII (1922), 605-38 and XXXVIII (1923), 57-81.

CHAMBERS, JOHN. "The Japanese Invasion," *Annals of the American Academy of Political and Social Science*, XCIII (1921), 23-29.

COOLIDGE, MARY R. "Chinese Labor Competition on the Pacific Coast," *Annals of the American Academy of Political and Social Science*, XXXIV (1909), 340-50.

CORBALLY, JOHN E. "Orientals in the Seattle Schools," *Sociology and Social Research*, XVI (September-October, 1931), 61-67.

DE FALLA, PAUL M. "Lantern in the Western Sky," *Journal of the Historical Society of Southern California*, XLII (1960), 57-88, 161-85.

DE MOTTE, MARSHALL. "California—White or Yellow," *Annals of the American Academy of Political and Social Science*, XCIII (1921), 18-23.

DRESSLAR, F. R. "Chinese Pedagogies in Practice," *Education*, XX (1899), 136-42.

EDHOLM, M. G. C. "A Stain on the Flag," *California Illustrated Magazine*, I (1891-92), 159-70.

ERICKSON, AL. "Los Angeles Nisei Today," *California Sun Magazine* (Summer, 1958), 3.

EVANS, ALBERT S. "From the Orient Direct," *Atlantic Monthly*, XXIV (1869), 543-47.

FUJITA, MICHINARI. "Japanese Associations in America," *Sociology and Social Research*, XIII (1929), 211-28.

GOATER, RICHARD A. "Civil Rights and Anti-Japanese Discrimination," *University of Cincinnati Law Review*, XVIII (1949), 81-89.

HAINE, J. J. F. "A Belgian in the Gold Rush. A Memoir by Dr. J. J. F. Haine Translated with an Introduction by Jan Albert Goris," *California Historical Society Quarterly*, XXXVII (1958), 311-46.

HAO, FU CHI. "My Reception in America," *Outlook*, LXXXVI (August 10, 1907), 770-73.

IWATA, MASAKAZU. "The Japanese Immigrants in California Agriculture," *Agricultural History*, XXXVI (1962), 25-37.

KEMBLE, JOHN, transcriber. "Andrew Wilson's 'Jottings' on Civil War California," *California Historical Society Quarterly*, XXXII (1953), 209-24.

KENNAN, GEORGE. "The Japanese in the San Francisco Public Schools," *Outlook*, LXXXV (June 1, 1907), 246-52.

LEE, ROSE HUM. "A Century of Chinese and American Relations," *Phylon—The Atlantic University Review of Race and Culture*, XI (1950), 240-45.

LEE, YAN PHOU. "The Chinese Must Stay," *North American Review* CXLVIII (1889), 467-83.

LOCKLEAR, WILLIAM R. "The Celestials and the Angels," *Historical Society of Southern California Quarterly*, XLII (1960), 239-56.

LOOMIS, AUGUSTUS. "Chinese in California, Their Sign-board Literature," *Overland Monthly*, o.s., I (1868), 152-55.

————. "Chinese Women in California," *Overland Monthly*, o.s., II (1869), 344-51.

————. "Holiday in California Quarter," *Overland Monthly*, o.s., II (1869), 148-49.

————. "How Our Chinamen are Employed," *Overland Monthly*, o.s., II (1869), 231-40.

————. "The Six Chinese Companies," *Overland Monthly*, o.s., I (1868), 221-27.

MACARTHUR, WALTER. "Opposition to Oriental Immigration," *Annals of the American Academy of Political and Social Science*, XXXIV (1909), 223-30.

McWILLIAMS, CAREY. "Once Again the Yellow Peril," *Nation*, CXL (June 26, 1935), 735-36.

MANN, ARTHUR. "Gompers and the Irony of Racism," *Antioch Review*, XIII (1953), 203-4.

MASTERS, FREDERICK J. "Among the Highbinders," *California Illustrated Magazine*, I (1891-92), 161-73.

————. "Opium and its Votaries," *California Illustrated Magazine*, I (1891-92), 631-45.

MILLIS, H. A. "California and the Japanese," *The Survey*, XXX (1913), 332-36.

MODELL, JOHN. "Class or Ethnic Solidarity: The Japanese American Company Union," *Pacific Historical Review*, XXXVIII (1969), 193-206.

MORRIS, ROLAND S. "The Background of the Relations Between Japan and the United States," *Annals of the American Academy of Political and Social Science*, XCIII (1921), 1-6.

MUELDER, WALTER G. "National Unity and National Ethics," *Annals of the American Academy of Political and Social Science*, CCXLIV (1946), 10-18.

NODERA, ISAMU. "Second Generation Japanese and Vocations," *Sociology and Social Research*, XXI (May-June, 1937), 464-66.

NORTH, HART H. "Chinese and Japanese Immigration to the Pacific Coast," *California Historical Society Quarterly*, XXVIII (1949), 343-50.

O'MEARA, JAMES. "The Chinese in Early Days," *Overland Monthly*, new series, III (1884), 477-81.

PAUL, RODMAN. "The Origins of the Chinese Issue in California," *Mississippi Valley Historical Review*, XXV (1938), 181-96.

ROSTOW, EUGENE V. "Our Worst Wartime Mistake," *Harpers*, CXCI (1945), 193-201.

ROWELL, CHESTER H. "Chinese and Japanese Immigrants—A Comparison," *Annals of the American Academy of Political and Social Science*, XXXIV (1909), 223-30.

SANDMEYER, ELMER C. "California Anti-Chinese Legislation and the

Federal Courts: A Study in Federal Relations," *Pacific Historical Review*, V (1936), 189-211.

SIENKIEWICZ, HENRYK. "The Chinese in California," *California Historical Society Quarterly*, XXXIV (1955), 301-16.

SMITH, BRADFORD. "Legalized Blackmail," *Common Ground*, VIII (1948), 34-36.

SPIER, ROBERT F. G. "Food Habits of the Nineteenth Century California Chinese," *California Historical Society Quarterly*, XXXVIII (1958), 79-81, 128-36.

STEARNS, MARJORIE R. "The Settlement of the Japanese in Oregon," *Oregon Historical Quarterly*, XXXIX (1938), 262-69.

WOLFE, TOM. "The New Yellow Peril," *Esquire*, LXXII (1969), 190-99, 322.

WORTHY, EDMUND H. JR. "Yung Wing in America," *Pacific Historical Review*, XXXIV (1965), 265-87.

YOSHIA, YOSABURO. "Sources and Causes of Japanese Immigration," *Annals of the American Academy of Political and Social Science*, XXXIV (1909), 157-67.

Glossary

Chinese Six Companies: District associations representative of areas from Kwangtung Province, China, banded together in San Francisco to coordinate common efforts.

Daimyo: Feudal landlords in Japan.

Golden Mountain: Cantonese name for California.

Haaka: Residents of Kwangtung Province who developed a culture different from earlier inhabitants of the Pearl River Delta.

Issei: First generation Japanese Americans who migrated from Japan to the United States.

Meiji Restoration: Japanese Emperor Meiji restored imperial rule in 1868 following the overthrow of the Tokugawa Shogunate.

Nisei: Children of Japanese immigrants, Issei, to the United States. Nisei, second generation Japanese Americans, were American citizens by virtue of being born in the United States.

Punti: Descendants of the indigenous residents of the Pearl River Delta, Kwangtung Province.

Samurai: Warrior class in feudal Japan.

Sansei: Third generation American Japanese.

Shogun: Title given to feudal lord placed in charge of all Japanese imperial troops.

Tanka: Chinese of Kwangtung Province who lived their lives on boats in the Pearl River Delta region.

Tokugawa Shogunate: Tokugawa family controlled the office of Shogun from 1803-1868. The Tokugawa Shogunate closed Japan to the outside world.

Tongs: Chinese organizations in the world of crime, drugs, and gambling.

Zaibutsu: Japanese cartels, organized during the Meiji Restoration, to launch industrial Japan.

Index